The Legacy of J. William Fulbright

The Legacy of
J. William Fulbright

Policy, Power, and Ideology

Edited by Alessandro Brogi,
Giles Scott-Smith, and David J. Snyder

UNIVERSITY PRESS OF KENTUCKY

Editorial and Sales Offices: The University Press of Kentucky
663 South Limestone Street, Lexington, Kentucky 40508-4008
www.kentuckypress.com

Cataloging-in-Publication data available from the Library of Congress

ISBN 978-0-8131-7770-0 (hardcover : alk. paper)
ISBN 978-0-8131-7772-4 (pdf)
ISBN 978-0-8131-7773-1 (epub)

This book is printed on acid-free paper meeting
the requirements of the American National Standard
for Permanence in Paper for Printed Library Materials.

Manufactured in the United States of America.

Member of the Association
of University Presses

Contents

Part 2.
The Fulbright Exchange in Historical Perspective

Introduction

Alessandro Brogi, Giles Scott-Smith, and David J. Snyder

J. William Fulbright's key role in the formulation and criticism of US foreign policy has long been recognized. To date, however, scholarship has been slow to assess his influence in relation to American power and global affairs in the decades after World War II. Save for Randall Woods's seminal biography, now a generation old, and fragmentary studies of the exchange program that bears the Arkansas senator's name,[1] an overall assessment of Fulbright's influence on the purpose and practice of US foreign policy is still lacking.[2] This volume critically evaluates his political role on both the domestic and the international fronts. It assesses his significance as a key architect of post–World War II liberal internationalism and as an advocate for cultural exchange, as well as his historic reversal from Cold War hawk to Vietnam dove.[3] Such a reassessment also addresses Fulbright's difficulties in maintaining his position as a national and a global voice on foreign relations while wrestling with the political controversies of the US South during the civil rights movement.

While focusing on Fulbright's career and his exchange program, this collection is not a biographical study. The aim here is rather to highlight Fulbright's life and legacy as a conduit for exploring American foreign policy in the Cold War and beyond, further assessing the possibilities and limitations of liberal internationalism. Our narrative follows a dual purpose. First, we offer a critical analysis of both Fulbright the politician and Fulbright the exchange program, linking the two in ways that indicate how the senator's outlook was not as straightforward or consistent as it may seem at first. Second, we frame this investigation within a wider reevaluation of liberal internationalism, addressing ongoing debates on ideology, consistency, and imperialism within US foreign policy throughout the twentieth century. Through a multidimensional exploration that covers issues of politics, culture, race, and gender, the contributors highlight

Fulbright's influence on foreign policy debates at home, the relevance of his exchange program in US foreign relations abroad, his involvement in domestic political controversies, and the broader implications of all these issues for US foreign policy in the second half of the twentieth century. In giving him this overdue attention, this collection recognizes that the liberal internationalism Fulbright aimed to represent for almost three decades also eluded his control. The views from the White House or the State Department on liberal internationalism differed from his at crucial times; so did those of New Left thinkers. Yet he stands apart as a legislator who could claim widespread public influence and considerable clout over (indeed, rivalry with) the presidency.

The ensuing essays are organized into two broad categories: Fulbright as an avatar of US foreign policy and the exchange program as a carrier of US diplomatic initiative and soft power influence. Across these two categories, the examination of Fulbright's remarkable career is conducted through three key themes. The first, the ideology of liberal internationalism, constitutes the common thread of all the contributions but is particularly highlighted in the opening essays, which argue that its global impact demonstrates its merits as much as its inconsistencies. No full understanding of Fulbright's legacy is possible without an appreciation of how his notions of liberal internationalism, whether idealist or pragmatic, were tested and transformed over time in a changing domestic and international political context that raised questions about the conduct and purpose of US foreign policy.

The second theme is the intersection of domestic and international issues that both expanded and limited the influence of the junior senator. Fulbright's political clout in particular owed much to his extended chairmanship of the Senate Foreign Relations Committee. His intellectual outlook and leadership gave him influence that helped reshape the contours of thinking on the Cold War, rebalancing the power between Congress and the executive, and establishing a connection with the media and the public that took on significant proportions during the years of growing dissent occasioned by the war in Vietnam. As a public intellectual, Fulbright also added luster and weight to the institutional role he played. Associated with his role as a powerful southerner in this long-standing institutional position was the all-pervasive influence of race in US politics and diplomacy. The realities of southern politics that Fulbright represented envisaged national interest according to ongoing racial or civilizational hierarchies, clashing with the enlightened promotion of freedom and democracy abroad that liberal internationalists ostensibly advocated.

For all its inconsistencies, Fulbright's liberal internationalism (and the shifts in public opinion he sought to represent) maintained its emancipatory potential and dissenting influential voice. The correlation between these two aspects constitutes the third theme under scrutiny here. It was particularly through the exchange program that bore his name that Fulbright pursued a foreign policy of development aid and cultural diplomacy. The championing of this double trajectory of foreign policy aimed at promoting peace and, at the height of the Cold War, complemented the senator's call for peaceful competition, if not coexistence, with America's Communist rivals. While the exchange program and the foreign policy it was meant to advocate ostensibly advanced cultural inclusiveness of all kinds, Fulbright's understanding of emancipation was limited in scope when it came to the involvement of women and people of color. Despite these limitations, the program underlined his celebrated position as dissenter and critic of US Cold War foreign policy, engaging with and questioning American nationalism, imperialism, and militarism in ways that still resonate in the debates on the US role in the world today.

The collection as a whole grapples with the question of to what degree Fulbright shifted his positions during his long career in the national spotlight. Previous work on Fulbright tends to stress the apparent shifts, especially later in his career when the sponsor of the Gulf of Tonkin Resolution transformed himself into the leading Washington critic of America's Vietnam policy. Yet, while there is no doubt that important shifts occurred, we also see durable consistencies that have remained largely hidden, passed over, or misunderstood. Throughout his long career, Fulbright remained wedded to a particular republican philosophy and a convinced Tocquevillian advocacy of elitism in foreign policy making. He felt a deep distrust of the uneducated, especially when ignorance was joined to idealism, as is often the case in American politics. Consistently battling the forces of demagoguery, he took center stage against the likes of Senator Joseph McCarthy, Governor Orval Faubus, and reactionaries within the US Army.[4] He scorned John Foster Dulles's millennial rhetoric as overheated and emotional, the superficial righteousness of the unsophisticated.

Though he was a loyal Democrat, party mattered less in his ideological view of the world than a kind of class sensitivity. When Johnson intensified American involvement in Vietnam, for example, Fulbright became convinced that the president was playing to a cruder populism in American political life. Despite his warm affinity for Henry Kissinger's strategic approach to foreign relations, he deeply distrusted the paranoid and crude calculations of the Nixon White House. Elitism was a constant in his political outlook. The new dimensions of American imperialism came to offend him since the exercise of imperial power risked the very democracy it was designed to protect, as McCarthy, Johnson, and Nixon had so evidently shown.

On the issue of race, Fulbright was on far less principled ground, but his consistencies nevertheless reveal broader patterns. That he shared the common racial assumptions of his era and his region is beyond doubt. He was, for example, an instigator and signer of the Southern Manifesto. But his was the racism of the South's upper crust, of the aloof local gentry whose assumptions of black inferiority were based not on contact with African Americans but on the lack thereof. It was a racism that informed his view of politics and of foreign policy. In keeping with his distrust of the rabble, he repudiated the crude race-baiting of vulgar politicians such as Faubus or George Wallace. But his casual racism informed his view of policy making. He did not consider the Global South nations to be key priorities for his beloved exchange program, as several of the essays in this collection make clear. He also came to his critique of Vietnam at least partially through a racial lens, reasoning that the stakes of fighting in a third-rate Asian country did not justify the damage being wrought to American prestige. He would retain his Europe-first orientation throughout his entire political career. When his political enemies began to mount a campaign against him based in part on allegations of anti-Semitism (he had consistently spoken out against the influence of foreign lobbies, including Israel's), it was a charge that resonated with the rural evangelical voters he had always distrusted. The claim also pointed to the racial elitism that marked the public careers of many liberal internationalists in the period, northern and southern.

Given the importance of the senator and the exchange program for American foreign relations, elitism and race provide vital clarifications for understanding Fulbright's career and his relationship with US foreign and domestic policies. They also help us reformulate the narrative on Fulbright outside the strict parameters of the Cold War, in which his philosophy, actions, and reevaluations were nevertheless deeply embedded. His liberal internationalism survived the vicissitudes of the Cold War, just as the program that bears his name has continued beyond that global ideological contest. Certainly, the Fulbright program has been institutionally and strategically reassessed since the end of the Cold War. Controversies surrounding the program's geopolitical scope, its presumed enduring role in promoting America's soft power, the effectiveness of educational and cultural exchange in reducing prejudice and promoting peace, and burden sharing in times when the United States has reconsidered its budget priorities have all plagued its long-term vitality.

Liberal internationalism had its permutations—or interpretations—ranging from largely peaceful and cooperative to hawkish and unilaterally interventionist. The main focus of this collection—largely in line with Fulbright's own views—is on how it was rooted in the vision of President Woodrow Wilson for a cooperative, rule-based international order. Under President Franklin Roosevelt, it increasingly emphasized the spread of free market economics and democracy and, through both, the cultivation of peace among nations. Following US participation in World War II, most liberal internationalists interweaved the promotion of international cooperation with the ideological confrontation with both fascism and communism. American interventionism—military, economic, or even cultural and political—informed the nation's pursuit of a liberal world order. During the Cold War, that interventionism often prevailed over the cooperative aspects of liberal internationalism. The United States embarked on an international role that, like that of its Communist counterpart, the Soviet Union, displayed a proselytizing fervor that was meant to accelerate the path of history—through development, modernization, emancipation, and rights—for the beneficiaries of its ideology. And, most assuredly, there was a messianic element—Randall Woods refers to this as *liberal imperialism*, the "evil twin" of Wilsonianism—that even Fulbright, the future champion of cultural exchange, embraced in his early career. Liberal internationalism's multilateral aspects, advocating the development of a community of nations based on the benefits of free trade, economic and political freedom, self-determination, and peace founded on mutual understanding and knowledge, would become increasingly evident in the political trajectory of the junior senator and the liberal democratic voices he represented.[5]

Indeed, Fulbright's early political posture provides an outline for tracking US foreign policy after World War II. For roughly four decades, a bipartisan consensus characterized the formulation of American foreign policy. And, while his Atlanticist and Europe-first outlook was typical of many liberal internationalists, Fulbright initially set out backing the United Nations as the basis for a new world order. How and why that shift occurred sheds light on the breakdown of the one-world/UN approach to international governance and the consolidation of a Cold War posture during the late 1940s and early 1950s. The new research presented here emphasizes that Fulbright's internationalism was never disconnected from American national interest—in fact, it strove to fit in and refine the correlation between international cooperation and the nation's internal priorities. The senator was also tied to his own electoral base and source of political power in the South. He was one of a select group of southerners who exerted an outsized influence in policy-making circles. And there was the rub: by becoming an authority on foreign policy for the New South, he also showed some limitations in his version of liberal internationalism and US cultural diplomacy; on race especially, whether from personal conviction or political expediency (most often a mix of both), he limited the emancipatory potential of his own exchange program.

Accounts of the Fulbright program too often underline its idealism and promise. The essays in this volume dealing with the Fulbright exchange program in action, showing its operations in places from Yugoslavia to China, Africa, and Australia, illustrate its merits as much as its limitations. Still, the program managed to associate exchanges with broad American geopolitical goals while also wrestling, in most cases with relative success, with conflicting demands and negotiated cultural and political challenges in specific locales. Perceptions from abroad further enrich our understanding of how Fulbright's thoughts, actions, reconsiderations, and, finally, legacy corresponded or failed to match the expectations of governments and peoples elsewhere. The research presented here is a harbinger of what could be achieved with a fuller study of the Fulbright program's long-term significance for US influence abroad, particularly concerning key allies such as Britain, France, (West) Germany, and Japan, or across the Global South.

This volume is far from an unquestioning celebration of Fulbright's internationalism. It provides a variety of opinions, inviting a deep reflection on the purposes of US foreign policy. The contributors highlight the inconsistencies and constant reassessment of that foreign policy and its pivotal role—beneficial or deleterious—in shaping global developments. This very reflection indeed evokes the ways in which Fulbright himself questioned, debated, and invited open discussion of ideas, in defiance of a stifling consensus. As he famously pondered, it was through America's extraordinary capacity for open debate and dissent, especially within the establishment that he represented, that the "arrogance of power" could best be addressed, challenging the "self-righteous" America in favor of the "self-critical one," castigating the morality of absolutes "fired by the crusading spirit" while advancing "the morality of decent instincts tempered by the knowledge of human imperfection."[6]

Randall B. Woods highlights the positive trajectory of the senator's evolving views on liberal internationalism, showing that his path was at times slippery and somewhat contradictory. Woods's conceptual and biographical sketch addresses the broad aspects of that trajectory. Through the prism of Fulbright's internationalism and his growing critique of Cold War interventionism, Woods invites further reflection on the evolution, legacy, and even distortions of liberal internationalism in its current neoconservative permutations. Fulbright started off within the liberal consensus that made anticommunism a "transcendent mission" for the United States. Yet, by the late 1950s, his unwavering faith in the role of international cooperation and collective security put a first dent in the most messianic aspects of that consensus. The exchange program that bore his name functioned, at least to the public eye, according to a cultural relativism that made it a more purist vision of Wilsonian internationalism than its original post–World War I incarnation. But that call for cultural relativism, tolerance, and flexibility was far from idealist. For Fulbright it was exactly idealism combined with militarism that plagued American foreign policy at the peak of the Cold War and, according to Woods, has continued to do so up to the present.

In contrast, Sam Lebovic and Justin Hart emphasize that Fulbright's liberal internationalism was not divested of a nationalist purpose. It remained fundamentally exceptionalist, maintaining certain missionary impulses that were sometimes hard to distinguish from Woods's liberal imperialism. Surely, throughout his career, Fulbright advocated an international order based on interpersonal connection and mutual understanding, and he saw programs of educational and cultural exchange as a necessary policy for the creation of such a world. It was a world in which the nature of the game would change, moving away from national advantage in the traditional competitive game of international relations. But intertwined with such universalist rhetoric was always an assumption that civilizing and humanizing international relations would benefit American interests. It was not just that doing so would benefit Americans insofar as they had to live in the world and would automatically and passively benefit from peace. Fulbright also imagined that the program would create a global elite attuned to American values and American interests. The soft elitism of his vision of educational exchange was no great secret. Lebovic unpacks the inherent conception of US national power at the heart of the Fulbright program's ostensible internationalism, thereby offering a critique of standard interpretations of the program's apolitical merits.

The Fulbright program, as Hart argues even more pointedly, largely sought to make Americans better imperialists, not undermine the imperial project itself. While Fulbright did indeed criticize US imperial practice, he was not a critic of US empire as such, understood as the American project to secure global hegemony. His principal complaints were about the failure to align means and ends and the inability to consider how the world might look through the eyes of other people. Despite his laments about the "arrogance of power" and the "price of empire" in response to the catastrophe in Vietnam, he never really questioned the need for US leadership in the world, even while offering strenuous critiques of various manifestations of the imperial impulse at home and abroad. In short, his criticisms of US foreign policy throughout his long career—both before and after 1964–1965—should be understood as tactical, not strategic, in nature.

Placing the debate over liberal internationalism within the specific context of the diatribe between Fulbright and President Lyndon Johnson, Benjamin Brady shows that Fulbright's reevaluation of the Cold War consensus occurred in the years immediately preceding America's escalation of the Vietnam War. To be sure, Presidents Kennedy and Johnson (and their key advisers) agreed about the futility of many aspects of the US-Soviet struggle and accepted many of the assumptions underlying

Fulbright's critique. Nonetheless, crises in Latin America and Vietnam ultimately ruined the possibility of ratcheting down the Cold War. As other scholars have argued, policy makers on both sides of the Iron Curtain often recognized that the US-Soviet global struggle was counterproductive.[7] Nonetheless, until the late 1980s, successive administrations chose continued competition over change. Senator Fulbright's internationalism offered an alternative, but his failure to persuade Presidents Kennedy and Johnson of its merits partly illuminates why the Cold War continued for so long. Focusing on his critique of US policy toward Cuba and the Dominican Republic in the early 1960s, Brady explains why these countries, and not Vietnam, drew the senator's increasing criticism of US Cold War foreign policy. Fulbright sought to restore the multilateral, less messianic form of liberal internationalism that still remained within the classic ideological dichotomy of the Cold War, only fought with other means.

Regarding the interplay of domestic and international factors, Frédérick Gagnon describes the senator's self-assigned roles as agenda setter, public educator, and presidential restrainer as the powerful chair of the Senate Foreign Relations Committee (SFRC). For all his elitist views on foreign policy leadership, Fulbright also reached out to the public like no other SFRC chair has done, through speeches, books, and media appearances. As he embarked on his role as public educator, he upheld one of the most shared beliefs among liberal internationalists—that "in a democracy dissent is an act of faith."[8] Yet, as much as he succeeded in educating the public at home, his views appeared in a different light when scrutinized by some of America's closest allies. Focusing on British and Australian reactions to Fulbright's critiques of the exhaustive worldwide commitments of the United States, especially in Vietnam, David L. Prentice notes that what worried US allies was not so much the arrogance of American power but its retreat. For British and Australian policy makers, Fulbright symbolized congressional neo-isolationism. They believed that his rhetoric and leadership threatened US defense commitments worldwide, undermining their own national security and the future of global stability. In response, Great Britain and Australia encouraged US policy makers to maintain the nation's commitments even as they adapted their diplomacy to accommodate the presumed American retreat represented by Fulbright's attack.

Fulbright the dissenter and critic of the old myths that marred Cold War strategies nevertheless did not fully evolve away from traditional Western notions of race and even rankings of modern civilizations. This was the result of both conviction and political expediency. As Neal Allen convincingly reminds us, the senator's political base was built on a white Arkansas electorate that largely rejected racial desegregation. With an almost perfect anti–civil rights voting record, Fulbright was able to craft a political career that fed his state constituents the racial conservatism they wanted in order to create the space for his forays into foreign policy. Yet his views on race did not stop at the water's edge. Nowhere was his prejudice more apparent than in the implementation of the Fulbright program in Africa. Hannah Higgin echoes Brady, arguing that Fulbright's criticism of US interventions in the Global South did not necessarily mean that, by contrast, he highly favored devoting attention, energy, and funds to public diplomacy in the developing nations. He simply showed little interest in the State Department's efforts to cultivate an educated elite in Africa. He remained skeptical of African "multipliers" as adding value for US liberal internationalism. The color line therefore bridled his conception of universalism at home and abroad. It also limited his conception of America's appropriate sphere of influence. Though the avowed internationalist believed that deeper intercultural understanding provided the best hope for preventing future conflagrations and that the American government had a duty to foster such understanding, he continued to view international affairs through a colonial prism, never championing, for example, education for elites from developing nations.

While the Fulbright program's emancipatory effects on the issues of ethnicity and civilizational diversity were limited, they were perhaps felt most directly in terms of gender and political human rights—or, more generally, political pluralism. Molly Bettie's broad investigation of Fulbright women entering the intellectual and political global elite adds a crucial perspective on both the merits and the paradoxes of gender advancement in the last seventy years. Unlike many other prestigious academic institutions, the Fulbright program has been open to female participants since its foundation. Women were admitted as Rhodes scholars only in 1976, and the Ivy League became fully coeducational only a decade later. The Fulbright program, on the other hand, has had female students, scholars, and administrators since its establishment in 1946.

Women Fulbrighters include Pulitzer and Nobel Prize winners as well as the first female president of an Ivy League University. Fulbright alumnae have also served as the first female heads of state of the Slovak Republic, the Bahamas, and Peru. Women have gradually had a powerful impact on the program as participants, as administrators, and even as accompanying spouses of Fulbright grantees. Overcoming gender subordination, combined with cultural clout, constitutes perhaps one of the main offshoots of the program's effects, at home and abroad.

Alice Garner and Diane Kirkby further illuminate the interplay between foreign perceptions of US motives and the role of women in reshaping those perceptions. Exploring the particular impact of female American scholars—and of male scholars' wives—in the Australian-US Fulbright program's first operational years, they point out that the scholars' contribution to the program's goals and reputation building was not necessarily recognized by Fulbright program administrators but was very evident in press and scholar reports. The academics negotiated their roles as multilevel unofficial ambassadors representing their universities, the program itself, and the United States. In particular, women's informal ambassadorships extended well beyond the academic world they inhabited to reach women and men in the broader community who were curious about US society and culture and about what kinds of professional opportunities were available to women in the postwar period.[9]

The soft power of the United States has grown out, to a large extent, from its promotion of political pluralism as much as from the advancement of social pluralism worldwide. Fulbright internationalism was prepared to reach out across Cold War ideological divides in the interests of laying small-scale but elite-sanctioned cultural and educational bridges. In this sense, the program stayed true to the senator's founding one-worldism. Its opening to Communist countries could mitigate, if not eclipse, the most tarnished record of the United States: the war in Vietnam. Two case studies here—on Yugoslavia and China—offer insights into the program's strategic instrumentality, its genuine promise of the new realities Fulbright advocated in the face of the Cold War's rigid assumptions, and the social effects this kind of engagement could trigger. Carla Konta illustrates how the Fulbright program in Yugoslavia was part of a general American effort of public diplomacy to exert an influence on that country's leadership and public opinion to sustain and reinforce the

Yugoslav turn to the West. Senator Fulbright himself attended the signing of the Fulbright exchange agreement in Belgrade in 1964, just days after Johnson's election as president. The senator's visit underlined the significance of the new paths for US foreign policy that he was at that time mapping out in his most influential speeches, a transition covered in the essays by Woods, Hart, and Brady. The Yugoslav regime represented a synthesis of communism and nationalism, with pragmatic qualities free of dogma, as the senator contended. This again confirmed Fulbright's turn away from America's dogma on the Communist monolith—and the willingness of the Yugoslav leadership to engage with the United States in a new way, despite the ideological risks.

The case of China also demonstrates the usefulness of the Fulbright program in expanding a bilateral relationship when an opening appears across ideological lines. It also confirms the risks involved in such processes of opening up. The first bilateral agreement for the program was signed between the United States and China in 1947. With the triumph of the Communist Party under Mao Tse-tung in 1949, the agreement was nullified. It would take thirty years, the Sino-Soviet split, and the Nixon-Kissinger "opening to China" before the agreement could be renewed as part of Deng Xiaoping's modernization program for a post-Mao China. Guangqiu Xu looks at both the early and the later Fulbright program in China to underline the importance of US-led educational exchange for China in the second half of the twentieth century and for the bilateral relationship in general. He also shows from a different angle the dilemmas faced by other powers when engaging with US liberal internationalism. The Chinese leadership understood the value of US knowledge and the desperate need to integrate Chinese institutions into the US circuits of knowledge production and circulation. At the same time, it wanted to keep these contacts within narrowly controlled ideological confines. Instead, the appeal of democratic ideals from outside fueled discontent of the country's young people with a one-party system, leading, ultimately, to the bloody 1989 crackdown to reinstate the Party line. The emancipatory potential represented by the program therefore challenged the assumption that foreign ideas could be kept within the walls of the lecture hall. The pervasive ideology of liberal internationalism, here represented through cultural and educational exchange, exposed the limits of cultural relativism.

Focusing on the early evolution and vicissitudes of the Fulbright program, Lonnie R. Johnson looks at both its philosophical underpinnings and its institutional developments. The program embodied Fulbright's thinking on a variety of fundamental issues related to his education and experience as a Rhodes scholar in Oxford and Vienna and his maturing views on international relations, executive powers, national sovereignty, the maintenance of world peace in the nuclear age, the role of educational and cultural exchange in preventing conflict and advancing cross-cultural tolerance, and the ironies of cultural relativism. Only the embedded bilateral or binational articulation of Fulbright program interests and objectives on a country-by-country basis, Johnson emphasizes, could guarantee the reciprocity of the exchange of citizens and, most important, a commitment to academic freedoms. But bilateralism also meant for host countries the burden of sharing costs that resulted from a diminished US interest. Johnson draws some alarming conclusions, charting the institutional development of the program, in particular its continuation beyond the Cold War and its current vulnerabilities to declining US government financial support. In many ways, his chronicling of the rise and gradual fall of the program mirrors the arc of American power itself.

Many scholars and pundits see liberal internationalism as never having fully recovered from its crisis during the Vietnam War years. Like its domestic equivalent, New Deal liberalism,[10] it is often mourned, whether as a victim of reaction or of its own contradictions—contradictions that Fulbright's own career so amply illustrates. The rise of global threats has rekindled a "Wilsonianism of fear," placing emphasis on the dangers more than the benefits of an interconnected world,[11] hence prompting unilateral actions from Washington. Its decline is also partly blamed on the enduring belief in American exceptionalism that ascribed a proselytizing role to the United States—a belief that sometimes marred the application, if not the philosophy, of the Fulbright exchange program as well. With this collection, we hope to recalibrate the narrative from quick assessments or even judgments of the fate of American liberal internationalism. The legacy of J. William Fulbright not only offers a prism through which to evaluate its merits and contradictions. It also shows the enduring impact of the most progressive notions of Wilsonianism in US foreign policy and the relevance of cultural exchange in mitigating the intoxicating abstractions of nation and ideology and promoting peace.

Notes

1. Notable individual country studies of the exchange program, which however do not integrate thematically into a broader conceptualization of the senator's influence, include Frank Salamone, *The Fulbright Experience in Benin* (Williamsburg, VA: College of William and Mary, 1994); Jan C. C. Rupp, "The Fulbright Program; or, The Surplus Value of Officially Organized Academic Exchange," *Journal of Studies in International Education* 3 (1999): 59–82; Guangqiu Xu, "The Ideological and Political Impact of US Fulbrighters on Chinese Students: 1979–1989," *Asian Affairs* 26 (1999): 139–57; Thomas König, "Das Fulbright in Wien: Wissenschaftspolitik und Sozialwissenschaften am 'versunkenen Kontinent'" (PhD diss., University of Vienna, 2008); Lorenzo Delgado Gomez-Escalonilla, *Westerly Wind: The Fulbright Program in Spain* (Madrid: LID Editorial Empresarial, 2009); Matt Loayza, "A Curative and Creative Force: The Exchange of Persons Program and Eisenhower's Inter-American Policies, 1953–1961," *Diplomatic History* 37 (2013): 946–70; Alice Garner and Diane Kirby, "'Never a machine for propaganda?' The Australian-American Fulbright Program and Australia's Cold War," *Australian Historical Studies* 44 (2013): 117–33; Juan José Navarro, "Public Foreign Aid and Academic Mobility: The Fulbright Program (1955–1973)," in *The Politics of Academic Autonomy in Latin America*, ed. Fernanda Beigel (London: Routledge, 2013), 105–18; and Giles Scott-Smith, "The Fulbright Program in the Netherlands: An Example of Science Diplomacy," in *Cold War Science and the Transatlantic Circulation of Knowledge*, ed. Jeroen van Dongen (Leiden: Brill, 2015): 128–53.

2. Institutional histories of the Fulbright program include Walter Johnson and Francis Colligan, *The Fulbright Program: A History* (Chicago: University of Chicago Press, 1965); and Sam Lebovic, "From War Junk to Educational Exchange: The WWII Origins of the Fulbright Program and the Foundations of American Cultural Globalism," *Diplomatic History* 37, no. 2 (April 2013): 280–312; and Molly Bettie, "Ambassadors Unaware: The Fulbright Program and American Public Diplomacy," *Journal of Transatlantic Studies* 13, no. 4 (October 2015): 358–72. There are a few anecdotal accounts, including Arthur Power Dudden and Russell Dynes, eds., *The Fulbright Experience, 1946–1986: Encounters and Transformations* (New Brunswick, NJ: Transaction, 1986); Leonard Sussman, *The Culture of Freedom: The Small World of Fulbright Scholars* (Lanham, MD: Rowman & Littlefield, 1992); and Richard Arndt and David Lee Rubin, eds., *The Fulbright Difference* (New Brunswick, NJ: Transaction, 1996).

3. On Fulbright and dissent, particularly during the Vietnam War, see esp. Randall B. Woods, *J. William Fulbright, Vietnam, and the Search for a Cold War Foreign Policy* (New York: Cambridge University Press, 1998) (an abridged version of Randall B. Woods, *Fulbright: A Biography* [New York: Cambridge University Press, 1995]); Haynes Johnson and Bernard M. Gwertzman, *Fulbright: The Dissenter* (New York: Doubleday, 1968); William C. Berman, *William Fulbright and the Vietnam War: The Dissent of a Political Realist* (Kent, OH: Kent State University Press, 1988);

Eugene Brown, *J. William Fulbright: Advice and Dissent* (Iowa City, IA: University of Iowa Press, 1985); and Randall B. Woods, "Dixie's Dove: J. William Fulbright, the Vietnam War and the American South," *Journal of Southern History* 60, no. 3 (August 1994): 533–52.

4. See Giles Scott-Smith, "Bill and Ed's Big Adventure: Cold Warriors, William Fulbright, and Right-Wing Propaganda in the US Military, 1961–62," *Histoire@ Politique*, no. 35 (May–August 2018), https://www.histoire-politique.fr/index.php?numero=35&rub=pistes&item=41.

5. On the origins and legacies of liberal internationalism, see, most recently, Tony Smith, *Why Wilson Matters: The Origins of American Liberal Internationalism and Its Crisis Today* (Princeton, NJ: Princeton University Press, 2017).

6. J. William Fulbright, *The Arrogance of Power* (New York: Random House, 1966), 245–46.

7. See, e.g., Vojtech Mastny, "The 1963 Nuclear Test Ban Treaty: A Missed Opportunity for Détente?" *Journal of Cold War Studies* 10 (2008): 3–25; Stephan Kieninger, *Dynamic Détente: The United States and Europe, 1964–1975* (Lexington: University Press of Kentucky, 2016); and Martin McCauley, *The Cold War, 1949–2016* (London: Routledge, 2017).

8. Fulbright, *The Arrogance of Power*, 25.

9. For a full exposition of the program's impact, see Alice Garner and Diane Kirkby, *Academic Ambassadors, Pacific Allies: Australia, America and the Fulbright Program* (Manchester: Manchester University Press, 2018).

10. For an argument connecting aspects of foreign policy and domestic politics in this type of assessment, see esp. H. W. Brands, *The Strange Death of American Liberalism* (New Haven, CT: Yale University Press, 2003). See also Smith, *Why Wilson Matters*.

11. For an explication of the "Wilsonianism of fear," see Frank Ninkovich, *The Wilsonian Century: U.S. Foreign Policy since 1900* (Chicago: University of Chicago Press, 2001).

Part 1

Fulbright's Liberal Internationalism in
Historical Perspective

Fulbright Internationalism

A Retrospective

Randall B. Woods

Aside from the international exchange program that bears his name, J. William Fulbright is best known as the avatar of Wilsonian internationalism during the three decades following the end of World War II. At the outset of the Cold War, with McCarthyism at its height, American liberals were forced to jump on the anti-Communist bandwagon. They became virulent Cold Warriors but with a transcendent mission—the United States would not only protect the world from the scourge of Communist totalitarianism but also bring the blessings of democracy and liberal capitalism to the developing world. Bill Fulbright was initially at the forefront of liberal anticommunism, but then, with the coming of the Vietnam War, he stepped forward to argue that militarists and true believers were perverting the Wilsonian ethic, siding with corrupt dictators in the name of liberty and justice. The Wilsonian vision was concerned not so much with the spread of democracy, he insisted, as with the building of a cooperative and rule-based international order. American imperialism whether liberal or conservative was anathema. Since 9/11, his commitment to and subsequent critique of liberal internationalism has become more relevant than ever. As the invasion of Iraq turned into a protracted war, the Bush administration increasingly invoked liberal internationalist ideas to justify its actions. "The survival of liberty in our land increasingly depends on the success of liberty in other lands," George W. Bush declared. The administration subsequently asserted the right to use force anywhere in the world against "terrorists with global reach." It would do so largely outside the traditional alliance system through coalitions of the willing. As Robert Jervis has observed, Wilson promised to make the world safe for democracy, while Bush seemed to be saying that the entire world had to be democratic for the United States to be safe.[1] An examination of Fulbright internationalism—its origin and evolution—is still instructive.

Wilsonian Origins of Fulbright's Liberal Internationalism

In no small part, the Arkansan's commitment to Wilsonian principles was an offshoot of his years at Oxford. The most important acquaintance he made at Pembroke College was his young tutor, Ronald Buchanan McCallum, whose guidance and instruction were crucial in shaping the young American's intellect and worldview. From that first autumn afternoon when they met and cycled together to view the tomb of William Lenthall of Long Parliament fame, the two men maintained a close personal and intellectual relationship that lasted until McCallum's death in 1973.

The Oxford don was an ardent admirer of Woodrow Wilson, revering both the man and his vision. During their tutorials, he and his young American charge spent long hours examining the former president's premises and policies. In a speech before a joint session of Congress in the spring of 1917, Wilson had declared that war against Imperial Germany was necessary so that the world could be "made safe for democracy." Underlying this statement was the notion that the internal characteristics of states are decisive in matters of war and peace. Autocratic and militarist states make war; democracies make peace. There was in the Wilsonian philosophy the corollary notion that the establishment of an enduring and peaceful world order depended on collective action by a community of democratic nations. No autocratic state could be trusted to act responsibly within such a community. Only a community of free peoples could be trusted to sacrifice for the greater good. Democracy and the rule of law, moreover, could not coexist with economic autarky. Political freedom required economic freedom, and that meant an international regime of free trade. Wilson believed that international law and agencies of cooperation in themselves bred understanding and tolerance. (Here, one can see a seed of the Fulbright exchange program.) His approach to progressive reform was conservative, stressing equality of opportunity rather than a growth in the federal power designed to foster a welfare state. His vision did not call for nation-states to relinquish their sovereignty except in one important instance. The Fourteen Points famously called for the establishment of a league of nations whose heart was Article X establishing a regime of collective security. The league charter included mutual guarantees of political independence and territorial integrity. When and if the council of the league called on members to impose sanctions and contribute to an international military force to halt aggression, member states would have to respond.

Wilsonian internationalism had an evil twin, however, in the form of liberal imperialism. At the outset of his administration, the Progressive president believed that he had a duty to spread democracy to other nations—especially in the Western Hemisphere—by the use of force if necessary. The United States twice sent troops to Mexico, once in 1914 and again in 1916, in support of political factions committed to popular sovereignty and the rule of law. Wilson would also order the military occupation of Haiti and dispatch troops to Nicaragua. "I will teach the South American Republics to elect good men," he declared.[2] Liberal interventionism proved counterproductive, of course, enabling the dictatorships he was trying to overthrow to pose as nationalists, defenders of their states against Yankee imperialism. By the end of his presidency, Wilson had learned his lesson; thus his great reluctance to intervene, if only temporarily, in the Russian Civil War.

In 1944, Ronald McCallum published *Public Opinion and the Lost Peace*, in which he challenged the long-standing view of John Maynard Keynes that the peace structure worked out at the Versailles Conference was predestined to fail. The concept of the League of Nations was sound, the Oxford don wrote; the organization had not worked because political figures on both sides of the Atlantic had never been willing to make a true commitment to the principles that underlay it and had attempted to use it for their own selfish, political purposes. Eventually, owing to ignorance, ambivalence, xenophobia, and especially a lack of leadership, Anglo-American public opinion became intensely disillusioned with the Versailles peace settlement. McCallum concluded his book with an appeal to Americans and Britons to rediscover and rededicate themselves to the principles of Wilsonian internationalism and specifically to resurrect the League of Nations. He voiced support for the International Monetary Fund (IMF) and the International Bank for Reconstruction and Development then under discussion at the Bretton Woods Conference. He warned against a revival of political isolationism in the United States, and he appealed for postwar cooperation with Russia. Above all, he wrote, if the modern world were to survive, there would have to be "some abnegation of formal state sovereignty."[3]

Realism Intrudes: The Dynamic Internationalism of World War II

Meanwhile, in the United States, J. William Fulbright, the practicing politician, began to develop and promulgate his own version of Wilsonian internationalism. In his speeches inside and outside Congress and in debates on the floor of the House and the Senate, the outline of his vision began to emerge. Like Wilson, Fulbright believed that it was imperative that American leaders develop a set of principles to guide their foreign policy, but, unlike Wilson, he advocated for the creation of a bipartisan coalition to support those principles. As it had been at the close of the Great War, the world in 1945 was battered, exhausted, horrified by the Holocaust and Hiroshima, and ready for a new world order. Underlying Fulbright's internationalism was the assumption that there existed a body of ideas and a constellation of economic and political institutions that together defined Western civilization, that the United States shared in these ideals and institutions, and that therefore it had an obligation to defend them. If it were true, he told the Senate, that Americans, Britons, Scandinavians, and Italians had in common "the love of family, the regard for contractual obligations, the abhorrence of torture and persecution, the distrust of tyrannical and oppressive government . . . then we should acknowledge them in order that a definite policy based upon sound considerations be firmly adopted."[4]

Fulbright was, like most internationalists, reacting to a particular interpretation of the immediate past, to what Gaddis Smith called a *great cycle theory of history*.[5] According to this view, the story of the twentieth century was largely a recurring pattern of American isolation, European aggression, and American intervention. It was up to the Greatest Generation to break this cycle. With the end of the struggle against the Axis impending, the United States and the world stood at a crossroads. The path selected would determine the shape of the future—tyranny or freedom, peace or annihilation. "We must," Fulbright told the George

Washington School of Law in 1943, "make this choice now while the minds and hearts of men are concerned with universal and fundamental problems, while danger and sacrifice give us humility and understanding." When the war ended, isolationists would sing their siren song once again, but the American people must turn a deaf ear. It was the nation's duty "to wage a creative war for a creative peace."[6]

Time and again, the former Rhodes scholar tried to demonstrate that isolationism was merely a facet of old-fashioned nationalism. Those of his contemporaries who posed as defenders of national sovereignty were in fact advocating a return to the policies of the interwar period, when the United States refused to acknowledge that its fate was tied up with those of other democracies. National sovereignty and its corollary foreign policy—unilateralism—were illusions in the modern world of airplanes, submarines, atomic weapons, and global economic integration. "If it means anything today," he told his Senate colleagues, "sovereignty as applied to a state surely means that a state is sufficiently independent economically, politically, and physically to defend itself and provide for the security and happiness of its own people." In this turbulent world, he asked, "can it be seriously contended that the vast majority of existing states are sovereign powers?"[7]

Initially, Fulbright's view of America's mission in the world took on the same messianic and parochial characteristics as Wilson's missionary diplomacy. In his early speeches, Fulbright argued that America must help other nations develop their own version of democracy. Implicit in this view was the assumption that, given the freedom to choose, all people would opt for a society characterized by popular sovereignty, individual liberty, the rule of law, and free enterprise. By late 1945, however, the junior senator from Arkansas seemed to be developing a sense of cultural relativity. He observed to the Senate that capitalism was not "divine and inviolable, something handed down by the Almighty from above."[8] It had worked for America because a particular set of circumstances and material conditions prevailed at a particular time in history. The peoples of the earth should be free to develop their own economic systems and political institutions.

But the principle of national self-determination would not in and of itself preserve the world from the deadly cycle of aggression and war. Something more was needed. What Fulbright had in mind was a new experiment in world government. In one remarkable address to the Foreign Policy Association in New York, he declared that the progress and welfare of modern humanity depended on the simultaneous and synchronized advance of technology and statecraft. While technology had produced machines that could fly above the earth and cruise beneath the sea and weapons that could destroy whole cities in the blinking of an eye, there had been no new developments in political theory and practice since the American and French Revolutions. The trend in economics had been toward larger and more complex units; the trend in government had not followed suit. What the freshman senator had in mind was an authentic international federation run on democratic principles. In a speech to the American Bar Association, he outlined his grand scheme: "The history of government over the centuries, which is largely the chronicle of man's efforts to achieve freedom by the control of arbitrary force, indicate [sic] that only by the collective action of a dominant group can security be obtained."[9] The hope of the world was the establishment of a global organization with a collective security mandate and a police-keeping force sufficient to enforce that mandate. The United States must participate and be willing to contribute to such a force. Participation required—indeed, necessitated—surrender of a portion of the national sovereignty. Once the UN Charter was ratified, it should be clearly understood that, through his delegate, the president would have the authority to commit American troops to military action authorized by the Security Council. Hopefully, would-be aggressors would be deterred by the mere existence of such a mechanism. Like Wilson, Fulbright believed that participation in international organizations had in and of itself a modernizing, civilizing effect on its participants. Moreover, was it not better to cooperate with the superpowers of the future, Russia and China, while they were still relatively weak? "It seems clear to me," he told an Arkansas audience in 1944, "that either we cooperate with Russia and the other nations in a system to preserve peace or we must look forward to a time when, in a chaotic world of warring nations we may have to compete for survival with an industrialized Russia of 250,000,000, or a China of 450,000,000."[10] To those of his conservative constituents who complained that the proposed world organization was so much globaloney, Fulbright argued that international cooperation was essential if the free enterprise system were to be preserved. Without a collective security organization, America would be forced to fight one costly war after another or at least be prepared to do so. This would require huge defense budgets and the regimentation of the economy. In such an environment, bureaucracy and red tape would choke the private sector to death.

J. William Fulbright was an economic as well as a political internationalist; that is, he, along with his friend Will Clayton, was a thoroughgoing multilateralist. Clayton, the Houston cotton broker Franklin Roosevelt appointed assistant secretary of state for economic affairs in 1944, was to be the chief architect of the Marshall Plan. These intellectual heirs of Adam Smith looked forward to the creation of an economically interdependent world free of tariffs, preferences, quotas, and currency exchange controls. They insisted that competition for the wealth of the world among national economies protected by high tariff walls restricted trade, wasted resources, and bred war. The multilateralists looked forward to the creation of a world market in which the citizens of each region concentrated on the commodities that they could produce most cheaply and efficiently. This specialization, coupled with the elimination of trade barriers, would mean the manufacture and distribution of the greatest number of goods at the cheapest possible price. To this end, Fulbright helped lead the fight in the Senate in 1945 for approval of the Bretton Woods Agreements, which established the World Bank and the IMF.

It was, of course, Fulbright's fate to experience the same disappointment and disillusionment that Woodrow Wilson had experienced in 1919 and 1920. In reality, neither FDR nor Harry Truman was committed to internationalism as either Woodrow Wilson or J. William Fulbright defined it. FDR was a devotee of realpolitik. His pet scheme for ensuring peace and prosperity in the postwar world had been the Four Policemen concept, in which the United States, Russia, China, and Great Britain kept the peace in their respective spheres of interest. Roosevelt, always the astute politician, had become a convert to internationalism in name only. In truth, as it turned out, the UN Security Council was nothing more than the Five Policemen (France having been awarded a permanent seat on the council) in internationalist clothing. At the UN Conference on International Organization (UNCIO) held in San Francisco in the spring of 1945, the attendees created an organization in which the great powers had the right of absolute veto, while Article 52 permitted regional alliances, and matters deemed purely internal were exempted from UN action. Fulbright watched with growing alarm as the United States refused to offer the Soviets a convincing strategy for the internationalization of atomic energy and supported the admission of Argentina, whose authoritarian governments had collaborated with the Axis. The rapid development of the Cold War, with the division of Europe and the communization of China, was a nightmare come true for him. Fulbright enthusiastically supported the Marshall Plan but voted for the Truman Doctrine only reluctantly, seeing it as potential overreach by the United States, a policy that would open the door to alliances with repressive and corrupt regimes in the name of fighting communism.

It was at this juncture that the idea of an international exchange program to train an educated and enlightened elite began to take shape in Fulbright's mind. On May 24, an Arkansas acquaintance of Fulbright's stationed in San Francisco wrote, bemoaning the tendency of the American delegation to the UNCIO to "operate like the backstage of a country convention." The friend, Lieutenant Commander Bernal Seamster, accused the United States of "playing up to the conflict between the capitalistic and communistic system on all sides" and blamed this tendency on "the lack of understanding and knowledge of the conditions other than in their own circle." The solution to the problem, he concluded, "might well be for the federal government to sponsor a major exchange of students from this country to other countries, and from other nations to our own colleges, universities, and trade schools," suggesting a minimum of 100,000 students each year.[11] That was an idea that Fulbright had been formulating in his own mind, and he responded enthusiastically. "Your views are in complete agreement with my own," he replied. "Your suggestion about the exchange of students is a very appropriate one."[12]

The Limits to International Activism: Fulbright as Critic

In 1959, after ten years as a member of the Senate Foreign Relations Committee (SFRC), Fulbright became its chairman and would remain so until his exit from the Senate in 1974. As such, he became not just a theorist and a debater but a partner in US foreign policy making. His commitment to liberal internationalism would lead him at first to support US involvement in Vietnam, but then as America assumed direct control of the conflict—in the process allying itself with a series of corrupt, autocratic military dictatorships—he became its most devastating critic. The activist foreign policies of the post–World War II era that produced the war in Southeast Asia were a product of the melding of conservative anti-Communists who defined national security in terms of bases and alliances and were basically xenophobic and liberal reformers who were determined to safeguard the national interest by exporting democracy and facilitating overseas economic development. Products of World War II, these internationalists saw America's interests as being tied up with those of the other members of the global community. They opposed communism because it constituted a totalitarian threat to the principles of cultural diversity, individual liberty, and self-determination that they hoped would prevail at home and abroad. Moreover, as a number of historians have pointed out, in the overheated atmosphere of the early Cold War period, anticommunism was a political necessity for liberals, whose views on domestic issues made them ideologically suspect. For them, the war in Vietnam was nothing less than a crusade to extend the blessings of democracy and individual liberty and guarantee stability and prosperity to a people threatened by the forces of Sino-Soviet imperialism.

Fulbright was initially not unhappy with the activist foreign policies of the Kennedy-Johnson administration. Its foreign policy team, composed as it was of classically educated foreign policy intellectuals, seemed a welcome change from the perceived vacuousness of the Eisenhower administration. Kennedy and Johnson—at least when the latter assumed the presidency—seemed committed to containing communism within its existing boundaries through alliance systems, foreign aid, and support for the non-Communist revolutionary Left in the developing world. Effective resistance against the forces of international communism involved not only military strength, JFK told the Senate in June 1961, but also a willingness to help developing nations "toward the fulfillment of their own highest purposes." The Arkansan was impressed. Noting that the principal Cold War antagonists were then focusing on the underdeveloped and newly emerging nations, Fulbright insisted that America's greatest contribution to the struggle was not "our affluence, or our plumbing, or our clogged freeways," but its values, "liberty and individual freedom . . . international peace, law and order, and constructive social purpose."[13] Following the Cuban Missile Crisis of 1962, both Kennedy and Johnson, with the SFRC chairman's enthusiastic support, pursued a policy of détente with the Soviet Union. In the spring of 1964, Fulbright delivered his famous "old myths and new realities" speech on the floor of the Senate. He declared that coexistence with the Soviet Union and even Fidel Castro was possible. He called for a realistic reassessment of US policy toward Latin America and the Far East, one based on the recognition that there were limits to American power and pressing domestic needs that demanded attention. In anticipation of the inevitable overthrow of "feudal oligarchies" in Latin America, the United States should consider opening communications with the revolutionary movements that would replace them. It should be ready to adopt a "more flexible attitude" toward Communist China and, indeed, the entire Communist world.[14] Treating different Communist countries differently would encourage diversity and independence that would inevitably work to America's advantage. As chair of the SFRC, Fulbright had shepherded the Tonkin Gulf Resolution through Congress in 1964 believing that it would strengthen LBJ's hand in his presidential contest with Barry Goldwater. But then in 1965 the Johnson administration unilaterally intervened in the Dominican Republic to block a left-leaning faction from coming to power and, at the same time, began a massive escalation of the war in Vietnam. In February 1966, Fulbright chaired a series of televised hearings on Vietnam that marked the beginning of a relentless crusade on his part to erode the consensus supporting the war.

Over the next two years Fulbright came to the conclusion that the war in Vietnam was essentially a civil war and that the United States was simply supporting one side against the other. And he was increasingly convinced that it was supporting the wrong side. The Communist insurgency in the South, he declared, was chiefly a response to the repressive policies of the Saigon government and its American ally. Johnson and his lieutenants claimed to be fighting for economic and social justice in South Vietnam and for the principle of national self-determination. But, like Wilson in Mexico, Johnson in Vietnam was enabling Ho Chi Minh and the National Liberation Front to cry Yankee imperialism and pose as the champions of Vietnamese nationalism. Whether the Second Indochinese War was a case of blind anticommunism or liberal internationalism gone terribly wrong, it had to be stopped.

Appalled by the carnage in Vietnam, the conversion of hundreds of thousands of sedentary villagers into homeless refugees, and the inability of the United States to raise up and work through any sort of broadly based political system in South Vietnam, Fulbright launched a devastating critique of American foreign policy. Addressing the Cold War interventionists— former isolationists who believed that, if America could not hide from the world, it would have to dominate it—he declared the war to be a monstrous strategic error. The domino theory had never been proved. Whenever a great power threatened to dominate a particular region, a coalition had always emerged to challenge it, regardless of ideological considerations. It just might be necessary, Fulbright suggested, for the United States to accept the legitimacy of an independent, nationalist, and united Vietnam, even one with a Marxist-Leninist government.

Implicit in Fulbright's philosophy of containment, developed in the late 1940s and early 1950s, was the notion that revolutions inevitably pass through stages, moving from an initial totalitarian, radical stage toward Thermidorean moderation. During his spring 1966 speaking tour, he reread Crane Brinton's *Anatomy of Revolution*.[15] Using that study of the French Revolution as a model, he argued that the Chinese Revolution, and, by extension, communism in Vietnam, would inevitably moderate. Like other revolutionary societies, China would become a "more or less normal society with a more or less normal relation with the outside world."[16]

Analogies from Thucydides's history of the Peloponnesian War, absorbed during his years at Oxford, continued to haunt the chairman of the SFRC. Decrying the Johnson administration's huge military budget and the militarization of American foreign policy, Fulbright told a joint congressional committee in 1967: "Contrary to the traditions which have guided our nation since the days of the Founding Fathers, we are in grave danger of becoming a Sparta bent on policing the world." But modern American imperialism—*welfare imperialism* Fulbright called it—was particularly pervasive and virulent because it combined militarism with idealism. America had decided to export its Athenian ideals using Spartan means. The United States, he told a college audience at Storrs, Connecticut, would have to decide which of the two sides of its character would prevail—"the humanism of Lincoln or the aggressive moralism of Theodore Roosevelt."[17] *The arrogance of power, the tragedy of American foreign policy, myth and reality in Soviet-American relations*—those and other phrases in Fulbright's rhetoric underscored his disillusionment with liberal internationalism. In the heat of war, frustrated by the nation's inability to win a clear-cut victory, Congress and the American people were deferring to an avaricious executive captivated by a burgeoning military-industrial complex whose existence was justified on the grounds that it was bringing social justice, a higher standard of living, and responsive government to those peoples of the world threatened by international communism.[18]

The Persistence of Old Myths

History does not repeat itself, but sometimes it comes awfully close. Where, some observers are beginning to ask, was the Second Gulf War's Bill Fulbright? In the wake of 9/11, the United States assaulted Iraq in the name of eliminating nonexistent weapons of mass destruction (shades of the Gulf of Tonkin incident), but the true motive was to establish a US base in the heart of the Middle East from which the Pentagon could project American power. Once it found that a large number of Iraqis viewed US soldiers as oppressive occupiers rather than selfless liberators, the Bush administration embraced nation building, a concept George W. and his advisers had derided during the 2000 election. The Bush-Cheney-Rumsfeld version of liberal internationalism harked back to the early Wilson and the missionary impulse that led to the disastrous Mexican policy of 1913–1916 and LBJ's tragic foray into Southeast Asia. Unlike his father, George W. acted unilaterally; he overthrew an autocrat who was a principal barrier against the expansion of Iranian Shia extremism and then attempted to reconstruct an occupied Iraq with no plan and no knowledge of Iraqi history or culture. One could almost hear Bill Fulbright weeping in frustration.

Notes

1. John Ikenberry, *The End of the West? Crisis and Change in the Atlantic Order* (Ithaca, NY: Cornell University Press, 2008), 1 (Bush quote), 7, 9 (Jervis quote).

2. Quoted in Thomas J. Knock, *To End All Wars: Woodrow Wilson and the Quest for a New World Order* (Princeton, NJ: Princeton University Press, 1992), 27.

3. George Herbert Gunn, "The Continuing Friendship of James William Fulbright and Ronald McCallum," *South Atlantic Quarterly* 83, no. 4 (1984): 417–19. See also Ronald B. McCallum, *Public Opinion and the Lost Peace* (Oxford: Oxford University Press, 1944).

4. *Congressional Record*, Senate, March 28, 1945, 2898.

5. Ibid., 2895.

6. Ibid.

7. Ibid.

8. Ibid., 2899.

9. Ibid., Senate, November 2, 1945, A4652–A46523.

10. Ibid., House, January 26, 1944, A412.

11. Seamster to Fulbright, May 24, 1945, BCN 24, F32, SPF, J. William Fulbright Papers, Special Collections, University of Arkansas.

12. Fulbright to Seamster, May 26, 1945, BCN 24, F32, SPF, Fulbright Papers.

13. *Congressional Record*, Senate, June 29, 1961, 11703–5.

14. Ibid., Senate, March 25, 1964, 6227–31.

15. Crane Brinton, *The Anatomy of Revolution* (New York: Vintage, 1938).

16. *Congressional Record*, Senate, March 25, 1964, 6227–31.

17. Ibid., Senate, March 25, 1966, 6749.

18. See Randall Bennett Woods, *Fulbright: A Biography* (Cambridge: Cambridge University Press, 1995), 418.

The Power of the One-Party South in National Politics

Segregation in the Career of J. William Fulbright

Neal Allen

As Senator J. William Fulbright was joining the segregationist filibuster to block open housing legislation in March 1968, he received a letter from an admiring Staten Island, New York, resident who found his positions on foreign and domestic issues inconsistent: "I and so many of my friends have been tremendously impressed over the years with your visions on foreign policy. Your 'Arrogance of Power' was especially influential. We are beginning to feel very disturbed by your civil rights record. We cannot understand one face to the world and one face to your fellow Americans."[1] This discordance that Fulbright's liberal, usually out-of-state, admiring correspondents noted was at the core of his power and influence. Fulbright could occupy the chairmanship of the Senate Foreign Relations Committee and use that position to criticize President Johnson's Vietnam policy only because he was a consistent supporter of segregation. In the one-party South, his only vulnerability was on the issue of race. Arkansas voters appreciated his relative moderation on domestic issues and consistently supported him and his Senate colleague John McClellan in bringing federal spending to Arkansas. Even if he had endorsed federal government action to support racial equality, his room to maneuver on racial issues would have been sharply limited. The political history of Arkansas, as his correspondence on civil rights shows, was one of his main sources of strength in maintaining his position as chairman of the Senate Foreign Relations Committee. The alternative was a different segregationist senator from Arkansas and a different committee chair.[2]

Fulbright's tenure as chairman encompassed much of the Cold War, and his opposition to the escalation of the Vietnam War added an establishment voice to the national peace movement. This cosmopolitan agenda, however, existed alongside his support for southern regional inegalitarianism on matters of race. Throughout the popular campaign for civil rights, Fulbright remained a loyal son of the white South and an integral part of the opposition to nondiscrimination legislation. These two incongruous commitments—to a balanced and vigorous American engagement abroad and to the continued subjugation of African Americans at home—worked together to produce the unique and consequential Fulbright legacy.

Fulbright served alongside nonsouthern senators, but he was the product of a political system fundamentally different from the modern two-party competition that characterized national and nonsouthern regional politics. He never faced significant general election opposition as the Republican Party was a nonentity in Arkansas during most of his career. The southern Democratic Party that supported Fulbright encompassed a wide variety of issue positions and representative types, as long as all its members supported and protected the system of racial exclusion in the region. Membership in this reactionary faction of the Democratic Party allowed for the accumulation of seniority and power. Elected Democrats like Fulbright were only potentially vulnerable in the Democratic primary. Until the post–civil rights movement transformation that occurred at the end of Fulbright's time in the Senate, such a challenge could come only from segregationists like Governor Orval Faubus and the grassroots populace that supported him. These local forces worked against his relative moderation and posed the most serious threat to his political career. His seminal contribution to international politics therefore emerged from this highly localized politics of race.

J. William Fulbright maintained a perfect anti-integration voting record in Congress from his first election to the House in 1942 until 1970, when he first deviated from the segregationist line with his vote to extend the Voting Rights Act (VRA). Prior to that moment of personal history, he had voted against the Civil Rights Acts of 1957, 1960, 1964, and 1968 and against the 1965 VRA. He was an active participant in various filibusters of nondiscrimination legislation between 1948 and 1964 and signed the Southern Manifesto of 1956. His only betrayal of the segregationist position was when he declined to join the doomed filibuster of the

1965 VRA, even though he voted against it on final passage. When the VRA came up for reauthorization in 1970 and for the first time he confronted an electorate with large numbers of black voters, he cast his only pro–civil rights vote in over three decades of public service. Otherwise, he stood with staunch segregationists such as James Eastland of Mississippi and Richard Russell of Georgia.

This essay analyzes the role of southern racial politics in the career and work of J. William Fulbright. The politics of the one-party Democratic South both empowered and limited his work as a liberal internationalist policy actor on the world stage. His adherence to segregationist politics and his support for the anti-integrationist project enhanced his influence within Congress. It even enabled him to rise to a position of national and international influence and maintain that position for a record period of time.

The Regional Foundations of National Power

The Arkansas that launched Fulbright onto the national stage in the 1940s was firmly a part of the one-party Democratic South. Republicans were not competitive in congressional or statewide elections. Even when the other states in the peripheral South—Florida, North Carolina, Tennessee, Texas, and Virginia—voted for the Republican Herbert Hoover, Arkansas stayed Democratic. In his classic 1949 study *Southern Politics in State and Nation*, V. O. Key argued that the state was an example of "pure one-party politics," with the pivotal Democratic primary organized around shifting factional alignments and the personal votaries of prominent politicians.[3]

While this Democratic dominance traced its lineage to post–Civil War white supremacist politics and continued to protect legal and customary segregation, Arkansas politics seemed to lack the stridency and racial demagoguery that characterized the politics of other states. Key found that "Arkansas—a state with relatively few Negroes, about one person in four—has no inexorable law that drives many of its political leaders to cap their careers by hysteria on the race question."[4] Fulbright's native northwest Arkansas was even further removed from militant segregationism, with the lowest black population in the state owing to its terrain, which was not conducive to plantation agriculture and thus did not host large enslaved populations before the Civil War. Unlike the mountainous Appalachian regions of other southern states like Tennessee or Virginia, however, the Ozarks of Arkansas did not support a Republican political tradition. Thus, when Fulbright won the 1942 Democratic primary for the US House on the strength of his mother's political influence and notoriety as a former president of the University of Arkansas, he could look forward to continued easy general election victories.

Fulbright's rather urbane segregationism would be tested in his first run for the US Senate. His adherence to segregation and white supremacy was challenged as he was portrayed as a supporter of integration. As the candidate of the relatively progressive faction led by former governor Carl Bailey, his chief rival was then governor Homer Adkins, who attacked Fulbright as a "nigger lover," and whose campaign distributed literature linking him to African Americans accused of being Communists.[5] The congressman responded by affirming his support for white-only political institutions and black inferiority, stating, during an election tour in the Delta region of eastern Arkansas: "I am not for Negro participation in our primary elections, and I do not approve of social equality." This rhetorical support for segregation, linked with an attempt to focus on foreign policy, was a persistent pattern in Fulbright's political career.

In the years before *Brown v. Board of Education* (1954) and the 1957 Little Rock integration crisis, this subtle strategy was a common means to gain statewide office. The same can be said about the initial victories of another midcentury Arkansan of national political stature, Governor Orval Faubus. Faubus also hailed from northwest Arkansas, although from a poverty-stricken rural area instead of the college town of Fayetteville. Rather than foreign policy, he focused on economic populism to defeat the business-friendly Governor Frank Cherry in 1954. This populist slant, combined with the required rhetorical fealty to segregation, remained a consistently successful strategy across the region.[6] Faubus was a relative moderate on racial issues, appointing black citizens to the Democratic Party state committee and even giving an "Arkansas Traveler" award to Daisy Bates, the state chair of the National Association for the Advancement of Colored People (NAACP). The militant segregationist state senator Jim Johnson unsuccessfully challenged Faubus's reelection in 1956. Faubus secured a victory thanks to huge majorities in his relatively moderate northwest Arkansas home district. As the political success of

Faubus and Fulbright both showed, moderate segregationism proved to be a winning strategy in Arkansas.

The racial politics of the region soon changed. When, in 1957, the federal district court ordered that the public Little Rock Central High School must admit black students, both Faubus and Fulbright gained new political incentives.[7] Faubus would transform himself from an economic populist and racial moderate into the most prominent national defender of segregation. By calling out the Arkansas National Guard to prevent integration, he made himself invulnerable to segregationist challenge and dominated state politics for a decade. The popular governor, who served until 1966, considered running against Fulbright in 1962, causing Attorney General Robert Kennedy and the powerful Democratic Oklahoma senator Robert Kerr to intervene personally to persuade Faubus to forgo the challenge and accept reelection as governor instead.[8] In 1967, Faubus continued to play maverick in national Democratic Party politics as he made his intention of running against Fulbright in 1968 public, criticizing the senator as a supporter of North Vietnam.[9] Throughout the 1960s, he served as a kind of demagogic segregationist challenger-in-waiting, a lurking threat to Fulbright's legislative power.

Fulbright took a different tack. While he was always a dependable vote against antilynching bills and the Federal Employment Protection Commission, he nevertheless exposed Arkansas to the nation as much as Faubus did, thanks to his rise to prominence in the Senate in 1956 and 1957. First, the Southern Manifesto of 1956 forced southern congressmen and senators either to sign a document arguing for a state's right under the federal constitution to segregate or to refuse to sign and risk electoral defeat. While initially uneasy with the stridency of the manifesto, Fulbright nevertheless dutifully signed the document after securing mainly cosmetic changes. Anthony Badger argues that, unlike several southern House members and Tennessee senator Albert Gore, Fulbright was following his electoral incentives even when they were discordant with his national and international progressive reputation:

> The news that Fulbright had signed the Manifesto disappointed many of those in the North and outside the US who admired his internationalist politics and his courageous stand against Joe McCarthy. His explanation, which he never disavowed, was: first,

that he had signed reluctantly and only after securing changes to the Manifesto that toned down the initial intemperate drafts; second, that he had no political alternative but to sign, otherwise he would have faced certain defeat; and third, that he was no racist and that the Manifesto was consistent with his doctrine of gradualism, promoting change in race relations through gradual economic and educational change rather than through legislative or judicial fiat.[10]

Faubus, still in the initial stages of his shift toward militant segregationism, came to Washington to lobby (ultimately successfully) the two more racially moderate members of Arkansas's House delegation, Brooks Hays and James Trimble, to sign the manifesto. Standing alone as a nonsigner would have left Fulbright running for reelection in 1958 as a symbol of capitulation to an unpopular Supreme Court.

When the Little Rock crisis thrust Arkansas into the international limelight in September 1957, Fulbright declined to play an active role in defusing racial tensions. He was in Europe when white mobs were preventing black children from attending Central High School. On his return, he did call for a return to social order, but he did not explicitly call for obeying the district court order to integrate. Only after he bested the segregationist James Johnson in the 1958 Democratic primary did he enter the Little Rock debate and only as a lawyer filing an amicus curiae brief with the Supreme Court in the *Cooper v. Aaron* (1958) case, in which the state of Arkansas challenged the decision of a federal appeals court that Central High School must proceed with desegregation immediately. He argued that the Court should reinstate a lower court ruling giving the state three years to prepare for integration, on the grounds that such a cooling-off period could lead to a reduction in tensions and peaceful compliance. The Court rejected the arguments of Arkansas and its senator, ruling that integration must proceed immediately. Fulbright's hope for gradual voluntary integration was not borne out by the next few years in the South, with significant public school integration occurring only after the 1964 Civil Rights Act empowered the federal government to intervene directly in school desegregation litigation.

Fulbright found further validation of his continued support of segregation in the defeat of the Democratic congressman Brooks Hays in 1958.

A reluctant signer of the Southern Manifesto, Hays was a consistent supporter of national Democratic priorities on nonracial issues. Representing
Little Rock, he attempted to mediate a resolution to the 1957 integration
crisis by arranging a meeting between Faubus and President Eisenhower.
His apparent moderation triggered a backlash in the increasingly acrimo-
nious racialized politics of the region after *Brown*. Thomas Alford waged
an explicitly segregationist write-in campaign against Hays, connecting
him to Eisenhower's use of federal troops to support judicial integration
orders, and criticized his chairmanship of the national Southern Baptist
Convention for the group's support of black rights. The highly unusual
write-in defeat of an incumbent congressman put others like Fulbright on
notice. Segregationist credibility was a necessary condition to continued
incumbency.[11]

Acquiring and Maintaining Influence over Foreign Policy

Having emerged electorally unscathed from the Little Rock crisis, Fulbright rose at the age of fifty-four to the chairmanship of the Senate Foreign Relations Committee in February 1959. The Democrats had just
gained sixteen seats, giving them a sizable majority. Their party had now
won a majority of nonsouthern Senate seats, but their overall majority was
unassailable because of their advantage of twenty-two to none in the
South. Since at that time the Senate granted committee chairmanships
reflexively to the member of the committee from the majority party with
the most years of continuous committee service, as long as Fulbright
remained the Democratic nominee for his seat, his position was assured.
He would serve as chairman of the Senate Foreign Relations Committee
for sixteen years, from 1959 to 1975, encompassing eight congresses. Until
his Democratic primary loss to Dale Bumpers in 1974, he avoided the
variability and broader accountability of partisan elections. As long as he
could avoid a segregationist challenge in the primary, he would remain
the senior Democrat on Foreign Relations.

The one-party electoral system of the South protected Fulbright and
other southern committee barons like Richard Russell, James Eastland,
and Harry Byrd from ever losing an election and thus their position of
national influence. The workings of competitive elections outside this

regional zone of noncompetitiveness increased the power of conservative southerners, eliminating those who might have ranked ahead in seniority. Table 1 lists nonsouthern Democrats who lost reelection prior to 1958 and were under eighty years old when Fulbright took the gavel. This sorting yields seven possible chairs in 1959. Six were defeated by Republicans, and Claude Pepper was defeated in a primary by the more conservative George Smathers. Four (Lee, Pepper, Lucas, and Duffy) would also have been likely chairs in 1967 when Fulbright began to oppose President Johnson's escalation of the Vietnam War publicly.

Having been elected to the Senate in 1944, Fulbright was thus immune to the Republican electoral landslides of 1946, 1950, and 1966. He benefited from the prior Republican landslide of 1938, which eliminated two potential chairs. His adherence to segregation and to conservative regional norms also protected him from the kind of right-wing primary challenge that defeated Pepper in 1950. To borrow categories from Great Britain, it was as if his seat was in the House of Lords but his rivals had to rise through the House of Commons. But, in the civil rights–era United States, the House of Lords equivalent was open only to segregationist southerners.

The work of Fulbright on Foreign Relations—especially his criticism of Vietnam policy—is the rare example of a liberal and progressive policy benefiting from the South's dominance of committee chairs. On domestic

Table 1. Defeated Democratic Members of Senate Foreign Relations Committee (SFRC) Pre-1959

Name	On SFRC	Defeated	Born	Died	Age, January 1959	Age, January 1967
Lee (OK)	1941	1942	1892	1967	68	74
Tydings (MD)	1949	1950	1890	1961	66	Dead
Pepper (FL)	1937	1950	1900	1989	58	66
Lucas (IL)	1945	1950	1892	1968	66	74
Gillette (IA)	1939	1944, 1954	1879	1973	79	87
Duffy (WI)	1933	1938	1892	1979	66	74
Bulkley (OH)	1933	1938	1880	1965	78	Dead

policy, the growth of the welfare state and civil rights legislation were sty-
mied by conservative Democrats like Senator James Eastland of Missis-
sippi on Judiciary and Representatives Howard Smith of Virginia on
Rules and Fulbright's fellow Arkansan Wilbur Mills on Ways and Means.
It was only through creative legislative maneuvering by House speaker
Sam Rayburn and President Lyndon Johnson, combined with the landslide of new nonsouthern liberal Democrats in 1964, that made possible
Great Society legislation. On Foreign Affairs, the opposite effect occurred:
Fulbright was protected from right-wing defeat by his good standing as a
southern segregationist Democrat. While fellow Vietnam War critics Earnest Gruening (D-AK) and Wayne Morse (D-OR) were going down to
defeat in 1968, Fulbright won his primary by 19 percent and his general
election by 18 percent. The power of the Arkansas Democratic Party, with
Fulbright as a member in good standing, was evident in his 59 percent
vote total in the general election, nearly equaling the combined 61 percent
of the Republican and Democratic presidential candidates in 1968. The
most hawkish region would still support "Dixie's Dove."

While support for southern segregation empowered Fulbright in Congress, it also complicated his movement into the executive branch. With
the election of fellow Democratic senator John F. Kennedy to the presidency in 1960, Fulbright appeared a perfect candidate for secretary of
state. His record of academic achievement paralleled that of the new president, and his established credibility as part of the foreign policy elite
would balance Kennedy's youth and relative inexperience. He had the
advantage over former Illinois governor and presidential candidate Adlai
Stevenson because he had not run a campaign against Kennedy for the
nomination. He also had the international status that career diplomats
like Chester Bowles and the eventual choice, Dean Rusk, did not possess.
But, while the liberal elements of the Democratic Party could stomach the
choice of Lyndon Johnson as the vice presidential candidate to hold the
South in the general election, a signer of the Southern Manifesto like Fulbright as secretary of state was a bridge too far after the election was over.

In his biography of Fulbright, Randall Woods details how the Arkansas senator emerged as the leading contender for secretary of state but was
blocked by critics of his civil rights record.[12] Outside pressure came from
NAACP leaders as well as United Auto Workers chief Walter Reuther.
Within the Kennedy inner circle, Robert Kennedy argued that Fulbright

would complicate efforts to retain the support of black voters who had swung the election to the Democrats. National liberals could not prevent the rise of segregationists like Fulbright or even of rabid race-baiters like James Eastland or Richard Russell to positions of power in Congress. Power in the Capitol flowed from seniority and state politics and was protected (at least until the onslaught of Johnson's Great Society) from the liberalism that was on the march in the national Democratic Party. But executive power could be denied to an otherwise eminently qualified and appropriate candidate like Fulbright.

While Fulbright, remaining in his chairmanship in the Senate, supported most of the Kennedy administration's agenda, he continued to part company with the Massachusetts liberal on civil rights. This split between parts of the Democratic coalition took on increased importance after the Birmingham demonstrations of 1963. Kennedy's impassioned televised address after the violent suppression of peaceful protest there and promotion of a strong civil rights bill to the top of his list of legislative priorities threatened continued southern regional autonomy on race. Fulbright continued to support filibusters of nondiscrimination legislation, as southern senators led by Richard Russell of Georgia attempted to block consideration of the bill that would become the 1964 Civil Rights Act. Fulbright would continue his opposition to nondiscrimination legislation when debate turned to housing, joining a successful filibuster of a strong open housing bill in 1966 and an unsuccessful filibuster of the weaker alternative that passed in 1968.

Fulbright and Citizen Opposition to Civil Rights

Fulbright's anti–civil rights legislative record was consistent with the opinions of his Arkansas constituents. While state-level polling was rare at the time, incoming correspondence from constituents reveals the force of statewide opinion. These letters show the increasingly vituperative perspectives that were driving citizen opinion on matters of race. Letters were also a readily available gauge of constituent opinion for legislators and their staff.[13] The public made it clear that the senator's popularity needed to rely on reactionary opinion in the state. As an Eldorado respondent put it, Fulbright needed to use his Senate leverage to "please stop that dangerous bill." "It would be the beginning of the end of the world," the letter concluded.[14]

In an interview with Randall Woods long after his departure from the Senate, Fulbright cast his record on racial issues as, in Woods's words, "a matter of political expediency." Focusing on his potential weakness outside his native northwest Arkansas, the retired senator argued that he lacked the opportunity to support integration and be reelected: "There's no mystery why the people from Georgia, Mississippi, and so on have been what they call bigots. They inherited an historical situation. You couldn't be elected if you didn't have that view. People in eastern Arkansas . . . couldn't see their daughter going to school with a black. They always imagined the black would rape their daughter. This was the worst possible thing. They were scared of them actually."[15] While Arkansans who wrote Fulbright usually did not put such fears of sexual violence in words, they validated his understanding of his electoral incentives. Of the 1,102 letters received by Fulbright concerning nondiscrimination legislation between 1963 and 1968, 976 (89 percent) opposed civil rights.[16] Not only did Fulbright's constituents overwhelmingly oppose nondiscrimination legislation; they did so on the basis of the belief that civil rights was a threat to fundamental American values.

Most letters connected opposition to nondiscrimination legislation to fundamental American values. Property and economic rights were prevalent as Fulbright's constituents focused on how the bill that would become the 1964 Civil Rights Act limited the rights of business owners and employers. One Little Rock resident asserted his opposition to the bill using a curious twist of the rhetoric on universal human rights: "Man should have the right to admit whomever *he wants* to his motel, restaurant, etc., even if he does lose the business because of this. It is a God-given right to refuse to serve somebody. Our constitution even protects us from it: the Thirteenth Amendment forbids 'slavery' and 'involuntary servitude.' If a person is forced to do something against his will, that is involuntary servitude."[17] The linkage of property rights to the Constitution was quite common. While not grounding his argument in specific constitutional language, a North Little Rock writer claimed that restrictions on business freedom infringed on constitutional rights: "We realize that a bill of this kind is unconstitutional and would destroy free enterprise—the one ingredient that has made this Country great. This Bill, if passed, instead of giving 'rights,' would take away personal liberty from all people."[18] The freedom of the business owner to choose his or her customers and to refuse to hire particular individuals is cast as a fundamental American liberty. If Fulbright wavered in his opposition to civil rights, his constituents would reevaluate his commitment to other values they found fundamental to American democracy.

The opposition to civil rights that motivated letter writers was not just an expression of issue positions. Constituents connected the fight over nondiscrimination legislation to Fulbright's position of influence in the Senate. The North Little Rock resident wrote: "With your seniority in Washington and the respect and influence that you command, we know that you can exert an unlimited force to defeat this Civil Rights Bill."[19] Fulbright's national role created an expectation that he could, and would, protect Arkansans from the threat posed by national prointegration legislation.

Letter writers also connected the civil rights bill to communism.[20] One McCrory resident argued: "If this Bill passes, we all will be like Russia and Cuba, then will be the beginning of tribulation our Bible tells about."[21] Not only would nondiscrimination legislation weaken America's opposition to communism; it would lead to the apocalyptic reckoning described in Revelation. An Eldorado resident concurred, imploring the senator: "Please stop that dangerous bill. It would be the beginning of the end of the world."[22]

While explicitly racist or white supremacist arguments were relatively rare in letters sent to Fulbright, a small fraction of writers who expressly discussed racial differences connected the opposition to nondiscrimination legislation to the segregationist backlash around the Little Rock school integrationist crisis of 1957. A Mt. Holly resident viewed the proposed legislation through the lenses of southern history and religiously derived racism: "This so called Civil Rights Bill is gradually to change into Civil War. Negroes aren't supposed to mix up with the white, the bible states so. Anyone knows this for a fact."[23] Such an expression of constituent opinion alerted Fulbright to the tenuousness of his electoral position if he departed from segregationist orthodoxy.

This virulent racism was expressed as unassailable truth. A writer from Osceola contended that civil rights action "will not make the Negro's skin white or make his hair straight or make him an A-1 citizen."[24] Another writer, from Mena, endorsed this apocalyptic biological determinism: "We must organize in force and fight to save our people from forced integration, mongrelization, degradation, sin and shame and to keep our beloved America from becoming a degraded mongrelized nation ruled by a communist dictator. I hope and pray that you and other good Senators will filibuster that rotten race mixing bill to death. We are counting on you Senator Fulbright, please don't let us down."[25]

Fulbright's seniority and the committee chairmanship that made him a power in world affairs were dependent on not letting down the white supporters of segregation who dominated the midcentury Arkansas electorate. If J. William Fulbright deserves credit for achievements like the scholar program that bears his name or his enlightened criticism of the escalation in Vietnam and other US misadventures around the globe, the southern segregationist one-party system must share in that credit as well. Fulbright emerged from a kind of Whiggish aristocracy, mostly protected from the threat of election defeat. A Republican could never beat him, and a Democrat could beat him only if he was seen as an opponent of segregation. Fulbright lost a race for reelection only after the emergence of New South politicians: Dale Bumpers would end the long career of the seasoned senator in 1974. For thirty years, Arkansas provided the foremost liberal internationalist in Congress. His power and stature, however, were built on the illiberal foundation of white supremacy.

Notes

1. Letter, March 8, 1968, Civil Rights Files, J. William Fulbright Papers, University of Arkansas Special Collections.

2. If Fulbright had been defeated for reelection in 1956, 1962, or 1968, the committee would have been headed by John Sparkman of Alabama, a strong proponent of the escalation of military action in Vietnam.

3. V. O. Key, *Southern Politics in State and Nation* (Knoxville: University of Tennessee Press, 1949).

4. Ibid., 183.

5. Randall Bennett Woods, *Fulbright: A Biography* (Cambridge: Cambridge University Press, 1995), 94.

6. See Earl Black, *Southern Governors and Civil Rights* (Cambridge, MA: Harvard University Press, 1976).

7. Anthony Badger, "The Forerunner of Our Opposition: Arkansas and the Southern Manifesto of 1956," *Arkansas Historical Quarterly* 56, no. 3 (Autumn 1997): 353–60, 358.

8. Woods, *Fulbright: A Biography*, 299–300.

9. "Faubus Says Fulbright Vulnerable," *Arkansas Democrat* (Little Rock), April 27, 1967.

10. Anthony Badger, "Southerners Who Refused to Sign the Southern Manifesto," *Historical Journal* 42, no. 2 (June 1999): 517–34.

11. See John Kyle Day, "The Fall of a Southern Moderate: Congressman Brooks Hays and the Election of 1958," *Arkansas Historical Quarterly* 59, no. 3 (Autumn 2000): 241–64.

12. Woods, *Fulbright: A Biography*, 255–59.

13. Letter writers are clearly not a representative group, those with strong opinions likely being overrepresented. They do, however, provide evidence of the content and relative strength of issue positions. Research on congressional behavior finds that members of Congress and their staffs believe that incoming correspondence reflects public opinion, irrespective of its inherent selection bias. See Douglas Harris and Amy Fried, "Governing with the Polls," *The Historian* 72, no. 2 (Summer 2010): 321–53.

14. Letter, May 16, 1963, Civil Rights Files, Fulbright Papers.

15. Woods, *Fulbright: A Biography*, 115.

16. This percentage is consistent with letters found in other southern collections of the period from the neighboring states of Texas, Louisiana, and Oklahoma. The percentage is consistent across the period as debate moved from employment and public accommodations in 1963–1964 to open housing in 1966–1968.

17. Letter, May 13, 1964, Civil Rights File, Fulbright Papers.

18. Letter, March 20, 1964, Civil Rights File, Fulbright Papers.

19. Ibid.

20. For a discussion of how the link between support for integration and communism was a regionwide concern for citizens, elites, and state governments, see Jeff R. Woods, *Black Struggle, Red Scare: Segregation and Anti-Communism in the South, 1948–1968* (Baton Rouge: Louisiana State University Press, 2003).

21. Letter, March 4, 1964, Civil Right File, Fulbright Papers.

22. Letter, May 16, 1963, Civil Right File, Fulbright Papers.

23. Letter, December 2, 1963, Civil Right File, Fulbright Papers.

24. Letter, March 20, 1964, Civil Right File, Fulbright Papers.

25. Letter, February 10, 1964, Civil Right File, Fulbright Papers.

J. William Fulbright on the US Senate Foreign Relations Committee

Foreign Policy Intellectual, Public Educator, Restrainer of Presidential Power

Frédérick Gagnon

The US Senate Foreign Relations Committee (SFRC) is one of the most prestigious and important committees on Capitol Hill.[1] Established in 1816 as "one of the original ten standing committees of the Senate,"[2] it has been the center of key congressional foreign policy debates and decisions over the last two hundred years. Various chairs of the SFRC have played a significant role in shaping US foreign policy since 1945. For instance, Arthur Vandenberg (D-MI) chaired the SFRC from 1947 to 1949 and was instrumental in helping President Truman secure the passage of the Truman Doctrine and the Marshall Plan at a time when isolationism was still a driving force on Capitol Hill.[3] More recently, Jesse Helms (R-NC), who chaired the SFRC during a highly polarized period (1995–2001), acted as a "foreign policy entrepreneur" determined to block President Clinton's initiatives (like the Kyoto Protocol and the Comprehensive Nuclear Test Ban Treaty) and to force the White House to accept conservative foreign policies such as the economic embargo on Cuba (the Helms-Burton Act of 1996).[4] However, when one considers that J. William Fulbright was a member of the SFRC from 1949 to 1975 and its longest-serving chair (from 1959 to 1975), one could argue that the senator from Arkansas easily ranks "among the upper house's influential members in its modern history"[5] and shaped the history of the SFRC like no other.

This essay examines the role and legacy of Fulbright as a member and chair of the SFRC. The senator's career has been documented extensively, and it would be a daunting task to highlight the many issues on which he was influential on Capitol Hill between 1949 and 1975.[6] He left his imprint on many key post-1945 international issues: the Marshall Plan budget extension of 1949, the Mutual Security Act, which launched a major US foreign aid program in 1951, the inclusion of Greece and Turkey in NATO in 1952, the Bricker Treaty Amendment debate of 1953 regarding congressional and presidential treaty powers, the 1955 Panama Treaty, which reaffirmed US influence in the Panama Canal, the Atomic Agency Treaty, which established the International Atomic Energy Agency in 1957, the 1960 Japanese Security Treaty, the proposed establishment of the Peace Corps by President Kennedy in 1961, the ratification of the Nuclear Test Ban Treaty in 1963, the deployment of US troops to the Dominican Republic in 1965, the establishment of the Arms Control Agency in 1968, the 1972 SALT Offensive Arms Agreement on American-Soviet armament control, and the 1973 Senate confirmation of Henry Kissinger as secretary of state.[7] Furthermore, he was among the most prominent voices in Washington on the war in Vietnam.

However, instead of telling an exhaustive story of his contribution to all these debates, this essay focuses on how Fulbright conceived of his role as a member and chair of the SFRC. Though his conception of his role evolved over the twenty years he sat on the committee, it seems fair to argue that three essential elements drove his action: he saw himself as a foreign policy intellectual and agenda setter, a public educator, and a restrainer of presidential power. This essay not only describes how he played these three roles. It also shows that one key aspect of his legacy as chair of the SFRC is that he used the public sphere more than any of his predecessors and immediate successors to try to influence US foreign policy. As such, he was not a textbook senator who limited his role to the activities that had been traditionally performed by US legislators (voting on bills, giving speeches on the Senate or House floors, making laws). He proved something that is still key to understanding how the SFRC and Congress work today: if a legislator wants to influence US foreign policy, he needs to be active not only inside Congress but also outside the walls of the Capitol. He needs to use his bully pulpit to try to affect how the American people see the world and rely on nonlegislative actions (media appearances, public speeches, public conferences, and the like) if he hopes to get noticed and actually make a difference.

Fulbright as a Foreign Policy Intellectual and Agenda Setter

As Fulbright noted in 1966: "The best way to assure the prevalence of truth over falsehood is by exposing all tendencies of opinion to free competition in the market place of ideas."[8] Accounts of his senatorial role and legacy often use the words *intellectual*[9] and *philosopher*[10] to highlight the fact that he had, to use a concept developed by Thomas Preston, a high degree of "cognitive complexity"[11] or, in other words, a pronounced curiosity and constant need for information about issues that mattered to him. He "never became intellectually curious" until he entered the University of Oxford in 1925, thanks to a Rhodes scholarship.[12] While he was an undergraduate student in history and political science, his tutor, the distinguished historian Ronald Buchanan McCallum, introduced him to the writings of Adam Smith and John Stuart Mill, among others.[13] He developed a passion for international relations during these years. As his biographer notes: "[Fulbright] became convinced . . . that the university had done for him what Cecil Rhodes intended that it do. He had been stretched intellectually and culturally. Fulbright would never be able to retreat into a cocoon of complacency. The march of civilizations across history had dazzled him. The complexities of other cultures and the rage of his tutors and his fellow students to learn about them left an indelible mark. Most important of all, those with whom he associated assumed that they were going to make a difference in the world."[14] This is exactly what Fulbright tried to do as a member and chair of the SFRC. Compared with other chairs of the committee of his time, he was "more studious," "more reflective," and spent "much more time in reading which others devote[d] to politicking and persuasion among their fellows."[15] Eleven years after he took the gavel of the SFRC, Senator Mike Mansfield of Montana compared him to his immediate predecessors (e.g., Tom Connally of Texas, Alexander Wiley of Wisconsin, and Theodore Green of Rhode Island) and concluded that he was "more knowledgeable, more interested and more concerned."[16] Another account argues that no man "since Henry Cabot Lodge brought such intellect, such vision, such ambition . . . to the position."[17]

Fulbright's high degree of "cognitive complexity" had a profound impact on his behavior on the SFRC. His strong desire to know more about international relations than most of his colleagues on Capitol Hill enabled Fulbright to challenge predominant foreign policy narratives that later came to be perceived as detrimental to US national interests. While he was a self-described bookworm at Oxford,[18] his SFRC chief of staff, Carl Marcy, notes that he never lost the habit of reading and of relying on intellectuals and professors to inform his views on current issues.[19]

The Vietnam example illustrates the habit. In interviews given to the historian Donald Ritchie, Marcy recalls that, at the end of 1964 and the beginning of 1965, Fulbright began to express doubts about US policy in Vietnam but did not feel he knew enough about the Far East to understand what was going on there clearly.[20] He thus directed Marcy to "pull information together" about the region, and gather books from the Library of Congress, usually French books about Indochina. He studied up on Vietnam and met with intellectuals such as Bernard Fall, a French-born expert on Southeast Asia who had made long trips to Vietnam in the 1950s and 1960s and repeatedly warned Washington about the complexities of the conflict and the risks of a military intervention.[21] According to Marcy, such meetings and his curiosity were among the key factors that led Fulbright to change his perspective on Vietnam.[22] Fulbright had supported Lyndon Johnson's decision to fight North Vietnam up until then, most famously by helping secure the passage of the Gulf of Tonkin Resolution in August 1964, which authorized the president to take "all necessary measures to repel any armed attacks against the forces of the United States and to prevent further aggression."[23] However, his study of the situation in Vietnam changed his views: he slowly became convinced that "the Vietnam War was not part of a Soviet world design, but was essentially a civil war."[24] Influenced by books such as Jean Lacouture's *Vietnam: Between Two Truces*, he felt the urge to challenge the Johnson administration's argument that the war was one of aggression, mounted by the North and the Soviet Union against the South.[25] He grew certain that Vietnam was a local conflict "whose roots were largely indigenous" and not fully understood in Washington, inside the White House in particular.[26] Blinded by their obsession with the Cold War, Johnson and his advisers had, in the senator's view, intervened for the wrong reasons in a war that could not be won.

Fulbright did not necessarily believe that Johnson did not have a great intellect. However, he thought that the president's decision to escalate the war in Vietnam illustrated an unfortunate tendency in Washington. As one account puts it, he argued that, through sheer intellectual slovenliness, "the nation and its leaders were unable to grasp the subtleties of world currents" and were guided by a "self-willed lack of nuance" that "raised the likelihood of relying on violent interventionism in a blind, misguided effort to shore up a presumably pro-American status quo."[27] He thus felt that he was better prepared to understand foreign policy issues than most other leaders, an attitude that sometimes drew the criticism that he was "intellectually arrogant."[28] Arrogant or not, he was certainly an elitist in the sense that he believed society should be led by its "most able" and "best prepared citizens"[29] or people who, like he himself, could bring "discernment and commitment to public affairs."[30] As the years passed, he developed the conviction that he was an intellectually gifted leader who should use his privileged position on the SFRC to try to set the agenda on issues on which he thought the United States was wandering like a lost soul, Vietnam first and foremost.

Just as Fulbright did, the academic literature on foreign policy agenda setting conceives of Washington as a marketplace of ideas in which myriad actors (the president, members of Congress, the media, think tanks, interest groups) rely on various strategies to try to influence US international priorities and "steer the discussion in a preferred direction."[31] The research of Ralph Carter and James Scott is among the best efforts to capture the different avenues by which members of Congress like Fulbright try to set the foreign policy agenda.[32] Carter and Scott discriminate between legislative and nonlegislative actions to highlight the "many ways for legislators to shape foreign policy." They argue that legislative actions "pertain to the passage of specific pieces of legislation," including legislation, appropriations, and treaties and votes on presidential appointments (both Senate responsibilities), while "nonlegislative actions do not involve a specific item of legislation" and can take the form of letters, phone calls, or person-to-person meetings with the president and/or members of his cabinet, public hearings, public speeches (inside and outside Congress), media appearances, public conferences, op-eds, or books.[33] Among these actions, all can be used to set the foreign policy agenda and steer national debates in one direction or another. For instance, a legislator can intro-

duce legislation in Congress to force the White House to pay more attention to an issue. Nonlegislative actions like television appearances or
public lectures can also be used to reach a similar goal.

Fulbright clearly understood how he could use his position on the
SFRC to try to set the foreign policy agenda. Furthermore, he relied on a
larger set of nonlegislative actions than had previous chairs of the SFRC.[34]
For instance, like Arthur Vandenberg, another key SFRC chair of the
post-1945 period, he relied on informal discussions with the president and
speeches in the Senate to make his views known inside the Beltway. More
particularly, Vandenberg and Fulbright advised Truman and Johnson,
respectively, on the best ways to secure Senate passage of the Truman
Doctrine and the Gulf of Tonkin Resolution. They also promoted these
same programs when they took the floor in the Senate and in the SFRC.[35]
However, one key aspect of Fulbright's legacy as chair of the SFRC is that
he seemed to understand more than any of his immediate predecessors
and successors how legislators can use the bully pulpit to try to influence
the American people. While the expression *bully pulpit* has usually been
used to describe how US presidents have taken advantage of the grandios-
ity of their office to appeal to public opinion and advocate for an agenda,[36]
Fulbright showed how the SFRC chair can, like the president, try to mold
the national mood by reaching out directly to the public. The SFRC chairmanship certainly is a less grandiose office than the US presidency. However, certain conjectures can make the public particularly attentive to the
discussions taking place on Capitol Hill, a growing popular sentiment
that the White House should change course, for instance.[37]

Vietnam gave Fulbright such an opportunity. The senator never fully
embraced the antiwar movement of the 1960s. As his biographer notes:
"He was much too conventional in his personal life to march or demonstrate, and he rejected draft card burnings, sit-ins, and other 'symbolic'
and frequently illegal forms of dissent." In the spring of 1966, convinced
that Johnson's escalation in Vietnam was a bad idea, he nonetheless
declared that there was wisdom, productivity, courage, decency, and
patriotism in the protest movement of students, professors, the clergy, and
intellectuals.[38] Having lost access to and influence with Johnson after he
gave a speech critical of the president's decision to launch a military intervention in the Dominican Republic, he still believed that he could feed
opposition to the war in Vietnam, set the Vietnam agenda, and force the

White House to reconsider his policy. As one account puts it: "[Fulbright] seized every opportunity afforded by his growing fame to rally opponents of the war and, in so doing, attempt to pressure the administration into a reversal of what he now regarded as an unrelieved disaster."[39]

At least four key nonlegislative tools were at the heart of this agenda-setting strategy.[40] First, Fulbright did what his academic background had taught him and what intellectuals often do: he published books. No SFRC chair has ever published more books than Fulbright did during his tenure. The Arkansan had already put out *Prospects for the West* in 1963, in which he encouraged President Kennedy to see the Soviet Union as the main threat to US national security.[41] This book was less critical of the White House than the ones that followed. It was published less than three years after Kennedy's election to the presidency, at a time when Fulbright was "excited about the new administration." Among the reasons that explain why Fulbright had a smoother relationship with Kennedy than he did with Johnson and Nixon, US difficulties in Vietnam were key. But he admired Kennedy for at least three other reasons. First, he saw him as an "educated" and "interested" president with a foreign policy vision similar to his (e.g., Kennedy believed that one key ingredient of the fight against communism was investment in educational, cultural, and economic development in the Third World). Second, he had played a key role in the composition of the Kennedy administration: he was responsible for the appointment of George Ball as undersecretary of state and had recommended many names to fill other key positions, such as Edwin Reischauer (ambassador to Japan) and Philip Stern (assistant secretary for congressional relations). Third, as his biographer notes, he had a "weakness for academics from prestigious institutions" and for intellectuals because of his own background as an academic. Kennedy's decision to surround himself with scholars like the historian Arthur Schlesinger (special assistant to the president) and John Kenneth Galbraith (ambassador to India) thus made Fulbright particularly sympathetic to this administration.[42]

However, as the titles *Old Myths and New Realities* (1964), *The Arrogance of Power* (1966), *The Pentagon Propaganda Machine* (1971), and *The Crippled Giant* (1972) show, Fulbright later relied on the books he wrote to express doubts and reservations about the executive branch and the choices made by the Johnson and Nixon administrations. For instance, he argued that US leaders look at the world in "moralistic rather than empirical terms" and are thus "predisposed to regard any conflict as a clash between good and evil rather than simply a clash between conflicting interests."[43] He also lamented that the war in Vietnam diverted US "energies from the Great Society program which began so promisingly,"[44] that the Pentagon's public relations campaign "directed at all of the American people" enabled the White House to propagandize in favor of dangerous policies like the escalation in Vietnam,[45] and that there was "no hope of either victory or peace" in Vietnam as long as the United States "continued to adhere to the war aims of Presidents Johnson and Nixon."[46]

The second nonlegislative tool used by Fulbright to set the foreign policy agenda was his public speech making, inside and outside the Senate. In one of his most famous speeches on the Senate floor, in September 1965, he argued that the US intervention in the Dominican Republic "was characterized by . . . overreaction[,] a lack of candor [and] exaggerated estimates of Communist influence in the rebel movement [based on] ambiguous evidence."[47] He emphasized similar themes in his Senate speeches on Vietnam. In July 1966, for instance, he challenged Johnson's policy, arguing that, in Vietnam, the United States was "fighting virtually alone and for undefined purposes in a war which is not an international conflict but an insurrection in one part of a divided country supported by the other part."[48]

His academic background also predisposed Fulbright to reach out to other intellectuals interested in foreign policy who could potentially embrace his agenda. For instance, he addressed a group of former Rhodes scholars at Swarthmore College in Pennsylvania in June 1965, faculty members and students at the University of Connecticut in March 1966, the American Newspaper Publishers Association in April 1966, and the American Bar Association in Hawaii in August 1967.[49] Some of the ideas he tested in his public lectures were later included in his books (e.g., his August 1967 address "The Price of Empire" certainly inspired the title of the conclusion of *The Crippled Giant* but also the title of another book he put out in 1989.[50]

The third nonlegislative tool with which Fulbright tried to set the foreign policy agenda was his frequent appearance in the media. Though he was able to reach his congressional colleagues and the country's intellectual elites with his public speeches inside and outside the Capitol, appearing in the media was a better way of exposing a larger public to his views.

He therefore published many op-eds in national newspapers and magazines. In April 1966, for instance, he wrote in the *Saturday Evening Post* that the United States should end the war and quickly negotiate peace in Vietnam.[51] A few months later, he lamented that Washington was relying on violence in the name of US imperial destiny in Southeast Asia while failing to end poverty at home.[52]

In addition to penning such articles, Fulbright thought that television was an ideal way in which to communicate directly with the American people. His ascension to the chairmanship of the SFRC coincided with a time when television was just starting to revolutionize American politics and the way in which politicians used this means of communication to attain their goals. While Kennedy was helped by his telegenic image and the contrast with Nixon on-screen during their famous 1960 debate,[53] Fulbright used television to gain a reputation as a foreign policy intellectual who could challenge narratives and policies he found detrimental to the nation.[54] During a *CBS News Special Report* broadcast on February 1, 1966, hosted by Eric Severeid and Martin Agronsky, he confessed his lack of judgment in the support he gave to the 1964 Gulf of Tonkin Resolution. As he put it: "At the time of the Bay of Tonkin I should have had greater foresight in the consideration of that resolution. That would have been a good time to have precipitated a debate and a reexamination and reevaluation of the involvement."[55] A few months later, in February 1968, shortly after the beginning of the Tet Offensive—an event that convinced many in Washington that the US effort in the region might be less successful than had previously been expected—he was a guest on the show *Issues and Answers* on the ABC network.[56] He took the occasion to announce to the American people that these new developments in Vietnam required public SFRC hearings aimed at completely reevaluating US policy in Southeast Asia.[57]

This is exactly what Fulbright did when he held SFRC hearings in February and March 1968 and invited his senatorial colleagues to discuss whether North Vietnam had attacked the USS *Maddox* in the Gulf of Tonkin and whether the decision to send out half a million American soldiers to the Vietnam jungle was justified.[58] Such hearings were the fourth type of nonlegislative tool he could use to try to change the national conversation about foreign policy issues that mattered to him. As he wrote in *The Arrogance of Power*: "To criticize one's country is to do it a service and pay it a compliment. It is a service because it may spur the country to do better than it is doing. . . . In a democracy dissent is an act of faith. . . . Criticism may embarrass the country's leaders in the short run but strengthen their hand in the long run."[59]

Fulbright as Public Educator

Fulbright's public SFRC hearings were not only aimed at raising doubts about US policy. The senator thought that they could also serve an educational purpose by fostering understanding of US foreign policy among the American people. Educating the public was one of the main purposes of what are now widely seen as some of the most important public hearings ever held by the SFRC: Fulbright's Vietnam hearings of January and February 1966.[60] As he explained in *The Arrogance of Power*: "I believe that the public hearings on Vietnam, by bringing before the American people a variety of opinions and disagreements pertaining to the war . . . , strengthened the country rather than weakened it."[61]

Fulbright believed that the SFRC chair should serve as a kind of public teacher and mentor. As one account of his legacy reminds us, his deep-rooted "faith in the power of education to solve our problems" explains many of the decisions he made during his senatorial career.[62] His conviction that the United States should create what is now called the Fulbright program—a government-sponsored exchange program enabling Americans to study or research abroad—not only stemmed from his perception that his Rhodes scholarship had had a transformative impact on him. It also originated from his belief that Americans in general did not know enough about the rest of the world and thus regularly supported ill-fated policies because of their prejudices and misconceptions regarding other countries and foreign peoples.[63]

The 1966 Vietnam hearings could serve this purpose. As one recollection puts it, Fulbright believed that education was one of the main responsibilities of the Senate, and he thought that the hearings were necessary to "inform the American people . . . about the implications of the war in Vietnam."[64] One of the factors that convinced him to hold the hearings was his belief that the Johnson administration's portrayal of the situation in Vietnam did not match accounts of troops on the ground and of journalists who had interviewed them.[65] When Secretary of State Dean Rusk addressed the issue of Vietnam at a closed SFRC hearing in January 1966 and told Fulbright and other members of the panel that a firm US commitment would eventually convince the Communists to give up in the region, the senator concluded that the Johnson administration probably painted a too-rosy picture of what was actually happening. Indeed, a few days before, Fulbright had read a letter penned by Clyde Pettit, a reporter who had interviewed more than two hundred soldiers in Vietnam and come to the following conclusion: "The war is not going well. The situation is worse than reported in the press and worse, I believe, than indicated in intelligence reports. A recent military buildup seemed to be having little effect."[66]

For Fulbright, the time had come for the SFRC to try to shed light on the situation and help the public decide whether Johnson's escalation policy was sound. When Fulbright and his SFRC chief of staff, Carl Marcy, planned to hold the hearings, they concluded that inviting establishment figures to testify before the committee would allow the senator, his colleagues, and other doubters to make their reservations known to the public. They also believed that they could affect the national conversation if the hearings were televised. Thus, after the January 28 session during which Secretary of State Rusk and Fulbright had already clashed on Johnson's policy in Southeast Asia, Marcy convinced major television networks (like CBS and NBC) to occupy Capitol Hill for the "real-life television drama" that the next sessions of the hearings would likely provide.[67] They did exactly that, and as Fulbright recalled a few weeks after the hearings: "I believe American news media performed a most worthwhile service in their complete coverage of the testimony of three pro-Administration witnesses (Secretary of State Rusk, AID Administrator David E. Bell, and General Maxwell D. Taylor, Ret.) and two non-Administration witnesses (Lieutenant General James M. Gavin) and Dr. George F. Kennan, former US Ambassador to the Soviet Union."[68]

Among these witnesses, the two nonadministration ones (Gavin on February 8 and Kennan on February 10) helped Fulbright expose the American people to very different narratives about the war than the ones that emanated from the White House. To the irritation of Johnson, Gavin made the case for an enclave strategy, which the Oval Office had already rejected.[69] Instead of supporting the president's escalation policy, Gavin told Fulbright and the American people that a defensive strategy could be more effective. What that strategy would have involved was US forces protecting the population within coastal enclaves while the South Vietnamese army fought the war against the Vietcong in the hinterlands.[70] It was, however, with the intellectual George Kennan that Fulbright and Marcy "pulled out their big gun." As Fulbright's biographer notes regarding the importance of Kennan's participation in the hearings: "No individual in or out of government had more prestige as a foreign policy analyst. As the father of containment policy, Kennan was hardly subject to criticism that he was soft on communism; at the same time he had endeared himself to cold-war liberals by his . . . advocacy of patience in dealing with the Soviets."[71] During his testimony, Kennan, like Gavin, challenged Johnson's assertion that escalating the war in Vietnam was mandatory. Here again, Fulbright's goal was clear: relying on the SFRC to educate the American people and raise public doubts about a policy that, according to the senator, left little room for discussion about the current state of US society.

Data gathered right after the hearings show that they did not instantly lead to a major increase in popular opinion against Johnson's policy. That said, many accounts conclude that Fulbright's efforts contributed to an important shift in public opinion. A seminal study about these hearings argues that they opened a crucial debate and made opposition to the war respectable. "No one could confuse Fulbright, Gavin, Kennan, or the SFRC with the long-haired, often disorderly protestors who marched on Washington or denounced the war on college campuses," writes one historian who has studied the hearings closely.[72] Fulbright himself did not exaggerate the influence of his 1966 hearings on public opinion, noting that, as with "any form of education," it is "hard to prove" the impact of such discussions even if one knows "it's there."[73] According to Fulbright's biographer, a key consequence of the hearings was to open a "psychological door for the great American middle class."[74] To everyday Americans, the hearings were a turning point in the sense that "Fulbright emerged as a key figure in the growing anti-war forces," demonstrating that it was possible to challenge Johnson's policy from the political center, including the mainstream media, and not only from the radical Left.[75]

Fulbright held additional SFRC hearings on Vietnam in the years that followed. None seemed to have greater resonance than the historic ones of 1966. However, the twenty-two hearings held between April 20,

1971, and May 27, 1971, were notable in the sense that they again allowed Fulbright to reach out to the American people in an attempt to foster public understanding about Vietnam. This time, Richard Nixon held the keys to the White House. Fulbright had initially welcomed Nixon's foreign policy realism compared with Johnson's more moralistic and "crusading style."[76] But he soon became frustrated with Nixon's mere continuation of Johnson's war effort in Vietnam. The 1971 hearings thus aimed at evaluating solutions to end the war.[77] Among the personalities testifying before the SFRC were many senators who, like George McGovern (D-SD), Mark Hatfield (R-OR), and Jacob Javits (D-NY), offered and debated legislation aimed at declaring a cease-fire in Vietnam, withdrawing US troops from the region, or setting a timetable for a termination of the war. But Fulbright also invited individuals from society in general to participate in the discussion. For instance, antiwar movement militants were given a seat at the table when representatives of the think tank Common Cause and of the group Students and Youth for a People's Peace testified before the committee. One of the highlights of these hearings certainly was the testimony of John Kerry, a Vietnam veteran who would later become a US senator (in 1985) and fill Fulbright's shoes as chair of the SFRC (from 2009 to 2013). Kerry echoed what Fulbright wanted the American people to hear at the time; his remarks were aimed at educating the public about the dark side of the war, the despicable violence of the actions of US soldiers on the front, and the fact that the White House was on the wrong track. As Kerry explained, veterans coming back home to the United States had to struggle with their demons as they had "cut off ears, cut off heads, . . . cut off limbs, blown up bodies [and] randomly shot at civilians" for a war that could not be won because it was not the "mystical war against communism" the White House was trying to sell to the American people but essentially a "civil war" by a people who would not abandon the fight because they had "for years been seeking their liberation from any colonial influence whatsoever."[78]

By the time Kerry gave his powerful testimony, public opinion about Vietnam had shifted toward his and Fulbright's conviction that the United States should have avoided the war. As Gallup data show, when asked, "Do you think the United States made a mistake sending troops to fight in Vietnam?" 61 percent answered yes in May 1971, while only 25 percent held this view in March 1966, a few weeks after Fulbright's previous hearings.[79] It would be an exaggeration to conclude that Fulbright and his SFRC hearings were the only factors that led to such a shift. However, President Johnson was certainly right to "become more and more distraught" with the attention Fulbright's efforts to challenge the White House were receiving.[80] The senator was among the most influential figures of a movement that brought key information about the war to the attention of the American people. This information was not readily or easily available before Fulbright used the SFRC to make it known to the public, and many Americans surely embraced his conviction that Washington needed to change course on this issue.

Fulbright as a Restrainer of Presidential Power

Vietnam also changed Fulbright's views about the role that the Senate and the SFRC should play in the formulation and conduct of US foreign policy.[81] In June 1959, a few weeks after taking the gavel of the SFRC, the senator told a television interviewer: "I think when you are dealing with foreign relations, you must have a very strong, assertive President who uses all the powers of his office to get his way in the international field."[82] He had often expressed this very same view since his first days in the Senate, including between 1945 and 1959, when he was a member of the SFRC but not yet its chair. As one account puts it: "Fulbright began his career as a champion of the executive's prerogatives in foreign affairs. He defended the Yalta Accords, the Bretton Woods Accords, the Dumbarton Oaks Conference, the Truman Doctrine, the Marshall Plan, and NATO; he identified executive domination of foreign policy with internationalism and congressional control with isolationism."[83] To be sure, he did not always defer to the executive branch and give a blank check to the president. In 1954, for instance, alarmed by the growth of the CIA and of US covert operations, he and Representative Mike Mansfield (D-NY) attempted to increase congressional control of the CIA by expanding the membership of a special subcommittee of the Senate Armed Services Committee to which the agency reported its activities.[84] However, key decisions that Fulbright made up until the mid-1960s show that his most profound conviction about the role Congress should play in foreign policy was the one he had described in his 1963 *Prospects for the West*. "The source of an effective foreign policy under our system is Presidential power," he wrote. "We must contemplate a further enhancement of Presidential authority in foreign affairs."[85] His decision to give President Johnson a blank check on the 1964 Gulf of Tonkin Resolution illustrates the extent to which he was content with conceding to the White House all the leeway it requested in the conduct of foreign affairs.

However, Fulbright later concluded that his approval of the Gulf of Tonkin Resolution was "his most humiliating moment in public life."[86] Indeed, he became convinced that Johnson had relied on the resolution to argue that the White House did not need further congressional approval to expand the US deployment in Vietnam. He also believed that Johnson had lied to him about his intentions in Vietnam and betrayed their friendship.[87] When they both served in the Senate, he admired no one more than Johnson, and the future president would often publicly "throw his arm around [the Arkansan] and say loudly to all present, 'Bill's *my* Secretary of State.'"[88] Recorded phone conversations between the two after Johnson became president show that Fulbright had good reason to believe that his Texan accomplice saw him as a close confidant and key adviser. In a conversation in December 1963, Johnson asked him what the White House should do in Vietnam. He responded that Vietnam was "an awful hell of a situation" and that going "all out in that kind of a situation" and in those "damn places [is] not worth it."[89] In March 1964, in another phone call, Johnson even laid out what he thought were the four options on the table for the White House regarding Vietnam.[90] Among the options were a "Barry Goldwater scenario" (named after the 1964 Republican presidential candidate) aimed at sending the US Marines and other US ground forces against North Vietnam. Fulbright thought that Johnson would not choose this option at the time but later realized that the president and his advisers had already veered toward it without admitting it. As he explained in his 1989 *The Price of Empire*: "I thought Johnson was a peacemaker. He had spoken against sending our young men to Vietnam . . . [and] was continually reassuring me. He spoke of his valiant efforts to resist extremist pressure for escalation."[91] By 1966, he had thus come to believe that Johnson's consultation methods were defective in the sense that they were "hastily arranged" and did not involve real "listening on the part of the President."[92] A few decades later, he explained that, before Vietnam, it had never occurred to him that presidents and their secretaries could deceive the Senate the way

Johnson and his team did on the war. He wrote: "I thought you could trust them to tell you the truth, even if they did not tell you everything. But I was naïve."[93]

Vietnam thus convinced Fulbright to launch a campaign aimed at recalibrating the balance of foreign policy powers between Congress and the White House. He described his new philosophy regarding congressional-executive relations on various occasions, for example, in *The Arrogance of Power*, where he argued that "the proper responsibilities of the Congress are those spelled out by [John Stuart] Mill": "to review the conduct of foreign policy by the President and his advisers, to render advice whether it is solicited or not, and to grant or withhold its consent to major acts of foreign policy." In his view, Congress had not been "fully discharging these responsibilities" since the 1940s. In the spring of 1961, for example, President Kennedy did not really consult members of Congress before launching the failed Bay of Pigs invasion against Cuba. Fulbright recalled that he was the only senator involved in the White House discussions preceding the intervention. He further noted that the Cuban Missile Crisis demonstrated that the Kennedy administration did not find it necessary to give Congress a key role in the foreign policy debate. He and other legislative leaders were convened at the White House on October 22, 1962, and briefed about the crisis that was unfolding. But, as Fulbright recalled, the president's goal was to inform key members of Congress about "the decisions *which had already been made*"[94] and not to request congressional advice or to engage in a serious evaluation of policy options with foreign policy intellectuals from Capitol Hill.

Convinced that Johnson had continued such a pattern with the Gulf of Tonkin Resolution and in Vietnam in general, Fulbright thus positioned himself as a restrainer of presidential power and became a champion of congressional foreign policy powers. In his view, members of Congress should never abdicate the "deliberative function" of the institution. Furthermore, when the White House claimed that a foreign policy emergency required swift action to protect national security, he insisted that members of Congress should not automatically comply with the president's demands but instead find a balance between complete deference to the executive branch and counterproductive and endless deliberation that could jeopardize the national interest and adopt the following attitude toward the commander in chief:

Mr. President, we will take your urgent request under immediate advisement; we will set aside our other legislative business and will proceed as rapidly as orderly procedure permits to hear testimony and to debate and act upon your request. We will not, however, except under conditions of national emergency, set aside the normal procedures of committee hearings and deliberation and debate on the Senate floor. We regret any inconvenience which this may cause you, but just as we are cognizant of your obligation to act, we know that you are cognizant of our obligation to inform ourselves and deliberate in order to be able to give you our best possible advice. We know you are aware that we render this advice not only in the hope that it will be a service to your Administration but also as an obligation to our constituents—an obligation, Mr. President, which we feel bound to meet even if, for one reason or another, our doing so subjects you to certain inconveniences.[95]

In July 1967, Fulbright relied on legislative action in his effort to reinforce the role of Congress in the making of foreign policy: he introduced the National Commitments Resolution in the Senate.[96] As one account puts it, the resolution aimed at "requiring explicit congressional approval of executive agreements with foreign countries."[97] It stated: "It is the sense of the Senate that a national commitment by the United States to a foreign power necessarily and exclusively results from affirmative action taken by the executive and legislative branches of the US Government through means of a treaty, convention, or other legislative instrumentality specifically intended to give effect to such a commitment."[98] The National Commitments Resolution was not adopted in 1967, but Fulbright had better luck when he reintroduced it in the Senate in 1969, during the Nixon presidency. By a roll call vote of 70–16, the Senate passed the resolution on June 25. During the floor debate, Fulbright termed the text "one of the most important of its kind that has ever been before the Senate since I have been here." He and his supporters—Frank Church (D-ID), for instance—were aware that the measure would not "by itself restore to Congress the war power now abdicated away," that it was meant only to "remind Congress of its responsibilities and to help create a new state of mind."[99]

Conclusion: Fulbright, the SFRC, and the "New State of Mind" in Congress

The "new state of mind" Frank Church was referring to in June 1969 soon gained traction on Capitol Hill. While Fulbright was one of the first of his legislative cohort to try expressly to limit presidential authority in foreign affairs, his nonlegislative and legislative actions such as the Vietnam hearings and the National Commitments Resolution undoubtedly inspired many of his colleagues. For instance, the famous War Powers Resolution—introduced in the Senate by Jacob Javits in June 1970 and passed in 1973 over Richard Nixon's veto—echoed Fulbright's view that the president should respect Congress's deliberative responsibilities in foreign affairs and consult the House and Senate before launching a foreign military intervention. The 1970s and 1980s saw many other members of Congress taking the lead on legislative initiatives that matched Fulbright's philosophy about congressional-executive relations in foreign policy. The Hughes-Ryan Act of 1974 stated: "No appropriated funds could be expended by the CIA for covert actions unless and until the President . . . provided the appropriate committees of Congress with a description and scope of each operation in a timely fashion."[100] The same year, the establishment of the Office of the Special Trade Representative by Congress was meant to make the executive branch more sympathetic and responsive to domestic interests than the State Department had been up until then.[101] These well-known initiatives have led many scholars to use expressions such as *cold war dissensus*[102] and *congressional resurgence*[103] to describe this new state of mind that led Congress to reaffirm its foreign policy prerogatives and fight what Arthur Schlesinger called *the imperial presidency*.[104]

Some of Fulbright's successors as SFRC chair have also followed his lead and echoed his views about what should be done from this position. Richard Lugar (R-IN) chaired the SFRC twice, from 1985 to 1987 and from 2003 to 2007, and believed, like Fulbright, that US legislators should play an active role in the making of foreign policy. As his biographer notes, Lugar was "perhaps the most influential US senator in the realm of foreign policy since Scoop Jackson" and enjoyed many accomplishments (promoting arms control, containing nuclear proliferation), demonstrating Fulbright's point that Congress can make a useful contribution to the formulation of US policy abroad.[105]

Joe Biden (D-DE), who chaired the SFRC from 2001 to 2003 and from 2007 to 2009, also behaved in a way reminiscent of what Fulbright had done forty years earlier. This should be no surprise. When Biden made his debut in the Senate in January 1973, he got a seat on Fulbright's SFRC as a freshman and saw the Arkansan as a mentor. His first discussions with Fulbright led him to believe that the SFRC had played a crucial role in educating the American people about Vietnam and turning public opinion against the war. In Biden's words: "The lesson I learned from Sen. Fulbright is that, if you inform the American public, they're pretty smart. . . . [T]hey can form their own opinions."[106]

After the 2006 midterm elections, Biden embarked on a Fulbright-like mission regarding George W. Bush's war in Iraq. He held SFRC hearings during which he tried to do exactly what Fulbright had done with his Vietnam hearings. On July 19, 2007, for instance, the US ambassador to Iraq, Ryan Crocker, gave testimony before the SFRC that was in many ways similar to that which Secretary of State Dean Rusk had given about Vietnam before the same panel in January 1966.[107] Crocker argued that the United States was making progress in Iraq and that the White House's strategy would eventually be a success.[108] Biden begged to differ. "Mr. Ambassador, I believe that the President's policy, which you are being asked to execute, is based on a fundamentally flawed premise," he lectured the ambassador. "If we just give the central government time, it will secure the support and trust of all Iraqis. In my judgment, that will not happen."[109] Here was a senator who, like his mentor in 1966, wanted to prove that an SFRC chair behaving as a foreign policy intellectual, public educator, and restrainer of presidential power could do great service to his country.

Compared to Lugar and Biden, however, most other senators who have chaired the SFRC since Fulbright's tenure have played a less significant and influential role. Sometimes it was because of personal factors: for instance, in the cases of John Sparkman (1975–1979) and Charles Percy (1987–1995), previous research shows that they were respectively "not inclined to challenge presidential leadership" and "too accommodating" when it came to a "deeply divided committee."[110] The fact that, because of the growing party polarization in the Senate and in the country in general, the SFRC has become more divided along party lines is also crucial to understanding the behavior of other senators who have chaired the committee since Fulbright. In a context were parties "have polarized

almost as much in the Senate as they have in the House,"[111] party identification weighs more on the decisions and actions of the SFRC chair than
it did in Fulbright's time. While Fulbright did not hesitate to challenge a
president from his own party, Democratic and Republican senators who
have chaired the committee in the same situation have tended to play a
more deferential and supportive role. For instance, the Democratic senators John Kerry (2009–2013) and Bob Menendez (2013–2015) tended to
rally around President Obama's foreign policies, while their successor, the
Republican Bob Corker (2015–2019), did not hesitate to call Obama an
"unreliable ally" and argue that the president's tergiversations in Syria and
Libya caused instability in the Middle East.[112] Jesse Helms was another
Republican who used the chairmanship of the SFRC to oppose a Democratic president, as was shown by his willingness to block ambassadorial
nominations, reduce US contributions to the United Nations, and reject
treaties negotiated by the White House (e.g., the Comprehensive Test Ban
Treaty of 1999).[113] J. William Fulbright's tenure on the SFRC is thus not
only memorable because of the considerable influence the senator had on
US foreign policy. It is also historic because Fulbright is the last influential
chair of the SFRC who did not hesitate to put personal convictions before
partisan considerations and clearly challenge a president of his own party
when the events required doing so.

Notes

1. David Farnsworth, *The Senate Committee on Foreign Relations* (Urbana: University of Illinois Press, 1961); Linda Fowler and Brian Law, "Parties, Executives and
Committee Prestige: The Eclipse of the Senate in National Security, 1947–2004"
(paper presented at the conference "Party Effects in the United States Senate," Duke
University, April 8–9, 2006).

2. US Senate Committee on Foreign Relations, "Committee History & Rules"
(n.d.), https://www.foreign.senate.gov/about/history.

3. Frédérick Gagnon, "The Most Dynamic Club: Vandenberg, Fulbright, Helms,
and the Activism of the Chairman of the US Senate Foreign Relations Committee,"
Foreign Policy Analysis 14, no. 2 (April 2018): 191–211, and *Les sénateurs qui changent
le monde: Le président de la commission du Sénat américain sur les relations extérieures
et la politique étrangère des États-Unis après 1945* (Ste-Foy: Presses de l'Université
Laval, 2013), 49–104.

4. Ralph Carter and James Scott, *Choosing to Lead: Understanding Congressional
Foreign Policy Entrepreneurs* (Durham, NC: Duke University Press, 2009), 199.

5. Naomi Lynn and Arthur McClure, *The Fulbright Premise: Senator J. William Fulbright's Views on Presidential Power* (Lewisburg, PA: Bucknell University Press, 1973), 75.

6. See, e.g., Haynes Johnson and Bernard Gwertzman, *Fulbright the Dissenter* (New York: Doubleday, 1968); William C. Berman, *William Fulbright and the Vietnam War: The Dissent of a Political Realist* (Kent, OH: Kent State University Press, 1988); and Eugene Brown, *J. William Fulbright: Advice and Dissent* (Iowa City: University of Iowa Press, 1985).

7. For a useful resource to learn more about Fulbright's role in these issues, see CQ Press, *CQ Almanac*, https://library.cqpress.com/cqalmanac.

8. J. William Fulbright, *The Arrogance of Power* (New York: Random House, 1966), 57.

9. David Lauter and Burt Folkart, "William Fulbright, Critic of Cold War Policy, Dead at 89," *Los Angeles Times*, February 10, 1995, http://articles.latimes.com/1995-02-10/news/mn-30368_1_james-william-fulbright.

10. Tristan Coffin, *Senator Fulbright: Portrait of a Public Philosopher* (New York: Dutton, 1966).

11. Thomas Preston, *The President and His Inner Circle: Leadership Style and the Advisory Process in Foreign Affairs* (New York: Columbia University Press, 2001), 9.

12. Brown, *Advice and Dissent*, 8.

13. Randall B. Woods, "Dixie's Dove: J. William Fulbright, the Vietnam War, and the American South," in *Vietnam and the American Political Tradition: The Politics of Dissent*, ed. Randall B. Woods (Cambridge: Cambridge University Press, 2003), 149–70, 160.

14. Randall B. Woods, *Fulbright: A Biography* (Cambridge: Cambridge University Press, 1995), 35–36. See also Randall B. Woods, *J. William Fulbright, Vietnam, and the Search for a Cold War Foreign Policy* (Cambridge: Cambridge University Press, 1998), 4.

15. Beverly Smith quoted in Brown, *Advice and Dissent*, 39.

16. Mike Mansfield quoted in Lynn and McClure, *The Fulbright Premise*, 74.

17. Woods, *The Search for a Cold War Foreign Policy*, 18.

18. Woods, *Fulbright: A Biography*, 28.

19. Carl Marcy, "Interview #5: Fulbright Breaks with Johnson," interview with Donald A. Ritchie, October 19, 1983, 155–56, http://www.senate.gov/artandhistory/history/resources/pdf/Marcy_interview_5.pdf.

20. Ibid., 156.

21. Woods, *Fulbright: A Biography*, 391.

22. Marcy, "Interview #5," 157.

23. Woods, *Fulbright: A Biography*, 354.

24. J. William Fulbright, *The Price of Empire* (New York: Pantheon, 1989), 17.

25. Johnson and Gwertzman, *Fulbright the Dissenter*, 233. See also Jean Lacouture, *Vietnam: Between Two Truces* (New York: Random House, 1966).

26. Woods, *Fulbright: A Biography*, 392.

27. Brown, *Advice and Dissent*, 100.

28. Woods, *Fulbright: A Biography*, 392.

29. Brown, *Advice and Dissent*, 9.

30. Woods, "Dixie's Dove," 159.

31. Martin A. Smith, *NATO in the First Decade After the Cold War* (Boston: Kluwer Academic, 2000), 11. See also Don Abelson, *A Capitol Idea: Think Tanks and US Foreign Policy* (Montreal: McGill-Queens University Press, 2006).

32. See Carter and Scott, *Choosing to Lead*. I have already used Carter and Scott's conceptions of legislative and nonlegislative actions to study Fulbright in Gagnon, "The Most Dynamic Club."

33. Carter and Scott, *Choosing to Lead*, 13–14.

34. I have already made this point in Gagnon, *Les sénateurs qui changent le monde*, and "The Most Dynamic Club."

35. Gagnon, *Les sénateurs qui changent le monde*, 270.

36. James Strock, *Theodore Roosevelt on Leadership: Executive Lessons from the Bully Pulpit* (New York: Three Rivers, 2001).

37. James Lindsay, "Deference and Defiance: The Shifting Rhythms of Executive-Legislative Relations in Foreign Policy," *Presidential Studies Quarterly* 33, no. 3 (September 2003): 530–46.

38. Woods, *Fulbright: A Biography*, 392 (quote), 423.

39. Brown, *Advice and Dissent*, 95.

40. I made a similar point in Gagnon, "The Most Dynamic Club," and *Les sénateurs qui changent le monde*.

41. J. William Fulbright, *Prospects for the West* (Cambridge: Cambridge University Press, 1963). See also Brown, *Advice and Dissent*, 50.

42. Woods, *Fulbright: A Biography*, 261, 263.

43. J. William Fulbright, *Old Myths and New Realities, and Other Commentaries* (New York: Random House, 1964), 6.

44. Fulbright, *The Arrogance of Power*, 131.

45. J. William Fulbright, *The Pentagon Propaganda Machine* (New York: Vintage, 1971), 28.

46. J. William Fulbright, *The Crippled Giant: American Foreign Policy and Its Domestic Consequences* (New York: Random House, 1972), 72.

47. *Congressional Record*, 89th Cong., 1st sess., vol. 111 (pt. 18), September 15, 1965, 23855.

48. *Congressional Record*, 89th Cong., 1st sess., vol. 112 (pt. 13), July 22, 1966, 16808.

49. Gagnon, *Les sénateurs qui changent le monde*, 156–57.

50. Fulbright, *The Price of Empire*.

51. J. William Fulbright, "We Must Negotiate Peace in Vietnam," *Saturday Evening Post*, April 9, 1966, 10, 12, 14.

52. J. William Fulbright, "The Great Society Is a Sick Society," *New York Times Magazine*, July 20, 1967, 30.

53. See Chris Matthews, *Nixon and Kennedy: The Rivalry That Shaped Postwar America* (New York: Touchstone, 1996), chap. 10 ("The Great Debate").

54. Gagnon, *Les sénateurs qui changent le monde*, 151–54.

55. "Fulbright, Advice and Dissent," *CBS News Special Report*, February 1, 1966. For a transcript of the discussion between Fulbright, Severeid, and Agronsky, see *Congressional Record*, 89th Cong., 2nd sess., February 2, 1966, 1941–43.

56. Gagnon, *Les sénateurs qui changent le monde*, 153.

57. Berman, *William Fulbright and the Vietnam War*, 95.

58. See Gagnon, *Les sénateurs qui changent le monde*, 168; and Brown, *Advice and Dissent*, 97–98.

59. Fulbright, *The Arrogance of Power*, 25.

60. US Senate Foreign Relations Committee, *The Vietnam Hearings*, with an introduction by J. William Fulbright (New York: Random House, 1966).

61. Fulbright, *The Arrogance of Power*, 56.

62. Brown, *Advice and Dissent*, 29.

63. Woods, *Fulbright: A Biography*, 129.

64. Joseph A. Fry, *Debating Vietnam: Fulbright, Stennis, and Their Senate Hearings* (Lanham, MD: Rowman & Littlefield, 2006), 31.

65. See US Senate, "Vietnam Hearings" (n.d.), https://www.senate.gov/artandhistory/history/minute/Vietnam_Hearings.htm.

66. Quoted in ibid. See also Woods, *Fulbright: A Biography*, 393.

67. Ibid., 402–3.

68. US Senate Foreign Relations Committee, *The Vietnam Hearings*, x.

69. Woods, *Fulbright: A Biography*, 404–5.

70. William R. Haycraft, *Unraveling Vietnam: How American Arms and Diplomacy Failed in Southeast Asia* (Jefferson, NC: McFarland, 2005), 138.

71. Woods, *Fulbright: A Biography*, 405.

72. Fry, *Debating Vietnam*, 79–80 (quote 80). Fulbright's biographer comes to the same conclusion when he writes that Kennan and other witnesses during the Vietnam hearings "were not irresponsible students or wild-eyed radicals but conservative, establishment figures." Woods, *Fulbright: A Biography*, 405.

73. Quoted in Fry, *Debating Vietnam*, 80.

74. Woods, *Fulbright: A Biography*, 411.

75. Julian Zelizer, "How Congress Helped End the Vietnam War," *The American Prospect*, February 6, 2007, http://prospect.org/article/how-congress-helped-end-vietnam-war.

76. Brown, *Advice and Dissent*, 108.

77. Woods, *Fulbright: A Biography*, 599.

78. "Transcript: Kerry Testifies before Senate Panel, 1971," NPR, April 25, 2006, http://www.npr.org/templates/story/story.php?storyId=3875422.

79. Mark Gillespie, "Americans Look Back at Vietnam War," Gallup News Service, November 17, 2000, http://www.gallup.com/poll/2299/americans-look-back-vietnam-war.aspx.

80. Woods, *Fulbright: A Biography*, 405.

81. I made a similar point in Gagnon, "The Most Dynamic Club," and *Les sénateurs qui changent le monde.*

82. Quoted in Lynn and McClure, *The Fulbright Premise*, 52.

83. Woods, "Dixie's Dove," 164.

84. Woods, *Fulbright: A Biography*, 430; Carter and Scott, *Choosing to Lead*, 112.

85. Fulbright, *Prospects for the West*, 112, 114, quoted in Brown, *Advice and Dissent*, 81.

86. Haynes and Gwertzman, *Fulbright the Dissenter*, 196.

87. Gagnon, *Les sénateurs qui changent le monde*, 135–38.

88. Haynes and Gwertzman, *Fulbright the Dissenter*, 6–7.

89. "Lyndon Johnson and J. William Fulbright on 2 December 1963," tape K6312.02, PNO 9, Presidential Recordings: Digital Edition, http://prde.upress.virginia.edu/conversations/9020029.

90. "Lyndon Johnson and J. William Fulbright on 2 March 1964," tape WH6403.02, citations 2320 and 2321, Presidential Recordings: Digital Edition, http://prde.upress.virginia.edu/conversations/9040288.

91. Fulbright, *The Price of Empire*, 105, 108.

92. Lynn and McClure, *The Fulbright Premise*, 131–32.

93. Fulbright, *The Price of Empire*, 106.

94. Fulbright, *The Arrogance of Power*, 44–48.

95. Ibid., 54–55.

96. Brown, *Advice and Dissent*, 98; Gagnon, *Les sénateurs qui changent le monde*, 170–71.

97. Woods, "Dixie's Dove," 169.

98. Brown, *Advice and Dissent*, 98.

99. "Senate Moves to Restrict Foreign Commitments," in *CQ Almanac 1969*, 25th ed. (Washington, DC: Congressional Quarterly, 1970), 177–81.

100. Marshall Curtis Erwin, "Covert Action: Legislative Background and Possible Policy Questions," Congressional Research Service, April 10, 2003, https://fas.org/sgp/crs/intel/RL33715.pdf.

101. James Lindsay, "Congress and Foreign Policy: Why the Hill Matters," *Political Science Quarterly* 107, no. 4 (Winter 1992–93): 607–28, 617.

102. Carter and Scott, *Choosing to Lead*, 115.

103. Randall Ripley and James Lindsay, eds., *Congress Resurgent: Foreign and Defense Policy on Capitol Hill* (Ann Arbor: University of Michigan Press, 1993).

104. Arthur Schlesinger, *The Imperial Presidency* (Boston: Houghton Mifflin, 2004).

105. John T. Shaw, "The Legacy of Richard Lugar," *National Interest*, May 9, 2012, http://nationalinterest.org/commentary/the-legacy-richard-lugar-6900?page=show.

106. Jonathan Broder, "White House Hopeful Biden Bets on Being a Global Expert," *New York Times*, January 19, 2007.

107. US Congress, Senate, Committee on Foreign Relations, "Iraq: An Update from the Field," 110th Cong., 1st sess., July 19, 2007, https://www.gpo.gov/fdsys/pkg/CHRG-110shrg40380/html/CHRG-110shrg40380.htm.

108. For a transcript of Ryan Crocker's testimony, see ibid.

109. Joe Biden, "Opening Statement in the Senate Foreign Relations Committee Hearing," in ibid.

110. James McCormick, "Decision Making in the Foreign Affairs and Foreign Relations Committees," in Ripley and Lindsay, eds., *Congress Resurgent*, 115–54, 142–43; Gagnon, "The Most Dynamic Club," 6–7.

111. Sean Theriault and David Rhode, "The Gingrich Senators and Party Polarization in the US Senate," *Journal of Politics* 73, no 4 (2011): 1011–24, 1011.

112. Bob Corker, "Obama Is an Unreliable Ally," *Washington Post*, August 5, 2014.

113. Gagnon, "The Most Dynamic Club," 16.

"A thorn in the flesh"

Fulbright, Latin America, and the Enduring Cold War

Benjamin Brady

On December 2, 1963, less than two weeks after assuming the presidency, Lyndon Johnson telephoned J. William Fulbright. "Spend some time on Cuba for me," the president told the Arkansas senator. "A little bit on Vietnam, too."[1] Cuba had proved the biggest foreign policy headache for Johnson's assassinated predecessor and had brought the United States and the Soviet Union to the brink of nuclear war. Disaster in Vietnam was still to come. But in 1964 and 1965, as Fulbright examined these and other Cold War battlegrounds, he developed an alternative internationalism that offered a path past "the terror and the tensions of the cold war."[2]

That alternative internationalism rested on a commitment to self-determination. While supporting continued US leadership against Soviet imperialism, Fulbright decried the "excessive moralism" that drove the United States to treat any and every conflict as a struggle between good and evil that admitted no compromise. Recognizing how difficult it was for the United States to impose its values on other states, he concluded that a nation's internal affairs—how it "organizes its internal life, the gods and doctrines that it worships"—should concern Washington only inasmuch as that nation sought to impose its beliefs and practices on others. Tolerating revolutionary nationalism would allow the United States to exploit divisions within the Communist bloc while opening the possibility of "normal relations" with the Soviet Union.[3]

But there was a dark side to Fulbright's willingness to rethink Cold War orthodoxy. His commitment to self-determination also motivated his opposition to federal civil rights legislation. Fulbright believed that the South must overcome segregation on its own terms, and he opposed what he saw as self-righteous and futile efforts to use outside federal power to transform the region. He overlooked common threads linking civil rights activists with revolutionary nationalists. Skeptical of Washington's power in the face of entrenched oligopolies in both the Global South and the American South, he accepted revolutionary nationalism abroad but resisted the civil rights movement at home.[4]

This irony was not lost on President Johnson. Rather than welcoming Fulbright's foreign policy ideas, he dismissed them in part by pointing to the senator's poor civil rights record. Fulbright's foreign policy views, like his stance on civil rights, revealed a spinelessness that exacerbated the president's deepest neuroses. As revolutionary change at home and abroad created new areas of Cold War confrontation, Johnson dismissed Fulbright as a cowardly, self-interested troublemaker.[5]

Before their falling out, however, Fulbright had been well positioned to educate the more hawkish president. As Congress's "resident intellectual" and "Arkansas and the Senate's link to the Establishment," he was free from the daily burdens that limited executive branch officials. He had a major voice in decision making, but he also had the freedom to think strategically. As Randall B. Woods has observed, his role as chairman of the Senate Foreign Relations Committee allowed him to "retain what he perhaps coveted most: independence of judgment and action, and, to a certain extent, control over his time."[6] His position was tricky, however. As an outsider, he could provide thoughtful analysis, but, as an insider and confidant, he risked antagonizing the president if he questioned too much.

In the end, Fulbright misplayed his hand. He grasped that relations with the Soviet Union were entering a new phase, and he saw self-determination as a principle that could keep the United States from being sucked deeper into a global Cold War.[7] But, even before he broke with the Johnson administration over the Vietnam War, his major speeches on Latin America antagonized the president.[8] By destroying their relationship, Fulbright missed an opportunity, though a remote one, to persuade Johnson to change course in Latin America and, perhaps, the wider Cold War.

The Bay of Pigs Memo and the Possibility of Détente

Fulbright's willingness to rethink US–Latin American relations dated from the early months of the Kennedy administration. As majority leader, Johnson had pushed aside the elderly Theodore Green and installed Fulbright as chairman of the Senate Foreign Relations Committee in 1959.[9] Having labeled Fulbright "my secretary of state," Johnson pressed Kennedy to appoint him to that role officially after winning the presidency. Fulbright's poor civil rights record and misgivings about taking the job led Kennedy to choose Dean Rusk instead.[10] Nonetheless, Fulbright enjoyed good relations with Kennedy, who passed him sensitive reports. According to Pat Holt, the Senate Foreign Relations Committee's Latin American specialist, such a collaboration was unprecedented.[11]

In the spring of 1961, Kennedy offered Fulbright a ride on Air Force One to Florida, where both planned to spend the Easter holiday. In the weeks before the trip, Fulbright and his staff had picked up signs that the administration was training Cuban exiles to topple Castro, a measure they feared would prove disastrous. Holt wrote a memo advising against it, and Fulbright passed it to Kennedy during the flight.[12]

The memo was prescient. Calling the training of the exiles an "open secret," it warned that the United States would be held responsible for an invasion even if the administration took steps to cover its involvement. Moreover, it emphasized that even a successful invasion would leave the United States with the difficult task of governing Cuba. Castro's revolution had popular support, and it was impossible to undo all the changes the dictator had made to Cuban society. As the memo put it: "One cannot completely unscramble the omelet." It also denounced an invasion in moral and legal terms. "To give this activity even covert support is of a piece with the hypocrisy and cynicism for which the United States is constantly denouncing the Soviet Union in the United Nations and elsewhere," it declared. "This point will not be lost on the rest of the world—nor on our own consciences for that matter."

Fulbright tried to convince Kennedy that the United States need not "fear competition from an unshaven megalomaniac." Cuba was not the threat the administration made it out to be. "[Remember] always this proviso," the memo counseled. "The Castro regime is a thorn in the flesh; but it is not a dagger in the heart." Most remarkably, it tentatively raised the possibility of what it termed the "reformation of the Castro regime." This was almost two years before Kennedy himself seriously considered US-Cuban accommodation, and the memo downplayed its likelihood as "more theoretical than real." Nevertheless, it advised Kennedy to make serious efforts to see whether the United States might find some basis to live with a Castro government: "Perhaps, however, it should not be rejected out of hand until the President has consciously satisfied himself, through whatever private channels are available, that it is a futile course to pursue."[13]

On their return to Washington a few days later, Kennedy asked Fulbright to attend a meeting at the State Department. Expecting a low-key discussion, Fulbright was startled to encounter the president's national security team. In fact, the meeting was the final major review before Kennedy approved the Bay of Pigs invasion. Fulbright was the lone dissenter, and he failed to dissuade the president. The ensuing fiasco justified Fulbright's misgivings.[14] Kennedy remembered Fulbright's advice, and he tried to explain to himself how Fulbright had been right while he had been so wrong. Arthur M. Schlesinger Jr. recalled his words: "There is only one person in the clear—that's Bill Fulbright. And he probably would have been converted if he had attended more of the meetings. If he had received the same treatment we received . . . it might have moved him down the road too."[15]

What Kennedy failed to realize was that Fulbright had already begun to move beyond what the senator soon termed the *old myths* that had long shaped US policy in the Western Hemisphere.[16] These myths had roots in an earlier era, when strategic, economic, and cultural imperatives drove US imperialism in Latin America.[17] After World War II, as policy makers "redefined the US strategic perimeter" in the face of the Soviet threat and extended US hegemony beyond the Caribbean, McCarthyism compounded traditional strategic, economic, and cultural motivations and left Democrats like Kennedy and Johnson wary of seeming weak.[18] By invading Cuba in 1961, Kennedy hoped to recover a country the United States had "lost" to the Communists and thereby remove any taint of responsibility.[19] As Fulbright later charged: "Underlying the bad advice and unwise actions of the United States was the fear of another Cuba. The specter of a second Communist state in the Western Hemisphere—and its probable repercussions within the United States and possible effects on the careers of those who might be held responsible—seems to have been the most important single factor in distorting the judgment of otherwise sensible and competent men."[20]

Fulbright himself was not immune from these assumptions, and his own outlook often coincided with Kennedy's and Johnson's more hawkish inclinations. He had condemned Eisenhower's policies toward Cuba, for example, and he supported Kennedy's efforts to isolate the Castro regime.[21] Most surprisingly, he advised Kennedy to attack Cuba during the 1962 missile crisis. According to Holt, Fulbright thought a "surgical" air strike would be "less provocative" than a blockade.[22]

While it seems puzzling that the prescient opponent of the Bay of Pigs in 1961 would readily endorse air strikes on Cuba in 1962, there was a consistency to Fulbright's thought. Though the senator would increasingly come to empathize with peoples in the Global South, his advocacy of better relations with Cuba stemmed in part from his sense that Cuba was a distraction from the *real* struggle against Soviet imperialism. Labeling Castro an unshaven megalomaniac in 1961 was a way of dismissing him and allowed Fulbright to take chances with Cuba that conventional thinking closed off. But a megalomaniac with nuclear weapons was a different story, and the presence of Soviet missiles in Cuba led Fulbright to assess Castro from the more conventional Cold War perspective of Soviet aggression. Self-determination was acceptable, he would say in 1964, until it "threatens us and other peoples of the non-Communist world."[23] In other words, his dissent from conventional thinking was "highly conservative," a fact that his admirers have often missed.[24]

But, at least on the surface, this conservatism also strengthened the force of Fulbright's opposition. His criticisms were not attacks from a "prophet with too much honor" such as Adlai Stevenson, who was widely (though unfairly) regarded as weak.[25] Thus, at least initially, his openness to diplomatic engagement did not entail a sweeping reassessment of American society and policy. The failure of his conservative critique in the early 1960s, combined with the deteriorating situation in Vietnam, pushed Fulbright to a more radical opposition in the late 1960s. His dissatisfaction "became not just strategic, or constitutional, or political, but moral as well."[26]

But, in 1962, the Cuban Missile Crisis created the possibility of a real thaw in US-Soviet relations, inducing Kennedy himself to seek détente.

The United States and the Soviet Union had come far too close to the nuclear abyss, and both Kennedy and Soviet premier Nikita Khrushchev had learned a great deal from the crisis. Kennedy had sought East-West accommodation at the 1961 Vienna Conference, but Khrushchev had rejected his overtures. It was not until the missile crisis that Kennedy, as Schlesinger put it, "was able to pick up the threads of his policy and try again to lead the world beyond the cold war."[27]

On June 10, 1963, Kennedy spoke at commencement exercises at American University, challenging Americans to consider their own responsibility for the Cold War: "But I also believe that we must reexamine our own attitude—as individuals and as a Nation—for our attitude is as essential as theirs." Moreover, he echoed Khrushchev's call for peaceful coexistence: "No government or social system is so evil that its people must be considered as lacking in virtue. As Americans, we find communism profoundly repugnant as a negation of personal freedom and dignity. But we can still hail the Russian people for their many achievements—in science and space, in economic and industrial growth, in culture and in acts of courage." He concluded with a concrete proposal for a limited nuclear test ban as a step toward a more comprehensive agreement.[28] Six months later, with a new president in the White House, it fell to Fulbright to take up these themes.

"Old Myths and New Realities"

On assuming the presidency in November 1963, Lyndon Johnson showed little sign of sharing Kennedy's willingness to rethink the fundamental assumptions of the Cold War.[29] But Fulbright was Johnson's loyal friend and confidant and eager to work with the new president.[30] The aforementioned phone call a few weeks after Kennedy's assassination illustrates the good relations between the two men—and Johnson's ability to flatter and manipulate. "You don't bother me," the president told Fulbright. "I always feel a little *better* after I talk to you. I learn something." Johnson wanted Fulbright's advice about "what we ought to do to pinch [the Cubans'] nuts a bit," and he asked him to produce a memo. Though busy, Fulbright could not refuse the request.[31] As his assistant Pat Holt recalled: "Fulbright complained once that the president called him at eleven o'clock at night or something and he said, 'Geez, he just won't hang up, and you can't hang up on him!'"[32]

In the first two years of Johnson's presidency, however, the relationship began to deteriorate. The Johnson-Fulbright split originated in the 1964 Panama crisis, which involved deadly riots over US sovereignty of the Panama Canal Zone.[33] In the 1950s and early 1960s, dictatorships collapsed across Latin America, and new leaders emerged through democratic elections. Fulbright and Holt felt that the United States should welcome them. As Holt explained: "A lot of people around the United States, including me, thought that it was very much in the national interest of the United States for these people to succeed in creating viable, open, liberal political systems, and that the alternative to this was social turmoil and probably Communism."[34] Fulbright therefore sympathized with Panamanian complaints of Yankee imperialism.

The senator had cause to think that Johnson did, too. In March 1964, Fulbright dined with the president at the White House. In addition to urging him to support cloture on the Civil Rights Act of 1964, Johnson discussed a range of foreign policy issues and revealed that the United States was secretly negotiating with Panama. Fulbright promised Johnson his full support in the run-up to the presidential election later that year.[35]

But, on March 25, 1964, during a Senate filibuster of the Civil Rights Act, Fulbright took to the floor of the Senate and delivered a major foreign policy address. Entitled "Old Myths and New Realities," the speech sought to move American foreign policy beyond the assumptions of the early Cold War. "We are clinging to old myths in the face of new realities and we are seeking to escape the contradictions by narrowing the permissible bounds of public discussion, by relegating an increasing number of ideas and viewpoints to a growing category of 'unthinkable thoughts,'" Fulbright declared. In particular, policy makers failed to realize that relations with the Communist world had moved into a new phase of peaceful coexistence. The "master myth of the cold war," Fulbright charged, was that of monolithic communism. He then addressed a number of specific issues, beginning with Panama: "We Americans would do well, for a start, to divest ourselves of the silly notion that the issue with Panama is a test of our courage and resolve."

Next, Fulbright called for a "candid reevaluation of our Cuban policy." He explained that US actions would not topple Castro: "It is necessary to weigh the desirability of an objective against the feasibility of its attainment, and when we do this with respect to Cuba, I think we are bound to conclude that Castro is a nuisance but not a grave threat to the United States and that he cannot be gotten rid of except by means that are wholly disproportionate to the objective." Echoing the memo he gave Kennedy before the Bay of Pigs, he suggested that the time had come for US-Cuban rapprochement: "Having ruled out military invasion and blockade, and recognizing the failure of the boycott policy, we are compelled to consider the third of the three options open to us with respect to Cuba: the acceptance of the continued existence of the Castro regime as a distasteful nuisance but not an intolerable danger." He complained that the United States had "flattered a noisy but minor demogog[ue] by treating him as if he were a Napoleonic menace." He concluded the speech with an assessment of US policy in Asia. He remained more cautious toward China and Vietnam than he had grown toward Latin America, urging fresh thinking while supporting existing policy.[36]

A week earlier, the Arkansas senator had addressed the Senate on the Civil Rights Act, confessing to "a certain sadness" and "a feeling of frustration and resignation at being forced to go through these biennial flagellations of our section and our people" as Congress debated a bill "designed to humiliate a proud and sensitive section of our country." Maintaining that there was "no more persistent prejudice in our country than that of one section against another," Fulbright lamented "a moral and legal absolutism" that ignored complexity. Citing the historian C. Vann Woodward, he complained that the South had been "left to its own devices" by Washington for almost a century. Now, guilty northerners hoped that "a few lines in a statute book" would upend deep cultural practices. Fulbright did not want "segregation in perpetuity," but the South's "particularly sensitive situation" could not be "speeded up beyond the capacity of a community." As he concluded: "Outside authority without the ultimate responsibility for living with the solution can be expected to spawn more turmoil and strife."[37]

Fulbright's old myths speech made many of these same points in the realm of foreign policy. Policy makers needed to recognize "a world in which neither good nor evil is absolute and in which those who move events and make history are those who have understood not how much but how little it is within our power to change." Countries like Panama had a long history of grievance, and the United States needed to understand "the profound social and economic alienation" between Panama and the wealthier US Canal Zone. Fulbright warned that violent social revolution was possible and that the United States needed to prepare for such a contingency. "It is wise and necessary for us to do all that we can to advance the prospects of peaceful and orderly reform," he declared. "At the same time, we must be under no illusions as to the extreme difficulty of uprooting long-established ruling oligarchies without disruptions involving lesser or greater degrees of violence. The historical odds are probably against the prospects of peaceful social revolution."[38]

Fulbright did not, however, acknowledge the parallels between his two speeches and betrayed no anxiety that his domestic complacency would undercut his foreign policy warnings. In fact, many pundits saw the old myths speech as an administration trial balloon.[39] But Johnson did not appreciate Fulbright's effort to create new space for diplomatic maneuver. "I'm not going to abandon our economic boycott [of Cuba], and I'm not going to negotiate, rewrite the 1903 treaty [with Panama]," he told National Security Adviser McGeorge Bundy.[40]

Johnson felt betrayed and assumed that Fulbright was seeking attention. As the notes from one meeting record: "The President observed that Senator Fulbright probably is enjoying the halo set on his brow by the *New York Times* and the *Washington Post* and will probably wish to retain the headgear."[41] If his friend Fulbright could give such a speech, the president wondered whom he could trust. During a conference call with Bundy and other advisers, he discussed the columnist Walter Lippmann's foreign policy positions. "Sunday night he seemed to be satisfied on Panama and Vietnam," he said. "But I thought Fulbright was, too."[42] Some of his advisers downplayed Fulbright's speech. Asked how it had been received abroad, George Ball responded that it might "give ammunition to those who do not favor our Cuba policy in the first place," but he otherwise minimized its impact. Bundy agreed. "It's a long speech, and the only parts where it gives us trouble are Cuba and Panama," he told Johnson.[43]

Nevertheless, the administration felt that the old myths speech warranted a response. According to the National Security Council (NSC) staffer Gordon Chase, the State Department believed that the "timing couldn't [have been] worse." The speech followed a major address on Cuba by George Ball to the North Atlantic Council, and it complicated efforts to pass a resolution in the Organization of American States addressing an arms cache discovered in Venezuela. "[The State Department's John

Crimmins] feels strongly that we have to knock this down hard (e.g. 'this is purely Senator Fulbright and the Administration doesn't agree with him')," Chase told Bundy. "John feels that either the President or the Secretary should knock it down."[44] The administration decided that Secretary of State Rusk would respond. Rusk would try to be "conciliatory" while emphasizing the administration's disagreement on Cuba, Panama, and China.[45]

The episode illustrates the president's discomfort with dissent. As his policies faced greater and greater opposition—especially when it came to the Vietnam War—Johnson became embittered. He saw Fulbright as driving criticism of his administration in once-friendly institutions like the Senate and the press. He expected his subordinates—and this included the chairman of the Senate Foreign Relations Committee—to support his agenda.[46]

Nonetheless, Johnson's friendship with Fulbright appeared intact, and, for the time being, the administration still considered the senator from Arkansas to be one of its "close allies." Gordon Chase even suggested that Fulbright's old myths speech could be used to deflect criticism if Johnson sought US-Cuban accommodation. If charged with going "soft," the administration could point to Fulbright's criticism that its approach was too "hard."[47] A month after Fulbright's speech, moreover, the Arkansas senator—to some surprise—represented Johnson in talks in Europe.[48] Perhaps the best proof of continuing good relations came in the late summer. Though he would later regret it, Fulbright steered the Gulf of Tonkin Resolution through the Senate, allowing Johnson to wage war in Vietnam.[49]

The Dominican Republic Speech

The friendship did not last. In the summer of 1965, the Senate Foreign Relations Committee held hearings on the recent US intervention in the Dominican Republic. The committee split and failed to produce a report, and Fulbright decided to publicize his own conclusions. On September 15, he rose on the floor of the Senate and launched into a scathing critique of administration policy. "US policy in the Dominican crisis was characterized initially by overtimidity and subsequently by overreaction," he said. "Throughout the whole affair, it has also been characterized by a lack of candor." Nevertheless, as Holt recalled, he changed initial drafts of the speech to take the blame off Johnson himself. According to Fulbright: "The principal reason for the failure of American policy in Santo Domingo was faulty advice given to the President by his representatives in the Dominican Republic at the time of acute crisis."

Fulbright nonetheless insisted that the administration had invaded on false pretenses. Johnson had claimed that he ordered troops to the Dominican Republic to save American lives. Yet, as Fulbright argued: "The danger to American lives was more a pretext than a reason for the massive US intervention that began on the evening of April 28. In fact, no American lives were lost in Santo Domingo until the Marines began exchanging fire with the rebels after April 28; reports of widespread shooting that endangered American lives turned out to be exaggerated." Instead, he alleged, the United States intervened to stop a Communist takeover: "On the basis of Ambassador Bennett's messages to Washington, there is no doubt that the threat of communism rather than the danger to American lives was [Bennett's] primary reason for recommending military intervention." He charged that policy makers had relied on "exaggerated estimates of Communist influence in the rebel movement." He laid ultimate blame on the fear of "another Cuba." As he said: "It is, perhaps, understandable that administration officials should have felt some sense of panic; after all, the Foreign Service officer who had the misfortune to be assigned to the Cuban desk at the time of Castro's rise to power has had his career ruined by congressional committees."

In mounting this critique, Fulbright developed many of the themes of his old myths speech. The United States, he maintained, was a conservative, status quo power whose own revolutionary origins had not upended American society: "We are not, as we like to claim in Fourth of July speeches, the most truly revolutionary nation on earth; we are, on the contrary, much closer to being the most unrevolutionary nation on earth." But Latin America had a very different history: "The dominant force in Latin America is the aspiration of increasing numbers of people to personal and national dignity." It was not easy for Americans to understand this point of view since the post–Civil War United States had never "experienced sustained social injustice without hope of legal or more or less peaceful remedy." Failing to acknowledge the civil rights revolution occurring within the United States, he urged Americans: "Give our understanding and our sympathy and support to movements which are alien to our experience and jarring to our preferences and prejudices. We must try to understand the social revolution and the injustices that give it rise because they are the heart and core of the experience of the great majority of people now living in the world."

Given such injustices, revolution was inevitable, and Communists would constitute some part of any revolutionary coalition. By intervening in the Dominican Republic, however, the United States aligned itself with a reactionary government and gave credence to more radical elements: "Since just about every revolutionary movement is likely to attract Communist support, at least in the beginning, the approach followed in the Dominican Republic, if consistently pursued, must inevitably make us the enemy of all revolutions and therefore the ally of all the unpopular and corrupt oligarchies of the hemisphere." A shrewder policy would ride the inevitable revolutionary tide, supporting non-Communist reformers as much as possible while otherwise staying out of the way.

Indeed, Fulbright argued that Latin America's future was not for the United States to make. He suggested that loosening the bonds linking the two regions might end up strengthening hemispheric solidarity. Giving the Latin Americans more leeway—leaving them "free . . . to maintain or sever existing ties as they see fit and, perhaps more important, to establish new arrangements, both among themselves and with nations outside the hemisphere, in which the United States would not participate"—would, ultimately, produce a friendlier relationship. Instead, the United States had intervened "unilaterally—and illegally," creating distrust, and undermining US credibility.[50]

The speech destroyed Fulbright's friendship with Johnson.[51] As Lee Riley Powell has pointed out, Fulbright's old myths speech "was primarily a theoretical attack on the mythical concept of a relentlessly expansionist, monolithic communist bloc." The Dominican speech, on the other hand, was a "specific denunciation" of an administration policy, something Johnson refused to tolerate.[52] The Johnson-Fulbright split over Latin America also opened the door for Fulbright's growing criticism of US policy in Vietnam. Given that the administration had made false statements about relatively minor turmoil in the Caribbean, Fulbright and his advisers wondered whether Johnson had lied to the American people about Southeast Asia. As Holt recalled: "[The Dominican intervention] ruptured the Johnson-

Fulbright relationship, but even more profoundly than that I think it opened the first crack in what later came to be the 'credibility gap' over Vietnam. It demonstrated to Fulbright and others that things were not always as Johnson and the administration were portraying them."[53]

The Johnson administration's reaction to Fulbright's speech was swift and vehement. Because it came after lengthy hearings, the administration had anticipated the thrust of his remarks and already prepared a response.[54] During the hearings, Johnson had asked allies in Congress to "stop this crowd from trying to prove that their country's wrong and the communists are right."[55] He now debated which senator should deliver the response to "this damn idiot of a Fulbright" for denouncing his administration as it was trying to set up a stable, non-Communist government in the Dominican Republic.[56] In the end, he settled on Thomas Dodd. The Connecticut senator answered Fulbright's charges and, according to Bundy, made "pretty good mincemeat of Fulbright."[57] Democratic senators Russell Long and George Smathers also defended the president in the wake of Fulbright's speech.[58]

Moreover, Bundy drafted a letter for Johnson to send to Fulbright. "I have tried to hit him with everything but the kitchen stove, and you will want to make your own judgment on whether in fact you wish to say these things to him directly," he told Johnson. In an especially biting passage, the letter condemned Fulbright's poor civil rights record: "You describe our people as 'the most unrevolutionary nation on earth,' although these are years of revolutionary advance in civil rights and in other fields where *some* of us have been working pretty hard."[59] And Bundy was right. In championing self-determination for Latin Americans and autonomy for white southerners, Fulbright ignored the claims of African Americans. To the Johnson administration, Fulbright's fear that the US government would end up strengthening extreme elements if it failed to respect local exigencies provided a cowardly excuse for inaction.

At the root of the administration's anger, however, was more a basic frustration. Fulbright was no longer acting like a member of the team. As one observer put it at the time: "The Fulbright speech was a drama simply because it was unique in this period of consensus."[60] As Rusk told Johnson the night of the speech: "I just don't understand that fellow. We've worked on him and he's had more facts thrown at him on this matter than on any subject that he's had in front of him for the last three months and why he just wants to go off on the Tad Szulc line and this kind of outburst I don't know."[61]

Wrong though he was on civil rights, however, Fulbright was right that fears of "another Cuba" plagued Washington. During a telephone conversation with Johnson, for example, Florida senator George Smathers, a Johnson ally, recounted how he had confronted Fulbright in the wake of the speech. "And I hate to see you go down in history as the man who was responsible for our losing the Dominican Republic," Smathers said he had told Fulbright. "[The Sinologist and State Department consultant] Owen Lattimore is given credit for having lost China, and Bill Fulbright is going to be given credit with having lost the Dominican Republic." According to Smathers, Fulbright was visibly shaken.[62] The conversation provides an example of exactly what Fulbright had charged on September 15. The stigma of losing another country to the Communists drove US policy.

Conclusion: The Enduring Cold War

In the end, Fulbright's deteriorating relationship with Johnson—over civil rights, Latin America, and, ultimately, Vietnam—illuminates why the Cold War continued unabated through the 1960s. Both men, in their different ways, perceived connections between the society they envisioned at home and the world they sought abroad. Fulbright developed a powerful critique of US interventionism abroad and made the case that self-determination would better advance American interests. But the commitment to self-determination underlying his alternative internationalism went hand in hand with his skepticism that federal power could transform the South. As a southerner shaped by the sectional divide with the North, he came naturally to his suspicion of Washington's power to effect change.[63] But he failed to recognize how "the aspiration of increasing numbers of people to personal and national dignity" applied equally to African Americans at home.

By contrast, worried that any slackening in the struggle to confront communism would imperil his vision for a better society at home, Johnson clung to "old myths."[64] But, though Fulbright was wrong on civil rights, his "new realities" and commitment to self-determination abroad would have better served Johnson's larger goals. Unfortunately, whereas Fulbright's private relationship with Kennedy from 1961 to 1963 fostered that president's openness to détente, his more public critique of Johnson in 1964 and 1965 foreclosed a similar process of development.[65]

Many of Fulbright's ideas would later animate—at least in part—the Nixon administration's policy of détente.[66] But the Arkansas senator's failure to win over Johnson meant that the United States missed a possible window to ratchet down or even end the Cold War.[67] By the mid-1960s, the United States and the Soviet Union had forged a de facto settlement in Europe, one based on respect for the status quo in Berlin and a non-nuclear West Germany defended by a large-scale American military presence, laying the groundwork for improved East-West relations.[68] But the Sino-Soviet split, decolonization, and the revolutionary activism of Cuba and Vietnam shifted the Cold War to the Global South. Newly independent states made inviting targets for the spread of socialism and capitalism, and the assertiveness of China, Vietnam, and Cuba in bringing revolution to these places made it difficult for the United States and the Soviet Union to allay their competition.[69] Thus, the Cold War did not just continue; it expanded, becoming truly global.

Fulbright's alternative internationalism resisted this globalizing impulse. The senator had become a chief spokesman within the Washington establishment for easing the Cold War in Latin America. Since 1961, he had argued privately and publicly that the United States was unlikely to overthrow Castro and that it needed a new policy in Latin America. He continued this theme in his 1966 *The Arrogance of Power*. "The greatest challenge in our foreign relations is to make certain that the major strand in our heritage, the strand of humanism, tolerance, and accommodation, remains the dominant one," he wrote. "It is of course reasonable to ask why *we* must take the lead in conciliation; the answer is that we, being the most powerful of nations, can afford as no one else can to be magnanimous."[70]

Johnson, however, could not afford to back down in the face of Fulbright's criticism, and he was in no mood to be magnanimous. Kennedy had turned to rapprochement in the wake of the Cuban Missile Crisis, when his reputation for standing up to communism was high. Johnson, on the other hand, was under attack from his own party over the Dominican Republic and Vietnam. Rather than enabling the president to overcome the legacy of old myths, Fulbright's critique put him on the defensive. It was, therefore, not just the evolving international system that carried the Cold War through the 1960s. The personalities and experiences of leaders also mattered.

As Melvyn P. Leffler has argued, policy makers on both sides of the Iron Curtain often regarded the US-Soviet struggle as counterproductive. Nonetheless, until the late 1980s, the policy makers chose continued competition over change.[71] The contrast between Johnson and Ronald Reagan is instructive. President Reagan's confidence and unquestioning faith in American ideals gave him the assurance to negotiate with Mikhail Gorbachev, creating space for Gorbachev to pursue domestic reforms. According to Leffler: "Ironically, Reagan's greatest contribution to ending the Cold War was not the fear he engendered but the trust he inspired." Reagan could inspire this trust because his self-assurance and reputation meant that he "*could* talk to the men from the evil empire with less fear of partisan recriminations and conservative criticism."[72] Gordon Chase had surmised that Fulbright's criticism from the left might insulate Johnson against attacks from the right, creating similar space for LBJ to maneuver.[73] Instead, isolated from liberals, Johnson embraced the more militant Cold War hawks. "During the brouhaha over the Dominican crisis," Woods has explained, "a number of observers noted that for the first time the administration seemed to be encouraging Russophobes and reactionaries in Congress."[74]

Meanwhile, the senator from Arkansas became persona non grata within the White House. He was no longer welcome at state dinners and was denied the use of government jets.[75] Intelligence reports "confirmed" that Fulbright's speeches had encouraged Castro.[76] The Washington press covered Fulbright's estrangement. "Winter has come early for Senator J. William Fulbright (D-Ark.) in the form of a sharp social chill from the direction of the White House," the *Washington Post* declared. "The Foreign Relations Committee Chairman, a ubiquitous figure in Washington's social whirl during the previous visits of foreign dignitaries, was conspicuously absent—and uninvited—to the White House party for Princess Margaret."[77] E. W. Kenworthy agreed in the *New York Times*: "It must be admitted that his advice—as for example, on Cuban policy—has more effect after the event than on it. And so it almost certainly will be with policy on the Dominican Republic and Vietnam—if, indeed, it has any effect at all."[78] Johnson continued to ignore Fulbright's advice on all three of these problems. If Fulbright and the other "Communists" in Washington supported rapprochement, then the president wanted nothing to do with the idea.

A minor incident illuminates how much had changed since Johnson became president. In the summer of 1966, Fulbright asked the White

House for a visa for Pat Holt, who wanted to make a tour of Cuba. It would be the first such visit by an American official since the United States and Cuba broke relations in 1961. According to the NSC staffer William Bowdler: "[Fulbright's request] spells trouble." As he wrote Walt Rostow, Bundy's successor as national security adviser: "I don't know the Senator's motives—but sending a Senate Foreign Relations staff man to make an on-the-spot survey of the Cuban situation will only stir up the quiescent Cuban problem for no useful purpose." Even worse, the visit would "lead to much speculation concerning accommodation with Castro, which will raise serious doubts in the minds of our Latin friends as to our intentions, and greatly excite the Cuban exile community." Along with the troubles in Vietnam, this would cause difficulties domestically.[79]

Two years earlier, in the summer of 1964, Bundy had sat in Rostow's chair, and Gordon Chase had handled matters now covered by Bowdler. Chase would have jumped at such an opportunity to find out what Castro was willing to do to improve relations with the United States. Of course, even he would have worried about publicity and, like Bowdler, would probably have recommended against a visit. But an opportunity that would have been tempting, if risky, in 1963 or 1964 was dismissed out of hand a few years later.[80]

Fulbright himself realized that his arguments would not sway Johnson, and he began to await a new president. In August 1968, he responded to a postcard from Havana sent by Edward Lamb, a famous labor lawyer and businessman active in liberal causes: "I am only hopeful that after this coming election something will prevail upon us to take a more tolerant attitude of other people, and follow a policy of reconciliation rather than antagonism." Seven years earlier, he had failed to persuade Kennedy that Cuba was a thorn rather than a dagger. In the intervening years, he had been far more successful in convincing Johnson that he himself was a bothersome thorn in the president's flesh.[81]

Notes

1. Max Holland, ed., *The Presidential Recordings: Lyndon B. Johnson*, 6 vols. (New York: Norton, 2005–2007), 1:81.
2. 110 *Cong. Rec.* 6228 (1964).
3. Ibid., 6227–29, 6232. Fulbright drew on the realism of George Kennan, whom he cited in the speech.

4. Randall Bennett Woods, *Fulbright: A Biography* (New York: Cambridge University Press, 1995), 118–19, 695–96.

5. Johnson could not tolerate dissent and was also driven by a machismo that left him worried about appearing unmanly. See, e.g., Fredrik Logevall, *Choosing War: The Lost Chance for Peace and the Escalation of War in Vietnam* (Berkeley and Los Angeles: University of California Press, 2001), 393–94. On domestic civil rights as a Cold War arena, see Mary L. Dudziak, *Cold War Civil Rights: Race and the Image of American Democracy* (Princeton, NJ: Princeton University Press, 2001).

6. David Halberstam, *The Best and the Brightest*, 20th anniversary ed. (New York: Ballantine, 1993), 29, 68, 415; Woods, *Fulbright: A Biography*, 245.

7. See generally Odd Arne Westad, *The Global Cold War* (New York: Cambridge University Press, 2007).

8. Contrast the way in which advisers like Jack Matlock and Robert McFarlane educated Ronald Reagan in the 1980s, outmaneuvering his more hawkish advisers. Melvyn P. Leffler, *For the Soul of Mankind: The United States, the Soviet Union, and the Cold War* (New York: Hill & Wang, 2007), 341, 359–62.

9. Halberstam, *The Best and the Brightest*, 416; Transcript, Pat M. Holt Oral History Interview 4, October 17, 1980, by Donald A. Ritchie, 129–33, Senate Historical Office, https://www.senate.gov/artandhistory/history/resources/pdf/Holt_interview_4.pdf; Woods, *Fulbright: A Biography*, 244–46.

10. On Fulbright's nearly becoming secretary of state, see Halberstam, *The Best and the Brightest*, 29–30, 416; Lee Riley Powell, *J. William Fulbright and America's Lost Crusade: Fulbright's Opposition to the Vietnam War* (Little Rock, AR: Rose, 1984), 73; Arthur M. Schlesinger Jr., *A Thousand Days: John F. Kennedy in the White House* (Boston: Houghton Mifflin, 1965), 139–40; Transcript, Pat M. Holt Oral History Interview 5, October 27, 1980, by Donald A. Ritchie, 147–49, Senate Historical Office, https://www.senate.gov/artandhistory/history/resources/pdf/Holt_interview_5.pdf; and Woods, *Fulbright: A Biography*, 256–60.

11. Holt Oral History Interview 5, 149.

12. Ibid., 149–51; Eugene Brown, *J. William Fulbright: Advice and Dissent* (Iowa City: University of Iowa Press, 1985), 47; Schlesinger, *Thousand Days*, 251; Woods, *Fulbright: A Biography*, 263–66.

13. Memo, March 29, 1961, ser. 48, subser. 14, box 38, folder 1, J. William Fulbright Papers, Special Collections, University of Arkansas Libraries, Fayetteville. The memo is published in Karl E. Meyer, ed., *Fulbright of Arkansas: The Public Positions of a Private Thinker* (Washington, DC: Robert B. Luce, 1963), 194–205. The possibility of rapprochement with Cuba is examined in William M. LeoGrande and Peter Kornbluh, *Back Channel to Cuba: The Hidden History of Negotiations between Washington and Havana* (Chapel Hill: University of North Carolina Press, 2014).

14. On Fulbright's role in the Bay of Pigs deliberations, see Brown, *Advice and Dissent*, 47–48; Halberstam, *The Best and the Brightest*, 67–68, 408–9; Powell, *J. William Fulbright and America's Lost Crusade*, 63–67; Schlesinger, *Thousand Days*,

251–52, 258, 289; Holt Oral History Interview 5, 151–55; and Woods, *Fulbright: A Biography*, 266–70.

15. Kennedy quoted in Schlesinger, *Thousand Days*, 289.

16. See the discussion below.

17. On strategic concerns, see, e.g., Richard H. Collin, *Theodore Roosevelt's Caribbean: The Panama Canal, the Monroe Doctrine, and the Latin American Context* (Baton Rouge: Louisiana State University Press, 1990), xiii–xiv; and Nancy Mitchell, *The Danger of Dreams: German and American Imperialism in Latin America* (Chapel Hill: University of North Carolina Press, 1999). On economic motives, see generally William Appleman Williams, *The Tragedy of American Diplomacy*, 50th anniversary ed. (New York: Norton, 2009); and Walter LaFeber, *The New Empire: An Interpretation of American Expansion, 1860–1898*, 35th anniversary ed. (Ithaca, NY: Cornell University Press, 1998). On cultural influences, see, e.g., Kristin L. Hoganson, *Fighting for American Manhood: How Gender Politics Provoked the Spanish-American and Philippine-American Wars* (New Haven, CT: Yale University Press, 1998); and Eric T. L. Love, *Race over Empire: Racism and US Imperialism, 1865–1900* (Chapel Hill: University of North Carolina Press, 2004).

18. See Melvyn P. Leffler, *A Preponderance of Power: National Security, the Truman Administration, and the Cold War* (Stanford, CA: Stanford University Press, 1992), 56–59.

19. Halberstam, *The Best and the Brightest*, 102–20.

20. 111 *Cong. Rec.* 23859 (1965).

21. Memo, Fulbright to George J. Robinson, January 17, 1961, ser. 48, subser. 14, box 38, folder 1, Fulbright Papers; Fulbright to J. M. Yantis, August 2, 1963, ser. 48, subser. 14, box 38, folder 3, Fulbright Papers.

22. Brown, *Advice and Dissent*, 47–48; Powell, *J. William Fulbright and America's Lost Crusade*, 67–68; Schlesinger, *Thousand Days*, 812; Holt Oral History Interview 5, 158–160; Woods, *Fulbright: A Biography*, 270–75.

23. 110 *Cong. Rec.* 6228 (1964).

24. Brown, *Advice and Dissent*, 2–3, 70–71.

25. On Stevenson, see Halberstam, *The Best and the Brightest*, 26–27. Stevenson played a pivotal role in efforts to reach an agreement with Castro. LeoGrande and Kornbluh, *Back Channel to Cuba*, 73–74, 84, 93–96, 102–3.

26. Woods, *Fulbright: A Biography*, 440.

27. Aleksandr Fursenko and Timothy Naftali, *One Hell of a Gamble: Khrushchev, Castro, and Kennedy, 1958–1964* (New York: Norton, 1997), 320–25; Schlesinger, *Thousand Days*, 405.

28. John F. Kennedy, *Public Papers of the Presidents of the United States: 1963* (Washington, DC: US Government Printing Office, 1964), 459–564.

29. See Lawrence Freedman, *Kennedy's Wars: Berlin, Cuba, Laos, and Vietnam* (New York: Oxford University Press, 2000), 419.

30. Woods, *Fulbright: A Biography*, 325.

31. Holland, ed., *Presidential Recordings*, 1:76–80.

32. Holt Oral History Interview 5, 164–65.

33. Ibid., 165–66; Powell, *J. William Fulbright and America's Lost Crusade*, 172. On the crisis, see Alan McPherson, "Courts of World Opinion: Trying the Panama Flag Riots of 1964," *Diplomatic History* 28 (January 2004): 83–112.

34. Holt Oral History Interview 4, 117–18.

35. Woods, *Fulbright: A Biography*, 334.

36. 110 *Cong. Rec.* 6227–32 (1964). Fulbright published the speech in J. William Fulbright, *Old Myths and New Realities, and Other Commentaries* (New York: Random House, 1964), 3–46. For discussion of the speech and the administration's reaction, see Brown, *Advice and Dissent*, 52–61; Robert David Johnson, *Congress and the Cold War* (New York: Cambridge University Press, 2006), 111; Powell, *J. William Fulbright and America's Lost Crusade*, 85–88, 96–97, 172; William O. Walker III, "The Struggle for the Americas: The Johnson Administration and Cuba," in *The Foreign Policies of Lyndon B. Johnson: Beyond Vietnam*, ed. H. W. Brands (College Station: Texas A&M University Press, 1999), 70; and Woods, *Fulbright: A Biography*, 334–39. On Fulbright's more conservative approach toward Asia, see Logevall, *Choosing War*, 139; and Woods, *Fulbright: A Biography*, 338.

37. 110 *Cong. Rec.* 5636–39 (1964).

38. Ibid., 6227–6231.

39. David Shreve and Robert David Johnson, eds., *The Presidential Recordings: Lyndon B. Johnson: Toward the Great Society: February 1, 1964–May 31, 1964*, vol. 5, *March 9, 1964–April 13, 1964* (New York: Norton, 2007), 467.

40. Recording of Telephone Conversation between Johnson and Bundy, March 25, 1964, 4:55 P.M., tape 2655, Recordings of Telephone Conversations—White House Series, Recordings and Transcripts of Conversations and Meetings, LBJ Presidential Library, Austin, TX.

41. Desmond Fitzgerald, Memo for the Record, April 1, 1964, "6 Jan. 1964–2 Apr. 1964," McCone Memoranda, box 1, LBJ Library.

42. Recording of Telephone Conversation, Conference Call, March 28, 1964, 9:30 A.M., tape 2683, White House Series, LBJ Library.

43. Recording of Telephone Conversation between Johnson and Bundy, March 25, 1964, 4:55 P.M., tape 2655, White House Series, LBJ Library; Fitzgerald, Memo for the Record, April 1, 1964, "6 Jan. 1964–2 Apr. 1964," McCone Memoranda, box 1, LBJ Library. See also Logevall, *Choosing War*, 139; Woods, *Fulbright: A Biography*, 338.

44. Memo, Chase to Bundy, March 25, 1964, "Contacts with Cuban Leaders," Country File, NSF, box 21, LBJ Library. The memo follows the "Fulbright Speech" tab. On Ball's speech, see US Department of State, *Foreign Relations of the United States, 1964–1968*, vol. 32, *Dominican Republic; Cuba; Haiti; Guyana* (Washington, DC: US Government Printing Office, 2005), 620–21 (editorial note, doc. 255).

45. Recording of Telephone Conversation between Johnson and Rusk, March 28, 1964, 3:30 P.M., tape 2697, White House Series, LBJ Library.

46. Halberstam, *The Best and the Brightest*, 623; Woods, *Fulbright: A Biography*, 385.

47. Memo, Chase to Bundy, April 7, 1964, and Chase, Memo for Record, April 13, 1964, "Contacts with Cuban Leaders," Country File, NSF, box 21, LBJ Library.

48. Memo, Bundy to Johnson, April 30, 1964, "Bundy, Vol. 3," Memos to the President, NSF, box 1, LBJ Library; "President Sends Fulbright to See Greeks and Turks," *New York Times*, May 4, 1964, 1; "The Fulbright Mission," *New York Times*, May 5, 1964, 42.

49. Brown, *Advice and Dissent*, 62–67; Johnson, *Congress and the Cold War*, 111–14; Halberstam, *The Best and the Brightest*, 416–20; Transcript, Pat M. Holt Oral History Interview 6, November 10, 1980, by Donald A. Ritchie, 177–78, Senate Historical Office, http://www.senate.gov/artandhistory/history/resources/pdf/Holt_interview_6.pdf; Powell, *J. William Fulbright and America's Lost Crusade*, 85, 89–97; Woods, *Fulbright: A Biography*, 349–55; Randall B. Woods, *LBJ: Architect of American Ambition* (New York: Free Press, 2006), 517.

50. 111 *Cong. Rec.* 23855–61 (1965). On the speech, see Brown, *Advice and Dissent*, 68–71; Johnson, *Congress and the Cold War*, 118–19; Powell, *J. William Fulbright and America's Lost Crusade*, 142–43, 160–68; Holt Oral History Interview 6, 171–76, 179–83; and Woods, *Fulbright: A Biography*, 381–85. On Johnson's primary responsibility for the intervention despite Fulbright's effort to deflect blame onto his advisers, see Alan McPherson, "Misled by Himself: What the Johnson Tapes Reveal about the Dominican Intervention of 1965," *Latin American Research Review* 38 (June 2003): 127–46.

51. On reaction to the speech, see Brown, *Advice and Dissent*, 71–74; Johnson, *Congress and the Cold War*, 118–19, 125; Halberstam, *The Best and the Brightest*, 415–16; Powell, *J. William Fulbright and America's Lost Crusade*, 93–94, 160–64, 168–76; Holt Oral History Interview 6, 173–76, 183–86; Walker, "The Struggle for the Americas," 70; and Woods, *Fulbright: A Biography*, 385–92, 474, and *LBJ*, 633.

52. Powell, *J. William Fulbright and America's Lost Crusade*, 172–73.

53. Holt Oral History Interview 6, 176.

54. Memo, Bundy to Johnson, September 14, 1965, "Bundy, Vol. 14," Memos to the President, NSF, box 4, LBJ Library.

55. Recording of Telephone Conversation between Johnson and Talmadge, August 23, 1965, 3:11 P.M., tape 8615, White House Series, LBJ Library.

56. Recording of Telephone Conversation between Johnson and Russell, September 14, 1965, 6:35 P.M., tape 8859, White House Series, LBJ Library.

57. Memo, Bundy to Johnson, September 16, 1965, "Bundy, Vol. 14," Memos to the President, NSF, box 4, LBJ Library.

58. 111 *Cong. Rec.* 23861–65 (1965); John M. Goshko, "Dominican Role of US Is Assailed," *Washington Post*, September 16, 1965, A1.

59. Memo, Bundy to Johnson, September 17, 1965, "Bundy, Vol. 14," Memos to the President, NSF, box 4, LBJ Library.

60. Eric Sevareid quoted in Brown, *Advice and Dissent*, 71.

61. Recording of Telephone Conversation between Johnson and Rusk, September 15, 1965, 7:20 P.M., tape 8877, White House Series, LBJ Library. Szulc was the

foreign correspondent for the *New York Times* who had broken the news of the Bay of Pigs invasion.

62. Recording of Telephone Conversation between Johnson and Smathers, October 1, 1965, 2:44 P.M., Tape 9002, White House Series, LBJ Library. On Lattimore, see Halberstam, *The Best and the Brightest*, 116.

63. Woods, *Fulbright: A Biography*, 695.

64. See Francis M. Bator, "No Good Choices: LBJ and the Vietnam/Great Society Connection," *Diplomatic History* 32 (June 2008): 309–40.

65. Fredrik Logevall has lamented that "those domestic and foreign voices who would have had the greatest potential impact on top officials were the most reticent to speak out" against escalation in Vietnam. Logevall, *Choosing War*, xxii. If Vietnam reveals the limitations of Fulbright's private approach, his speeches on Latin America show the pitfalls of a more public campaign.

66. See, e.g., Transcript, Pat M. Holt Oral History Interview 7, November 19, 1980, by Donald A. Ritchie, 226–28, Senate Historical Office, http://www.senate.gov/artandhistory/history/resources/pdf/Holt_interview_7.pdf. Woods describes a short-lived "honeymoon" with the incoming Nixon administration. Woods, *Fulbright: A Biography*, 519.

67. See Leffler, *For the Soul of Mankind*, 151–233.

68. Marc Trachtenberg, *A Constructed Peace: The Making of the European Settlement, 1945–1963* (Princeton, NJ: Princeton University Press, 1999), 285–86, 352, 398–99.

69. Westad, *Global Cold War*, 158–59.

70. J. William Fulbright, *The Arrogance of Power* (New York: Random House, 1966), 254–55.

71. Leffler, *For the Soul of Mankind*, 452.

72. Ibid., 448, 462–64. See also n. 8 above.

73. See n. 47 above and accompanying text.

74. Woods, *Fulbright: A Biography*, 380–81.

75. Ibid., 385.

76. Watson, Memo, April 29, 1964, "Vol. A: Chase File," Country File, NSF, box 18, LBJ Library.

77. "Winter Comes Early for Fulbright," *Washington Post*, December 18, 1965, A1.

78. E. W. Kenworthy, "Fulbright: Dissenter," *New York Times*, October 31, 1965, E4.

79. Memo, Bowdler to Moyers and Rostow, August 3, 1966, "Bowdler File, Vol. 2," Country File, NSF, box 19, LBJ Library.

80. By contrast, the Nixon administration readily granted the request. Pat M. Holt Oral History Interview 7, 226.

81. Fulbright to Lamb, August 20, 1968, ser. 48, subser. 14, box 39, folder 1, Fulbright Papers. On Lamb, see "Edward Lamb Is Dead at 84," *New York Times*, March 25, 1987, B5.

J. William Fulbright and the Retreat of American Power

Anglo-Australian Views of Fulbright and US Neo-Isolationism

David L. Prentice

The 1960s and 1970s witnessed simultaneous American social, political, diplomatic, economic, and military crises. Interventionism abroad had produced unrest in the streets, grave economic and financial strains, a military stalemate in Southeast Asia, and doubts about the nation's moral capability to lead the world. As in other periods of American interventionism, groups and leaders arose to question their nation's role in the world and demand a reordering of its domestic and foreign priorities. Liberal intellectuals and establishment figures like George Kennan and Walter Lippmann argued for a return to the prudent containment that had served America well in the 1940s.[1] They criticized America's role as a global policeman even as they shunned the New Left's radicalism and dissent. As much as the antiwarriors dominated the headlines, the liberal internationalists retained the power to move the middle.[2]

Like other liberal internationalists, Senator J. William Fulbright had grown restive over American foreign relations and society. He had long challenged notions of rigid anticommunism and containment, but, by the mid-1960s, he increasingly worried that continuing the war in Vietnam as well as maintaining dangerous commitments and expensive troop deployments abroad risked grave domestic problems and military overstretch. Arrogant interventionism eroded the American people's faith in the democratic system, invited social unrest, and frittered away scarce resources in overzealous Cold War commitments when domestic programs required greater attention. Under the senator's leadership, the Senate Foreign Relations Committee (SFRC) increased its oversight of US foreign policy and authored resolutions to scrutinize American commitments abroad. Fulbright considered these actions necessary "efforts to bring about a reordering of our national priorities." He argued that the "responsibilities of power" that US policy makers defended often resulted in debilitating displays of "the arrogance of power."[3]

In his widely read publications and his televised hearings, Fulbright became one of the most prominent critics of US foreign policy. His books and articles sold hundreds of thousands of copies and introduced ideas others would embrace. The journalist Ronald Steel observed: "*The Arrogance of Power* marks the passage of Senator Fulbright from a relatively orthodox supporter of the liberal line on foreign policy to a spokesman for the post-cold-war generation." Yet many radicals remained wary of Fulbright both for his liberalism and for his southern identity.[4] For them, he never went far enough. Conversely, his views drew much attention and praise abroad, evidenced by the brisk sale of translated editions of *The Arrogance of Power* overseas. His biographer Randall Woods noted: "He endeared himself to Europeans . . . in the 1960s and 1970s by working to save the world from America and America from itself." Woods pointedly added: "Fulbright was better known and respected abroad than in the United States." Although foreign news media and intellectuals lauded Fulbright, behind the scenes his statements and actions sent shock waves throughout the network of Cold War alliances. Key allies fretted that he was becoming the leading voice of a growing movement to reshape American power.[5]

What such allied officials and observers feared in the late 1960s and early 1970s was not the arrogance of American power but its retreat. This alarm extended beyond the targets of Fulbright's hearings and statements. The South Vietnamese naturally took his influence seriously; as will be shown here, so did Great Britain and Australia. These two nations were among America's closest allies. Both saw their national security bound up with US leadership in their respective regions—Europe and Asia—so they often explained how Fulbright's ideas could undermine their foreign policy goals and regional interests. They were not zealous, ideological Cold Warriors driven by a "crusading spirit" but powers aware of their national interest.[6] Leaders in both nations appraised the Communist military and political threat to global peace and stability and concluded that, some strategic retrenchment notwithstanding, American power would have to remain preponderant worldwide. With American institutions and internationalism under attack at home, foreign officials worried that retrenchment would become retreat.

For British and Australian policy makers, Senator Fulbright symbolized congressional neo-isolationism—a latent tendency to scrutinize US foreign aid, treaty commitments, and troop deployments overseas.[7] *Neo-isolationism* was (and is) a fraught term that derived from an already overused and poor historical analogy—interwar isolationism.[8] Nevertheless, it had contemporary meaning and use from the mid-1960s through the 1970s. It appeared in editorials, the news media, and official debates and analysis. Allied policy makers found utility in using it to describe the internal challenges to America's Cold War containment. They used it broadly, often labeling any person who scrutinized commitments a *neo-isolationist*. Charges of neo-isolationism were absurd; no prominent US politician advocated economic protectionism or an end to America's alliances. Instead, allied fears spoke to the instability of the postwar order. It was feared that, if the roots of American power—domestic tranquility, a strong economy, a sound dollar, and national self-confidence—continued to deteriorate, the supposed neo-isolationists could tip the balance toward a global retreat from American power.

British and Australian officials believed that Fulbright's rhetoric, actions, and Senate leadership challenged US defense commitments worldwide and thereby threatened their national security as well as global stability. Already, his Vietnam hearings had given legitimacy and attention to the antiwar movement. It was feared that he and the SFRC could do the same for those policies they considered neo-isolationist. Great Britain and Australia encouraged US presidents to maintain existing security commitments even as they adapted their foreign policies to accommodate American retrenchment and admonished Fulbright for weakening US Cold War internationalism.

In short, while Fulbright enjoyed respect and accolades among intellectuals and the news media overseas, his positions ironically reinforced allied policy makers' perceptions of congressional unpredictability and fears of neo-isolationism. This essay, then, is less about whether Fulbright was a neo-isolationist than it is about allied perceptions of neo-isolationism during a period of crisis for American society and foreign relations. It tackles not only liberal internationalism but also the "global Fulbright" as an international figure and political celebrity who was useful, in this case, as a foil for advocates of American power abroad.[9]

Fulbright, foreign officials, and domestic observers recognized that America's role in the world was at a tipping point. Allies sought to help the United States survive the traumas of Vietnam and construct a durable, American-led international order. For his part, Fulbright rebuffed his critics and continued to argue that America served the world best when its liberties and prosperity were not compromised by interventionist overreach.

Fulbright, the Arrogance of American Power, and Neo-Isolationism

Fulbright's shift from Cold War liberal internationalism toward neo-isolationism preceded the 1965 Americanization of the conflict in Vietnam. By the early 1960s, the senator advocated a complete reappraisal of US foreign policy. American foreign aid had come to emphasize military expenditure rather than the educational, cultural, medical, and political investments he had long championed. America's military and political commitments worldwide threatened to "overextend the United States" and embroil the nation and its scarce resources in "peripheral struggles." Even in core strategic areas like Europe, Fulbright and his staff noted that American troop deployments created balance-of-payments problems that could weaken the dollar. The United States was not the omnipotent superpower Americans believed and US allies hoped it to be. Finally, Fulbright sought reduced Cold War tensions and urged Americans to assess Soviet interests rather than blindly assume that the United States and the Soviet Union were mortal ideological foes. He declared: "We must dare to think about 'unthinkable' things. We must learn to explore all of the options and possibilities that confront us in a complex and rapidly changing world."[10]

By January 1965, Fulbright had established himself as one of America's preeminent advocates of strategic retrenchment. In a piece on Fulbright, *Time* magazine observed: "As the current foreign-policy debate progresses, it may seem odd that liberals—so strongly interventionist before World War II and so strongly internationalist after World War II—talk about American 'self interest' in a manner that in some quarters now means 'isolationism.'" Liberal internationalists like Fulbright sought to move the US budget back to domestic needs and the Cold War back to economic, political, and social competition. Yet Fulbright disputed those who accused him of embracing neo-isolationism. His interventionist critics were wrong: the United States did not have an interest everywhere, America's finite resources (in talent, attention, and money) meant that policy makers had to be selective in their commitments, and the nation could not place foreign concerns over domestic needs. He explained: "It should be very clear that what is called for is not a wholesale renunciation by the United States of its global responsibilities. That would be impossible even if it were desirable." But he warned that to fixate on foreign policy and postpone domestic needs "is exactly the same as saying that the price of security is the slow erosion of the foundations of security."[11]

Even before Vietnam, Fulbright saw the balance between domestic and foreign needs as dangerously favoring the latter. In 1964, he lamented: "We have had to turn away from our hopes in order to concentrate on our fears and the result has been accumulating neglect of those things which bring happiness and beauty and fulfillment into our lives." He argued that America needed to devote its talent and resources toward the improvement of education for all, infrastructure development, urban renewal, the reduction of crime, full employment, and substantive antipoverty initiatives. As the costs of foreign commitments and conflict rose in the late 1960s, he wondered how President Lyndon Johnson could spend $20 billion a year in Vietnam and only $4 billion a year on antipoverty programs or how President Richard Nixon could defend expensive Cold War commitments and weapons while suspending more than $50 million for needed rural water and sewage systems. Given the social tumult of the 1960s, this overemphasis on foreign policy could also undermine American democracy. He ever more stridently warned: "The price of empire is America's soul and that price is too high."[12]

The Johnson administration's progressive escalation of the war in Vietnam, along with the rising antiwar dissent and mounting racial riots, confirmed Fulbright's fears. The senator sharpened his rhetoric. After five years of internal strife at home and war abroad, he wrote: "The early restoration of peace matters enormously because every day that this war goes on the sickness of American society worsens."[13] From the perspective of a patrician conservative, Fulbright believed that the war was eroding the country's liberties and institutions as young protestors and moderates alike found their voices shut out of foreign policy decisions.[14] He feared that, as they lost faith in the system, the resulting unrest would fuel a polarization and extremism that would tilt the nation toward authoritarianism. Even as the protests and riots waned, he argued that Cold War commitments had become an unbearable burden. He stated in 1973: "I do not consider myself remotely isolationist, but this nation has severe domestic problems of crisis proportions; our national debt is astronomical; inflation is rampant, and the dollar is in trouble. It is high time we paid some attention to our own problems at home and ceased squandering our limited resources abroad."[15]

The SFRC became a forum for these new realities and a tool for applying pressure on the White House to recast America's role in the world. Fulbright backed resolutions and hearings to reassert congressional oversight of these commitments. Although he had first thought a resolution on US commitments should wait until the nation returned to "a non-crisis atmosphere," the Vietnam War's continuation led to the early 1969 creation of the Ad Hoc Subcommittee on United States Security Agreements and Commitments Abroad, with Senator Stuart Symington (D-MO) as chair. The SFRC's initial focus was on commitments in Southeast Asia, but Fulbright was increasingly open to "rehearings" on other security treaties, including NATO. Indeed, Fulbright added his weight to Senate majority leader Mike Mansfield's (D-MT) perennial call to reduce American troops in Europe through a congressional resolution. He believed that the Soviet threat had diminished and that, in Western Europe, "the United States provides a defense umbrella that frees resources of other rich nations which, in all likelihood, might otherwise be spent for military purposes." American defense commitments amounted to a "subsidy" that allowed foreign governments to focus their budgets on the very domestic improvements US taxpayers were having to sacrifice in the name of global Cold War security. Hence, he wrote that a reduction in American forces stationed abroad "was not isolation": "It is a prudent reduction of our armed forces at a time when our balance-of-payments situation is critical."[16] For Fulbright, all these commitments and deployments added up to "a kind of indiscriminate internationalism" that "not only exceed but positively detract from the requirements of American national security." The "real American influence" was the nation's values and culture, not the deployment of its military power abroad.[17]

Great Britain and the Retreat of American Power from Europe

Foreign diplomats and officials listened to Fulbright's pronouncements with growing alarm. The August 1968 Soviet invasion of Czechoslovakia raised the value of American troops in Europe, while the proposed Mansfield amendment and the 1969 congressional hearings on US commitments seemed to herald reductions.[18] What constituted a credible deterrent and what Congress would support appeared out of balance. In Europe and Asia, America's allies concluded that Fulbright's voice and vision lent weight to the liberal and New Left critiques of US Cold War internationalism. They feared that the influential senator from Arkansas could tip the scales toward neo-isolationism. Global policy makers could not remove American politics and society from their geopolitical calculations.

In Britain, Her Majesty's Government, including Prime Minister Harold Wilson, closely followed Fulbright, the SFRC, Mansfield's resolution on American troops in Europe, and the Symington subcommittee on US commitments abroad. British policy makers still considered the Soviet Union and Warsaw Pact forces a serious threat to their country's national security and one that only a decided US presence in Europe could deter. They believed that US presidents understood this threat while senators ignored it, to Europe and America's mutual peril. They feared that defeat in Vietnam could drive Americans into an irrational isolationist lobby led by the SFRC.

In the 1960s, Great Britain had adjusted its own international commitments. It accommodated global calls for decolonization and accepted its economic limits as the pound sterling faced constant weakness and devaluation.[19] Despite demands from the United States and its Asian allies that it maintain its military presence in Asia, Britain announced in January 1968 that it would curtail its empire east of the Suez Canal. Thereafter, British policy makers fixed their attention on Europe as the key theater of British defense. In the long term, they recognized that imperial retreat from Asia would reduce their influence with American leaders, but they also feared the immediate psychological and political effects the decision would have on the United States. As American officials vainly tried to persuade Prime Minister Wilson to maintain British defense commitments in Asia, they warned that, by forsaking their global responsibilities, the British would precipitate "a swing of isolationism in America." Wilson worried that Washington might be right even as he continued Britain's retreat from empire.[20]

As British officials tracked American public opinion and the SFRC, they believed that the domestic and congressional mood was moving toward neo-isolationism. In July 1968, British ambassador Patrick Dean cabled: "There is growing determination in Congress to limit the overseas commitments of the United States by all means possible." Dean doubted that America would renege on its commitments, but he did believe that the Senate would force troop reductions worldwide. As Richard Nixon assumed office in 1969, he wrote: "Congressional opinion is by no means favourable to Europe or to the European Allies at the moment, and could very easily neutralize any efforts which Nixon might make to strengthen NATO and to improve relations with de Gaulle. We must not forget, moreover, that it is Fulbright's aim to establish a degree of control by the Senate over foreign policy." While he hoped Fulbright would work better with Nixon than he had with LBJ, he noted: "[Fulbright's] ideas have not changed." The Foreign and Commonwealth Office (FCO) concurred, arguing that, while a return to "fortress America" was dubious, "the desire for disinvolvement from burdensome political and physical commitments overseas" would restrain US foreign policy in the near term. Dean's replacement, John Freeman, understood that events in America, Vietnam, and the world were fluid: military defeat, economic problems, and unrest at home could all push Americans toward neo-isolationism. Freeman also observed that détente itself "could greatly reinforce the neo-isolationist cause" by making it harder to justify containment. British officials in London and Washington agreed that, should America suffer another year like 1968, Congress—particularly Fulbright's SFRC—could move public opinion and US foreign policy toward global disengagement.[21]

Britain's chief concern was the Soviet threat in Europe and the possibility that Fulbright could galvanize votes against US troop commitments there. The British government maintained: "NATO is the basis of the United Kingdom's security." In the wake of the 1968 Soviet invasion of Czechoslovakia, the conservative former prime minister

Alec Douglas-Home expressed the sentiment shared by his successor, Harold Wilson, and Whitehall: "An absolute condition of the survival of Western Europe—and this will be so for many years ahead—is the presence of United States power."[22] America's military presence was not an arrogant display of Yankee imperialism but the essential foundation of Western security. The FCO noted in February 1969: "In the foreseeable future the US alone can provide the necessary degree of security against the military threat directed by the Soviet Union against Western Europe." Moreover, British officials believed that threat was growing as the Warsaw Pact expanded its military power so that it had a "substantial advantage in overall military capabilities in Central Europe." Conversely, NATO's conventional forces were "just sufficient" to maintain the flexible response strategy. Any major reduction would undermine deterrence and have "alarming consequences." With NATO's military credibility on the line, US Senate support for American troops in Europe was critical.[23]

The situation appeared equally grave in the psychological sphere. The FCO worried that American reductions, especially if they came through congressional fiat, would badly damage US credibility in the eyes of its allies and enemies and "reinforce existing tendencies . . . to unravel NATO." Another official explained: "The confidence of the European members in N. A. T. O. rests on their faith in the commitment of the United States to the Alliance." If American troops departed, British policy makers feared that Western Europeans might seek to accommodate rather than contain the Soviet Union. In response to perceived rising neo-isolationism, European NATO members considered ways to educate the American public and Congress about the value of the US commitment to American as well as European security. The United Kingdom increased its troop commitment on the Continent to counter the congressional charge that Europeans were not bearing the burden of their own defense. NATO and British officials also wanted to get the Soviets moving on mutual and balanced force reductions (MBFR) before Congress dictated a unilateral US reduction. They valued the potential for MBFR talks for the "propaganda aspect" "of heading off domestic pressures" on these reductions rather than as a means to reduce Cold War tensions. British policy makers believed that unilateral reductions were "probably inevitable in the long run" and that preventing them was dependent on American leaders' ability "to hold their internal situation for a greater period of time."[24]

Indeed, British diplomats and analysts were anxious about America's domestic situation and appreciated the need for US retrenchment, but their criticism centered on what they considered an unreasoning isolationist lobby in Congress. They believed that Fulbright, Mansfield, and their peers were not interested in facts, preferred posturing, and continued to use mistaken information even after the State Department and foreign governments provided accurate intelligence. Ambassador Freeman wrote: "Congressional opinion is based on a mixture of fact and prejudice." He identified Mansfield and Fulbright as part of a group of twenty-five "hard core . . . liberal doves" who "question the need for large conventional forces at all": "Both the hard core supporters of Mansfield and the less committed proponents of US reductions doubt the existence of a meaningful current Soviet threat to Western Europe." To British defense and diplomatic officials, such ideas remained ludicrous as they continued to see Soviet foreign policy as aggressively seeking world power. Yet these policy makers accepted the contingency of America's commitments. In the right circumstances, budget hawks could join with antiwar doves to cut US foreign aid and commitments worldwide.[25]

Prime Minister Wilson shared these official views, and he became increasingly anxious of American neo-isolationism in 1969–1970.[26] Wilson had opposed Johnson's escalation of the war in Vietnam and disputed the president's contention that US credibility was on the line in Southeast Asia. But, by 1970, his fears of neo-isolationism, Hanoi's intransigence in the Paris peace talks, and Richard Nixon's steady withdrawal of US forces from Vietnam changed his position. He and top British officials became convinced that America must "keep its nerve" in Vietnam lest defeat roil American politics and undermine any desire for continued Cold War deterrence and commitments. With his party and much of his cabinet demanding that Her Majesty's Government condemn Nixon's 1970 incursion into Cambodia, Wilson resisted, arguing that condemnation would "risk provoking a reaction in the United States in favour of isolationism, which would be very damaging to our interests in the longer term."[27] Such fears were fanciful, but they partly explain the allied fascination with Fulbright. With campus unrest and congressional dissent reviving that spring, Wilson feared nascent neo-isolationism and its perceived impact on British national security.

Australia and the Retreat of American Power from Asia

Australian policy makers shared British fears of an American retreat. By the late 1960s, South Vietnam, South Korea, Thailand, Taiwan, Japan, and Australia all had growing doubts about US resolve even as each still considered America their chief protector.[28] As a key regional ally with armed forces fighting in Vietnam, Australia particularly tried to predict how rising US neo-isolationism would affect American strategy throughout Asia. Not only do Australian sources illuminate this Asian context; unique Australian interactions with Fulbright and his aides further demonstrate how allied officials grappled with Fulbright's ideas and influence.

When Senator Fulbright asserted, "I think the presence of the United States in [Southeast Asia] is the greatest incitement to the difficulties that afflict that part of the world, [more] than any other thing," many Australian officials fundamentally disagreed.[29] With the Soviets increasing their naval presence in the Indian and Pacific Oceans, the British abandoning their commitments east of Suez, and the Chinese likely to take advantage of any regional instability or vacuum, Australian officials continued to assert: "It is vital to us and to the prosperity and stability of the region that United States power should continue to be preponderant." Debates about the presumed arrogance of American power were not academic affairs; developments in Southeast Asia were critical to Australia's national security interests. In concurrent speeches, the Australian and New Zealand leaders affirmed the region's importance. Australian prime minister John Gorton declared: "We cannot fail to be affected by what happens in our neighbors' countries." New Zealand prime minister Keith Holyoake similarly noted: "This is where our own security is at stake."[30]

Australia had long held that it needed a great power to protect its strategic and economic interests in Asia as well as ensure its national security. In the 1950s and 1960s, Australians wanted both Great Britain and America to maintain a strong military presence in Asia in order to deter Chinese aggression and manage regional insurgencies. Although they recognized the limits of British power, they felt betrayed by Britain's decision to end its presence east of Suez. Yet, like their British counterparts, they feared the impact that this decision, along with America's domestic troubles, would have on US internationalism. Losing one protector, they grew more apprehensive about losing the other.[31]

Even before President Nixon began America's withdrawal from Vietnam or announced the Nixon Doctrine of regional self-help in 1969, Australian policy makers understood the growing political trend toward US disengagement from the Asian mainland and sought to staunch this retreat. They believed that a decisive number of Americans would remain committed to internationalism if US allies contributed their fair share to regional defense. Hence, Australian officials concluded: "Australia's influence, and to the extent of United States assistance in time of need, will [in the future] depend to an important extent on the degree to which Australia helps itself." The Australian government accepted this responsibility and announced, along with New Zealand, in February 1969 that it would maintain forces in Singapore and Malaysia. Critically, this commitment was intended to demonstrate to the American people and Congress that the region was willing and able to carry a greater proportion of the defense burden so long as the United States remained committed to collective security. Regionalism required increased US economic assistance and aid as well as a credible, symbolic reaffirmation of US defense commitments. As the SFRC increased its attacks on foreign aid and commitments, Australians worried that the Nixon Doctrine could become the guise of American retreat.[32]

Whereas British attention focused on US forces in Europe, Australians fixated on the SFRC's ad hoc subcommittee on American commitments. British and Australian officials alike interpreted its creation not as an act of prudent congressional oversight but as a product of Senator Fulbright's vindictive nature. One British official called it "Senator Fulbright's hobby horse" and argued that it was "directed more against the high-handedness of previous Democrat Presidents" than the Nixon administration. The Australian embassy in Washington similarly considered Fulbright's efforts to challenge preexisting commitments part of his personal "vendetta against President Johnson over Vietnam." Regardless of his motive, Fulbright's scrutiny of treaties, commitments, and contingency plans could become a means of limiting the American military presence in Asia, restricting presidential flexibility, and either repudiating existing commitments or forcing countries to alter their understanding of when and how America might intervene on their behalf.[33] Australians believed that their most sacrosanct commitment with the United States—the Australia, New Zealand, United States Security Treaty (ANZUS)—would fall under the committee's purview. The State Department tried to reassure the Australian ambassador that ANZUS was "not a very sexy issue" and that Symington and Fulbright's intent was "to find ammunition with which to belabor" the Nixon administration, not worry stalwart allies. Nevertheless, Australian officials recognized that the White House would have great difficulty reaffirming past understandings publicly. They would also have to conduct joint military planning with the utmost "delicacy" lest the SFRC demand oversight and so cause needless headaches.[34]

Given the SFRC's rhetoric and actions, Fulbright's aide Jim Lowenstein should have been little surprised when he encountered these concerns on a trip to Australia. He observed: "Some of those in the government with whom I talked regard the Committee as a maverick element in American political life, causing the American Government great problems." Lowenstein sought to impress on Australian officials that the US treaty commitments to Southeast Asia represented a "dead letter," that "America should pull out of Vietnam," and that, despite the growing Soviet presence there, "the Indian Ocean could not matter less to the United States." The Australian official recorded: "All in all, Mr. Lowenstein showed scant appreciation of, and very little interest in, the strategic desiderata that influence our own policy and that we assess should influence America's policy." Thereafter, the Australian government characterized Lowenstein and other SFRC staff as "itinerant scavengers" committed to attacking Nixon's foreign policies and thereby hurting Australia's strategic interests and security. Effectively blacklisting SFRC staff, the Australian government strongly discouraged its embassies worldwide from welcoming or discussing foreign affairs with them.[35]

Prime Minister John Gorton and Australian officials did see the SFRC as "itinerant scavengers" and a "maverick element" in US foreign relations, and Gorton's May 1969 trip to Washington perfectly captured Anglo-Australian views of Fulbright and the SFRC. Gorton had been anxious about an American retreat from Asia since early 1968, frequently traveling to the United States to secure presidential reassurances of America's commitment to Australia. On this trip, he had the temerity to accept Fulbright's offer to speak before and have lunch with the SFRC.

Addressing the SFRC on May 8, Gorton acknowledged that he stood "before experts" as he tried to impress on them America's essential role in Asia and the world. He stated: "Too few of us pause to remember that your nation has spread an umbrella of aid all over the world and that today many millions of men and women are free because the United States has stood by them in their hour of need and with the support of like-minded nations has held the aggressor in check." He summarized Australia's efforts to be a responsible regional power and exhorted the United States to maintain forces in Asia after the Vietnam War had ended. He declared: "The continuing interest of America is of first importance. Without that the risks in the region will enlarge and the opportunities for growth and self-help will be limited." He ended: "We look to America as the keystone of the arch in the Pacific and South East Asia."[36]

The Arkansas senator's reaction was predictable. One witness reported to the British embassy in Washington that, at the subsequent lunch, Fulbright "treated Mr. Gorton to an exposé of his well-known views about Vietnam": "Mr. Gorton listened for a while, but he finally turned on Senator Fulbright and told him exactly where he got off, explaining that his views of the Vietnam situation may seem entirely sound as seen from Washington but to those like the Australians who live rather closer to the scene, they made absolutely no sense." The British doubted those strong words "in any way chastened" the senator.[37]

Conclusion

This exchange reflected one of the era's real tragedies: the relationship between Fulbright's SFRC—the most significant legislative body on foreign affairs—and two of America's closest allies had become a dialogue of the deaf despite the fact that they were remarkably close on the solutions for excessive US interventionism. All recognized a need for America to shift its attention and resources back to domestic affairs. All agreed on the need for strategic retrenchment abroad. But they differed on the scale, timing, and publicity of this retreat. In short, all upheld American liberal internationalism, but Australian and British officials wished that Fulbright and his followers would temper their liberal internationalism with enough realism to moderate the swings between liberal Wilsonian crusades and isolationism.

As US allies saw it, the arrogance of American power was that it could leave as fast as it arrived with little consideration for allied fears and concerns. In 1959, Fulbright had noted that the US government was beholden to American voters and, because of Cold War internationalism, foreign allies as well; no one could be quite sure what would happen when those two constituencies disagreed. By the late 1960s, Fulbright was clear: "It is for the people of the United States, and not [any foreign power], to determine what is in our national interest." He also became less interested in discussing these issues with foreign officials.[38] American allies recognized Fulbright's strident rhetoric and his role in bringing heavy congressional pressure "to move faster and farther" on US reductions worldwide. For British and Australian policy makers, America's military presence and defense commitments in Europe and Asia were not products of an "arrogance of power" or imperial hubris; they were products of the complex and often difficult geopolitical realities great powers faced in a hostile world. These allies desired American patience and cooperation as all sides adjusted to the change from the old myths of American hegemony to new geopolitical realities. But they felt rebuffed by Congress. One correspondent observed that, among European officials and experts, Fulbright had earned the title "America's No. 1 neo-isolationist."[39]

Still, Fulbright was no neo-isolationist; he never pressed for a radical reduction of American troops or influence abroad, and he remained a fervent supporter of US engagement in international institutions. In his 1972 article "Reflections: In Thrall to Fear," he wrote that *neo-isolationism* is a word invented by "people who confuse internationalism with an intrusive American unilateralism, with a quasi-imperialism." He understood that America was "inextricably involved with the world politically, economically, militarily, and—in case anyone cares—legally." He continued: "Those of us who are accused of 'neo-isolationism' are, I believe, the opposite: internationalists in the classic sense of that term. . . . We believe in international cooperation through international institutions." Anglo-Australian officials sympathized with this lofty sentiment but believed that they were not living in a fear-free world—real threats existed, and only the permanence of American power could allow such idealism to come into being.[40]

Notes

1. Campbell Craig and Fredrik Logevall, *America's Cold War: The Politics of Insecurity* (Cambridge, MA: Belknap Press of Harvard University Press, 2009), 240–42.

2. On the larger context, see Jeremi Suri, *Power and Protest: Global Revolution and the Rise of Détente* (Cambridge, MA: Harvard University Press, 2003); Niall Ferguson, Charles Maier, Erez Manela, and Daniel Sargent, eds., *The Shock of the Global: The 1970s in Perspective* (Cambridge, MA: Belknap Press of Harvard University Press, 2010); and Melvin Small, *Antiwarriors: The Vietnam War and the Battle for America's Hearts and Minds*, Vietnam: America in the War Years, vol. 1 (Wilmington, DE: Scholarly Resources, 2002).

3. J. William Fulbright, *The Arrogance of Power* (New York: Random House, 1966), 16–20; Letter, J. William Fulbright to C. E. Jewell, October 1, 1969, folder "1969," box 9:4, subser. 1 Foreign Relations Committee (General), ser. 48, Foreign Relations Committee, J. William Fulbright Papers, University of Arkansas, Fayetteville (hereafter Fulbright Papers); and Address, J. William Fulbright, "The Price of Empire," August 8, 1967, reprinted in *Concern*, October 1967, in folder "1967–1969," box 23:4, subser. 5 Articles by J. William Fulbright, ser. 78 Press, 1943–1974, Fulbright Papers.

4. Robert Tomes, *Apocalypse Then: American Intellectuals and the Vietnam War, 1954–1975* (New York: New York University Press, 1998), 154–55.

5. Small, *Antiwarriors*, 15, 41–42; Randall Bennett Woods, *J. William Fulbright, Vietnam, and the Search for a Cold War Foreign Policy* (New York: Cambridge University Press, 1998), 143–44, 284–85.

6. Address, J. William Fulbright, "The Cold War in American Life," April 5, 1964, folder "1964–1965," box 2:1, ser. 74 Published Statements and Speeches, 1943–1974, Fulbright Papers.

7. For two contemporary explanations of the term *neo-isolationism*, see Dispatch, Patrick Dean, "Neo-Isolationism," July 16, 1968, FCO 7/778, Public Records Office, Kew, Great Britain (hereafter PRO); and Cable, Australian Embassy (Washington), "United States Foreign Policy," July 19, 1968, item 582683, USA—Relations with Australia—Developments in USA Policy Affecting Australia, ser. A1838, National Archives of Australia, Canberra (hereafter NAA).

8. Defining fluid and politically laden terms like *isolationism* and *internationalism*, much less *neo-isolationism* and *liberal internationalism*, is difficult. Andrew Johnstone rightly distinguishes between pre-1945 internationalism and postwar or Cold War internationalism, with the former representing a "cooperative and multilateral internationalism." The latter was less concerned with such lofty goals, instead prioritizing international stability and US interests. See Andrew Johnstone, "Isolationism and Internationalism in American Foreign Relations," *Journal of Transatlantic Studies* 9, no. 1 (March 2011): 7–20. Fulbright consistently exhibited cooperative internationalism. In a 1973 address, he reaffirmed: "*I remain a Wilsonian*—a seeker of a world system of laws rather than men, a believer in the one great new idea in this century: an international organization for peaceful settlement of international disputes." The United Nations and diplomacy were the means to international arbitration and justice. See Address, J. William Fulbright, October 8, 1973, folder "Major Speeches, 1970–1974," box 30:1, ser. 5 Speeches and Articles, Fulbright Papers.

9. For a treatment of an American political figure as a global celebrity, see Richard Carwardine and Jay Sexton, eds., *The Global Lincoln* (New York: Oxford University Press, 2011).

10. J. William Fulbright, "The Fatal Obsession in US Foreign Policy," *The Progressive*, September 1958, 14–17; Memo, Carl Marcy to Art Kuhl, April 10, 1963, folder "1963," box 29:2, subser. 8 (A.I.D.), ser. 48 Foreign Relations Committee, Fulbright Papers; Letter, J. William Fulbright to Rusk, October 6, 1964, folder "1964," box 29:3, subser. 8 (A.I.D.), ser. 48 Foreign Relations Committee, Fulbright Papers; Memo, Carl Marcy to J. William Fulbright, December 27, 1960, folder "1960," box 1:2, subser. 1 FRC (General), ser. 48 Foreign Relations Committee, Fulbright Papers; Address, J. William Fulbright, "Our Means and Our Ends," July 24, 1961, reprinted in *Dialogue Magazine*, November 1961, in folder "1961," box 22:5, subser. 5 Articles by J. William Fulbright, ser. 78 Press, 1943–1974, Fulbright Papers; Memo Prepared for Lecture, J. William Fulbright, "The United States in World Affairs," ca. January 24, 1963, folder "1963," box 5:1, subser. 1 FRC (General), ser. 48 Foreign Relations Committee, Fulbright Papers; Address, J. William Fulbright, "Old Myths & New Realities," March 25, 1964, reprinted in *Concern*, April 15, 1964, in folder "1963–1964," box 23:1, subser. 5 Articles by J. William Fulbright, ser. 78 Press, 1943–1974, Fulbright Papers.

11. "US Foreign Policy: How to Relate Self-Interest and the Preservation of Freedom," *Time*, January 22, 1965; Address, J. William Fulbright, "Putting Our Own House in Order," April 3, 1965, folder "1964–1965," box 2:1, ser. 74 Published Statements and Speeches, 1943–1974, Fulbright Papers.

12. Fulbright, "The Cold War in American Life"; "US Foreign Policy: How to Relate Self-Interest and the Preservation of Freedom"; Fulbright, "Putting Our Own House in Order"; Address, J. William Fulbright, "Why Are We Fighting in Vietnam?" January 26, 1967, folder "Major Speeches, 1967–1969," box 29:6, ser. 5 Speeches and Articles, Fulbright Papers; J. William Fulbright, "Vietnam Has Forced Distortion of Our Foreign Policy," *US News and World Report*, June 28, 1971; and Fulbright, "The Price of Empire."

13. J. William Fulbright, "Vietnam: The Crucial Issue," *The Progressive*, February 1970, 16–18.

14. Address, J. William Fulbright to Melvin Laird, March 21, 1969, folder "Published Statements and Speeches, January 21 68–December 22, 1970," box 2:3, ser. 74 Published Statements and Speeches, 1943–1974, Fulbright Papers; Address, J. William Fulbright, "Dimensions of Security," May 19, 1969, reprinted in *Foreign Service Journal*, July 1969, in folder "1967–1969," box 23:4, subser. 5 Articles by J. William Fulbright, ser. 78 Press, 1943–1974, Fulbright Papers; Memo, Hoyt Purvis to J. William Fulbright, June 27, 1970, folder "1970," box 14:4, subser. 4 Office Memos, ser. 95 Office Files, Fulbright Papers. On Fulbright's conservatism, see Randall B. Woods, "Dixie's Dove: J. William Fulbright, the Vietnam War, and the American South," in *Vietnam and the American Political Tradition: The Politics of Dissent*, ed. Randall B. Woods (New York: Cambridge University Press, 2003), 149–70.

15. Fulbright, "The Price of Empire"; Statement, J. William Fulbright, February 19, 1973, folder "1973," box 31:4, subser. 8 (A.I.D.), ser. 48 Foreign Relations Committee, Fulbright Papers.

16. Fulbright, "Vietnam Has Forced Distortion of Our Foreign Policy."

17. Fulbright, *The Arrogance of Power*, 4, 232–37; Memo, National Committee for an Effective Congress, "Senate Emerges as Counter-Force: NCEC Sees Foreign Policy Curbs Forming around President," August 28, 1967, folder "1967," box 44:3, subser. 17 Vietnam (General), ser. 48 Foreign Relations Committee, Fulbright Papers; Letter, J. William Fulbright to Richard Russell, July 14, 1967, folder "1967," box 16, subser. 3 Committee Administration, ser. 48 Foreign Relations Committee, Fulbright Papers; Reports from the United States Senate, J. William Fulbright, "Constitutional Power of the Congress," August 4, 1967, folder "1966–1967," box 2:2, ser. 74 Published Statements and Speeches, 1943–1974, Fulbright Papers; Statement, J. William Fulbright, February 3, 1969, folder "1969," box 17, subser. 3 Committee Administration, ser. 48 Foreign Relations Committee, Fulbright Papers; Memo, Carl Marcy to J. William Fulbright, January 19, 1971, folder "1971," box 18:1, subser. 3 Committee Administration, ser. 48 Foreign Relations Committee, Fulbright Papers; Letter, J. William Fulbright to Philip Geyelin (editorial page editor at the *Washington Post*), November 16, 1971, folder "1971," box 31:2, subser. 8 (A.I.D.), ser. 48 Foreign Relations Committee, Fulbright Papers; Handwritten Notes, J. William Fulbright at Japanese-American Parliamentary Group Meeting, January 24–25, 1969, folder "Meeting, Japanese-American Parliamentary Group, Santa Barbara, CA," box 36:2, subser. 11 Asia, ser. 48 Foreign Relations Committee, Fulbright Papers; J. William Fulbright, "The Wars in Your Future," *Look*, December 2, 1969, in folder "1969–1976," box 23:5, subser. 5 Articles by J. William Fulbright, ser. 78 Press, 1943–1974, Fulbright Papers; J. William Fulbright, "For a New Order of Priorities at Home and Abroad," *Playboy*, July 1968.

18. On America's bearing on the broader European context, see Geir Lundestad, *The United States and Western Europe since 1945: From "Empire" by Invitation to Transatlantic Drift* (New York: Oxford University Press, 2003), 142–96; and Lawrence Kaplan, *NATO Divided, NATO United: The Evolution of an Alliance* (Westport, CT: Praeger, 2004), 30–68.

19. See Ronald Hyam, *Britain's Declining Empire, 1918–1968* (New York: Cambridge University Press, 2006); John Young, *The Labour Governments, 1964–70*, vol. 2, *International Policy* (2003; reprint, New York: Manchester University Press, 2009); and Alex Spelling, "'A Reputation for Parsimony to Uphold': Harold Wilson, Richard Nixon and the Re-Valued 'Special Relationship,' 1969–1970," *Contemporary British History* 27, no. 2 (2013): 192–213.

20. Draft, FCO, "Underlying Elements in Anglo-US Relations," 3rd Draft, February 21, 1969, PREM 13/3016, PRO; Telegram 54, Secretary of State from UK Mission (NYC) to Foreign Office January 11, 1968, CAB 129/135/22, PRO; Cabinet, January 12, 1968, 5th Conclusion, CAB 128/43/5, PRO; and Report, Patrick Dean to Mr. Stewart, "United States and British Foreign Policy," July 31, 1968, FCO 7/778, PRO.

21. Dean, "Neo-Isolationism"; Dean to Mr. Stewart, "United States and British Foreign Policy"; Dean to Sir Paul Gore-Booth, October 1, 1968, FCO 7/742, PRO; Memo, Patrick Dean, "The Presidential Election, 1968," Washington, DC, November 22, 1968, FCO 63/331, PRO; Letter, Dean to Denis Greenhill, Washington, DC, February 5, 1969, PREM 13/3018, PRO; FCO, "Underlying Elements in Anglo-US Relations"; Dispatch, John Freeman, December 15, 1969, FCO 15/1095, PRO; and Memo, John Freeman, "United States: Annual Review for 1969," January 1, 1970, FCO 7/1803, PRO.

22. Address, Alec-Douglas Home, October 31, 1968, *Hansard Parliamentary Debates*, Commons, 5th ser., vol. 772, col. 201.

23. Memo, Western Organisations Department, Background Information for Lord Chalfont's Meeting with Congressman Farbstein on 27 January, January 23, 1970, FCO 41/675, PRO; FCO, "Underlying Elements in Anglo-US Relations"; Chiefs of Staff Committee, Defence Policy Staff, "The Security Implications of East/West Balanced Force Reductions," November 26, 1969, DEFE 13/877, PRO; Secretary of State for Defence, "Statement on the Defence Estimates, 1970," January 27, 1970, CAB/129/147, PRO; Letter, D. V. Bendall to Private Secretary, February 9, 1970, FCO 41/676, PRO.

24. FCO, "Underlying Elements in Anglo-US Relations"; Dispatch, A. M. Wood, "US Force Levels in Europe," January 22, 1970, FCO 41/675, PRO; Memo, Bernard Burrows, "NATO: Annual Review for 1969," Brussels, January 13, 1970, FCO 41/607, PRO; Chiefs of Staff Committee, Defence Policy Staff, "The Security Implications of East/West Balanced Force Reductions," November 26, 1969, DEFE 13/877, PRO; Western Organisations Department, Background Information for Lord Chalfont's Meeting with Congressman Farbstein 27 January; Letter, Illegible Author, February 17, 1970, FCO 41/675, PRO.

25. Letter, J. A. Thomson, "Some Impressions of Washington," March 17, 1969, PREM 13/3548, PRO; Burrows, "NATO: Annual Review for 1969"; Wood, "US Force Levels in Europe"; GMV (70) Second Meeting Extract, "NATO and European Defence," March 3, 1970, PREM 13/3383, PRO; Telegram 40, John Freeman, "The Congress and US Troops in Europe," Washington, DC, June 12, 1970, FCO 41/678, PRO; and Memo, "Appreciation of the Military Situation as It Will Affect NATO through 1980," January 1973, DEFE 25/299, PRO.

26. For a longer treatment of Wilson and Vietnam, see David Prentice, "A Sympathizing Ear: Harold Wilson and the Vietnam War, 1968–1970" (paper presented at the annual meeting of the Society for Historians of American Foreign Relations, Lexington, KY, June 2014).

27. Alexander Banks, "Britain and the Cambodian Crisis of Spring 1970," *Cold War History* 5, no. 1 (February 2005): 92–98; and Cabinet, May 5, 1970, 20th Conclusion, CAB 128/45, PRO.

28. See, e.g., Sean Fear, "Saigon Goes Global: South Vietnam's Quest for International Legitimacy in the Age of Détente," *Diplomatic History* 42, no. 3 (June 2018): 428–55; James Llewelyn, "Steadfast yet Reluctant Allies: Japan and the United King-

dom in the Vietnam War," *Diplomacy and Statecraft* 22 (2011): 608–33; and Gregg Brazinsky, *Nation Building in South Korea: Koreans, Americans, and the Making of a Democracy* (Chapel Hill: University of North Carolina Press, 2007).

29. Transcript, *Meet the Press*, March 8, 1970, folder "Published Statements and Speeches, January 21 68–December 22, 1970," box 2:3, ser. 74 Published Statements and Speeches, 1943–1974, Fulbright Papers.

30. Memo, Jim Lowenstein to J. William Fulbright, "Trip to Australia for Asian Development Bank Meetings," April 18, 1969, folder "International Finance," box 31:6, subser. 8 (A.I.D.), ser. 48 Foreign Relations Committee, Fulbright Papers; Memo, External Affairs, "Talking Points for the Prime Minister's Visit to the United States, 6 and 7 May 1969," April 28, 1969, item 582710, USA—Relations with Australia—Visit by Prime Minister of Australia, ser. A1838, NAA; Statements, Prime Minister Gorton and Prime Minister Keith Holyoake, February 25, 1969, item 1728504, Australian Strategic Interests and Defence Policies in the Southeast Asia Area, ser. A1838, NAA.

31. On Australia's strategic and imperial calculations and environment, see David Goldsworthy, *Losing the Blanket: Australia and the End of Britain's Empire* (Carlton South: Melbourne University Press, 2002); and Andrea Benvenuti, "A Parting of Ways: The British Military Withdrawal from Southeast Asia and Its Critical Impact on Anglo-Australian Relations, 1965–1968," *Contemporary British History* 20, no. 4 (December 2006): 575–605. On the immediate strategic response and planning, see Defence Committee Report, "The Strategic Basis of Australian Policy—1968," August 19, 1968, item 3161508, ser. A5882, NAA.

32. Memo, "United States Defence Posture in Asia and Possible Future Attitudes," 1968, item 1725133, Australian US Relations—Developments in US Policy Affecting Australia, 1968, ser. A1838, NAA; Memo, Defence Committee, "Strategic Basis of Australian Defence Policy," March 1971, item 3188732, The Strategic Basis of Australian Defence Policy—1971, ser. A5619, NAA; Memo, Defence Committee, "The Roles of Australian Forces in South East Asia," ca. February 8, 1969, item 6977965, The Role of Australian Forces in South East Asia, ser. A7942, NAA; Speech Notes for the Prime Minister, "Senate Foreign Relations Committee," April 29, 1969, item 582710, USA—Relations with Australia—Visit by Prime Minister of Australia, ser. A1838, NAA; Memo, MRB, "United States Attitude towards Asia," Last Draft, April 3, 1969, item 582710, USA—Relations with Australia—Visit by Prime Minister of Australia, ser. A1838, NAA.

33. Memo, Pat Holt to Symington, October 7, 1969, folder "1969," box 9:4, subser. 1 FRC (General), ser. 48 Foreign Relations Committee, Fulbright Papers.

34. Memo, A. J. Williams, "Back to Politics," July 2, 1969, FCO 7/1418, PRO; Telegram, Australian Embassy (Washington), January 8, 1969, item 555489, USA—Relations with Australia—Defence—General, ser. A1838, NAA; and Telegrams, Keith Waller (Washington), April 25 and October 8, 1969, item 555489, USA—Relations with Australia—Defence—General, ser. A1838, NAA.

35. Memo, Lowenstein to J. William Fulbright, "Trip to Australia for Asian Development Bank Meetings"; "Discussion between Mr. J. Lowenstein (Staff of

USFRC) and Mr. W. B. Pritchett," April 9, 1969, item 582683, USA—Relations with Australia—Developments in USA Policy Affecting Australia, ser. A1838, NAA. On official attitudes toward SFRC fact-finding missions, see the following exchange: Cable, Australian Embassy (Washington), May 4, 1970, then Cable, Feakes at Australian Embassy (Phnom Penh), May 5, 1970, and, finally, Australian Embassy (Washington) to Embassy (Phnom Penh), May 5, 1970, all in item 555235, United States—Political—Congress—General Senate, ser. A1838, NAA.

36. Speech Notes for the Prime Minister, "Senate Foreign Relations Committee."

37. Letter, K. M. Wilford, Washington, DC, May 20, 1969, FCO 24/398, PRO.

38. Indeed, Fulbright agreed to have lunch with Japanese prime minister Eisaku Satō only because the Japanese "seem to be making such a fuss about it, and since Japan is a very important country." Henceforth, he ordered his staff to "make it as difficult as possible" for foreign dignitaries to meet with him. See J. William Fulbright to Marcy, November 6, 1969, folder "1969," box 17, subser. 3 Committee Administration, ser. 48 Foreign Relations Committee, Fulbright Papers. That this directive came in the context of the meeting with Satō is telling since, like Wilson and Gorton, Satō was concerned about US commitments and reliability. See Llewellyn, "Steadfast yet Reluctant Allies."

39. Address, J. William Fulbright, "What Makes US Foreign Policy," April 16, 1959, folder "1953–1961," box 1:4, ser. 74 Published Statements and Speeches, 1943–1974, Fulbright Papers; Letter, J. William Fulbright to Robert Hay, November 16, 1967, folder "H," box 51:3, subser. 18 Vietnam (Correspondence), ser. 48 Foreign Relations Committee, Fulbright Papers; GMV (70) Second Meeting Extract, "NATO and European Defence," March 3, 1970, PREM 13/3383, PRO; Ray McHugh, "Germany 1972 I: A Hope for US Support in Time of Danger," ca. February 1972, folder "1971–1974," box 37:4, subser. 13 Europe, ser. 48 Foreign Relations Committee, Fulbright Papers.

40. J. William Fulbright, "Reflections: In Thrall to Fear," *New Yorker*, January 8, 1972.

The Price of Imperial Thinking

J. William Fulbright as Critic of US Empire

Justin Hart

On March 25, 1964, Arkansas senator J. William Fulbright rose on the floor of the US Senate to speak as part of the filibuster on the civil rights bill pending in Congress. Although he was a well-known opponent of the bill and of racial equality, he really had minimal interest in discussing civil rights, so he gave instead a long foreign policy speech entitled "Old Myths and New Realities." This speech became something of a sensation; it was reprinted in full by the national wire services and received attention—mostly positive—from the national punditocracy. It launched what the columnist Max Frankel called *the Fulbright phenomenon* and provided the centerpiece and title for one of three highly successful books that Fulbright published in the mid-1960s.[1]

In the speech itself, Fulbright focused on the excessive moralism of American attitudes toward the world, detailing the ways in which America's myths about its foreign policies prevented the nation from confronting the "new realities" in the nature of the Cold War and from aligning means and ends in its dealings with the Soviet Union, China, and Cuba. Near the end, he turned to the growing predicament the United States faced in Vietnam. Although he would eventually become one of the staunchest and most consequential establishment critics of US policy toward Vietnam, he had not yet reached that point. In March 1964, he argued simply that the United States must "support the South Vietnamese Government and Army by the most effective means available," concluding that this meant either increased funding to the government in South Vietnam or the escalation of the American presence.[2]

This essay adopts Fulbright's evolving position on Vietnam as a jumping-off point for an examination of his reputation as a putative public critic, first, of US imperial practices and, ultimately, of US empire itself. My argument is that, while Fulbright did indeed criticize US imperial practice, he was not a critic of US empire as such, if we are to understand *empire* as a description of the US project to secure global hegemony that achieved broad consensus in the post-1941 period.[3] Over his long career as an official critic of US foreign policy, Fulbright's principal complaints were about the failure to align means and ends and the inability to consider how the world might look through the eyes of other people. Despite his laments about "the arrogance of power" and "the price of empire" in response to the catastrophe in Vietnam, Fulbright never really questioned the need for US leadership in the world, even while offering strenuous critiques of various manifestations of the imperial impulse at home and abroad. One can even argue—as Sam Lebovic has—that the Fulbright program, which the senator continually listed as the best hope for improving the US approach to international relations, largely sought to make Americans better imperialists, not undermine the imperial project.[4] In short, his dissent from official orthodoxy on US foreign policy—both before and after the mid-1960s—should be understood as tactical, not strategic, in nature.

To be sure, it is important not to dismiss Fulbright's contributions to the public conversation on the direction of US foreign policy or to suggest that his outlook never evolved. Certainly, it is a laudable endeavor, this effort to limit foolhardy adventurism and wanton destruction on behalf of US domination, to imagine ways in which the United States might take the lead in crafting a new approach to international relations. Ultimately, then, the question at hand is, How—and how effectively—can one criticize imperial practice from within the parameters of empire? How much of a difference can it really make if one seeks to repudiate imperial practice without repudiating empire as such? After all, if we are to endorse the fairly uncontroversial position that American public life would benefit from more modern-day Fulbrights, we should also consider just how much finding what might be described as a usable Fulbright would provide a useful counterweight to the predominant assumptions of the US approach to the world.

Saving Liberal Internationalism from Itself

Although Fulbright has, over the years, become associated with the Vietnam War–era critique of the United States as *empire*, he was, for most of his career, decidedly reluctant to apply that term to his own country. In his three book-length indictments of US foreign policy written during the Vietnam War—*The Arrogance of Power* (1966), *The Pentagon Propaganda Machine* (1970), and *The Crippled Giant* (1972)—he scarcely used the word *empire*. In the first, there was a brief section entitled "American Empire or American Example?" in which he portrayed the urge to empire as a minority attitude that had been turned back throughout US history and must continue to be resisted. In the second, he never used the word *empire* at all. And, in the third, the only place in which he applied the term to the United States was in the conclusion, entitled "The Price of Empire." Even here, however, his warnings about the dangers posed by behaving as an empire were interspersed with qualifications such as "we have not become a traditional empire yet"; he also expressed optimism that America as a whole would not succumb to the "false and dangerous dream of an imperial destiny."[5] Only in his final book, written in 1989 and also entitled *The Price of Empire*, did he actually treat the United States as a practicing empire. However, the title was a bit of a misnomer. There was almost no attention to what made the United States an empire or how the empire came to be; the creation and existence of the empire was implied more than analyzed. Instead, Fulbright focused on the modes of thought that enabled, or perhaps encouraged, the United States to behave in an imperious fashion. A better title might have been *The Price of Imperial Thinking*.

It was always the imperial thinking that bothered Fulbright the most—not the basic fact of US hegemony and certainly not the quest to marshal and acquire the material resources necessary for hegemony.[6] In *The Arrogance of Power*, his first sustained critique of the attitudes that fueled America's imperial excursion in Vietnam, he focused not on the economic rationale for the war (which went unmentioned entirely) but on what he described as the "psychological need that nations seem to have in order to prove that they are bigger, better, or stronger than other nations." The primary consequence of this attitude, he argued, was an inability to see the world through the eyes of other people and a corresponding desire to impose one's beliefs on others. This was the arrogance of power that so concerned him—"the tendency of great nations to equate power with virtue and major responsibilities with a universal mission." Even so, he reassured his readers that he did not "think for a moment that America, with her deeply rooted democratic traditions, is likely to embark upon a campaign to dominate the world in the manner of a Hitler or Napoleon."[7]

Vietnam did not shake Fulbright's faith in American power itself, which in his mind still held the "principal, though not exclusive, responsibility for world peace and stability" and provided the best hope for affecting "a fundamental change in the nature of international relations." Even after accounting for the arrogance that he so lamented, the senator still believed that the root of America's difficulties in Vietnam and elsewhere stemmed from "drifting into commitments which, though generous and benevolent in intent, are so far-reaching as to exceed even America's great capacities." It was, as always for Fulbright, a question of means rather than ends, tactics rather than strategy: "If America has a service to perform in the world—and I believe she has—it is in large part the service of her own example."[8]

The Vietnam War's main effect, rather, was to undermine the binary logic of the Cold War—a logic that Fulbright had largely endorsed going back to the 1940s—which required policy makers to treat communism "as a kind of absolute evil": "The view of communism as an evil philosophy is a distorting prism through which we see projections of our own minds rather than what is actually there." If only the United States could find a way to divorce the political and military trappings of empire from the quest for economic influence abroad, perhaps a new course could be charted: "Maybe—just maybe—if we left our neighbors to make their own judgments and their own mistakes, and confined our assistance to matters of economics and technology instead of philosophy, maybe then they would begin to find the democracy and the dignity that have largely eluded them, and we in turn might begin to find the love and gratitude we seem to crave."[9] If anything, as one of the most remarkable passages of the book suggested, "affection is more likely to be won by an American 'absence' than by a conspicuous American presence."[10]

Ultimately, Fulbright's approach to US foreign policy from roughly 1964–1965 forward should be understood as saving liberal internationalism from itself. It is often said that the Vietnam War fractured the liberal consensus—and this makes sense if we understand Vietnam as a classic outgrowth of liberal internationalism rather than a deviation from it.[11] In any case, Vietnam certainly played this role for Fulbright. It is striking that, although he attributed much of his rationale for rethinking US Cold War policy to the danger of a nuclear holocaust, his breaking point as an uncritical advocate for the containment policies of the early Cold War came not with the Cuban Missile Crisis but with the debacle in Vietnam.[12]

Liberal internationalists had always wrestled with what is often described as *the Wilsonian dilemma*: balancing a professed commitment to self-determination with the quest to make the world "safe for democracy."[13] For Wilson, the League of Nations was the key to squaring this circle. Fulbright, in turn, sought to graft realist principles onto liberal internationalism—jettisoning the desire to remake the world in America's image while maintaining the commitment to self-determination guaranteed through empowering international organizations.[14] As he put it in *The Arrogance of Power*: "The inconstancy of American foreign policy is not an accident but an expression of two distinct sides of the American character. Both are characterized by a kind of moralism, but one is the morality of decent instincts tempered by the knowledge of human imperfection and the other is the morality of absolute self-assurance fired by the crusading spirit." From this premise, he reached the damning conclusion: "The problem of excessive ideological zeal is our problem as well as the communists."[15]

The historian Arthur Link would have described Fulbright's approach to Wilsonian liberal internationalism as exhibiting a "higher realism." Link's argument about Wilson was that his commitment to self-determination and international law in the face of the breakdown of the international system was actually more attuned to the realities of the unprecedented destruction unleashed by World War I than was the balance-of-power approach of classical realism.[16] Fulbright made essentially the same argument about his attempt to reconceptualize international relations for the nuclear age.

Contesting Nixinger Realism

This was not, to be sure, the sort of Nixon-Kissinger "realism" that supplanted the "pay any price" vision of the Kennedy-Johnson years. In *The Crippled Giant*—written against the backdrop of Nixon's cold-blooded approach to the Cold War in which he escalated bombing in Southeast Asia while pursuing détente with the Soviet Union and China—Fulbright declared classical realism to be an acceptable description of a certain historical mind-set but woefully inadequate as a contemporary guide to the conduct of US foreign policy: "This conception [realism] is false not in the sense of misrepresenting human experience but in the more important sense of its dangerous obsoleteness, and its utter irrelevance to valid human needs."[17]

Interestingly, Fulbright regarded détente as the fulfillment of the sort of conservative approach to foreign policy that, back in 1966, he had advocated as the best alternative to the arrogance of power damaging his nation's image in the world. Much like the historian William Appleman Williams, who continually urged policy makers to embrace the conservative foreign policy tradition of John Quincy Adams and Herbert Hoover as the only realistic alternative to the liberal internationalist compulsions that drove the United States to impose its ideology on the world, he summarized his vision as follows: "The kind of foreign policy I have been talking about is, in the true sense of the term, a *conservative* policy. It is intended quite literally to conserve the world. . . . [I]t is an approach that accepts the world as it is, with all its existing nations and ideologies, with all its existing qualities and shortcomings."[18] Six years later, he saw Nixon as fulfilling his hope that conservatives would reject their identity as "relentless crusaders against communism" and instead "come to terms with the world as it is." (He did find it somewhat ironic that the particular conservative who embraced his plea was Nixon, the indefatigable apostle of early Cold War anticommunism; however, he would take his victories where he could get them.)[19]

Yet the Nixon-Kissinger approach to foreign policy did not meet all, or even most, of Fulbright's objectives. While better than its predecessor in terms of aligning ends and means through disengaging from some areas, it represented little improvement in terms of the arrogance that so concerned the senator. Moreover, its relentless advocacy of amorality led to what many, including Fulbright, regarded as immoral outcomes— especially in Vietnam, Cambodia, and Chile. In short, Nixon-Kissinger realism rejected what Fulbright regarded as the salvageable parts of liberal internationalism even more vigorously than it jettisoned what he saw as the irredeemable parts. He was particularly incensed that some, including Nixon, attached the label *neo-isolationism* to his attempts to modify and thus redeem Wilsonianism: "The people who are now being called 'neo-isolationists' are by and large those who make a distinction between the new internationalism and the old, who welcome the reversion to the old power politics as an improvement on the ideological crusade but regret it in all other respects."[20] If only the foreign policy establishment could figure out how to divorce Wilson from himself, liberal internationalism might be saved.

By the end of Nixon's first term, Fulbright had developed a full-blown critique of the entire logic of the Cold War going back to the Truman administration: Stalin may have "started the cold war," but the "Truman Administration seemed to welcome it," he concluded. When "a few brave individuals like former Vice President Henry Wallace offered dissenting counsel," they "paid dear for it." Most importantly, the United Nations—the best hope for a new world order—"was orphaned at birth . . . like the League of Nations before it" because Truman abandoned Franklin Roosevelt's commitment to nurturing an international organization.[21] In short, while the Truman Doctrine "may have made sense for its time and place . . . as the charter for twenty-five years of global ideological warfare and unilateral military intervention against Communist insurgencies, [it] has a different set of implications altogether. It represents a view of communism and of our role in the world which has had much to do with the disaster of our policy in Indochina."[22]

Although much of *The Crippled Giant* was devoted to this full-throated denunciation of the Truman Doctrine and the ways in which its application led to the Vietnam War ("the futile crusade") and ultimately domestic disaster, Fulbright's primary goal in the book was to prevent future Vietnams by redefining the nation's "vital interests." Continuing his efforts to square the circle of the Wilsonian dilemma, Fulbright argued that Vietnam was the result of a *misreading* of Wilson's pledge to make the world safe for democracy. "The prevailing interpretation of that statement," he suggested, was that "America, acting if need be entirely on its own, has an obligation to defend existing governments which, even though they may be dictatorships, are deemed to be defenders of democracy because of their opposition to communism." The tortured logic by which a dictatorship could widely be viewed as a "defender of democracy" said a lot about the ambiguities and contradictions of liberal internationalism in the first place, but this was not how Fulbright saw it. He proposed, instead, a narrower interpretation of Wilsonianism, "one which [he] believe[d] to be much closer to Wilson's own understanding of it":

"That is that the security of American democracy requires the United States to be prepared to join in an international organization with other democracies for the *collective* defense of their political independence and territorial integrity against acts of overt foreign aggression."[23]

Even if we accept this alternate reading as the correct one, however, it was still not clear who would get to determine which territories had integrity and deserved independence and what constituted the sort of foreign aggression that demanded a response from nations that considered themselves democracies. Certainly, the UN Security Council never could have come to a consensus on those questions as they related to Vietnam. Moreover, since the United Nations was not composed solely of "other democracies," it is hard to understand exactly what international organization Fulbright had in mind. The closest thing to what he described was NATO, but NATO's members had turned into some of the staunchest critics of the US escalation in Vietnam. This was particularly ironic since it was the desire to support America's NATO allies in their efforts to shore up their colonial endeavors in the region that prompted the initial US intervention in Southeast Asia. In short, NATO, too, provided an imperfect model for what Fulbright sought.[24]

Indeed, the most glaring oversight in this attempt to redefine Wilson in order to salvage liberal internationalism was the failure to interrogate America's motives for a series of policies that, by 1972, even Fulbright was willing to label *quasi imperialism*. Because of this, he could never really explain *why* Wilson had so consistently been applied in a manner he regarded as wrongheaded. In Fulbright's mind: "Our proper concern is not with what we can make of the world but what must be done in the world to create the conditions under which we will be free to make what we want of ourselves." And that was all well and good, but during the Cold War countless US officials repeatedly used the exact same argument, filtered through the prism of global political economy, to justify what Fulbright denounced as "intrusive American interventionism."[25]

After the Chinese Revolution in 1949, Japan became the last, best hope for the United States to maintain a strategic and economic foothold in Asia. In turn, the stability of Japan depended on finding places for it to do business in Asia, and, with the limitations on the market in Communist China, Indochina mattered more than ever before. As President Eisenhower put it in a public address in June 1954: "Japan cannot remain in the free world unless something is done to allow her to make a living. . . . [I]f we will not try to defend in any way the southeast Asian area where she has a partial trade opportunity, what is to happen to Japan?" Behind closed doors with Republican legislators, Ike was even more specific: "If we don't assist Japan, gentlemen, Japan is going Communist. Then instead of the Pacific being an American lake, believe me it is going to be a Communist lake." Thus, the dots were connected in such a way that the United States had to replace the French in Vietnam in order to preserve its half-century-long project of securing access to Asian markets. At the end of the day, then, how different was Fulbright's sense of the "proper concern" of US foreign policy ("what must be done in the world to create the conditions under which we will be free to make what we want of ourselves") from Eisenhower's argument that the United States needed to expand its presence in Vietnam "to build up for the United States a position in the world of freedom of action"?[26]

The Limits of Fulbright's Dissent

The closest Fulbright ever came to attacking the existence of the empire itself was in his largely ignored and thoroughly underappreciated 1970 book, *The Pentagon Propaganda Machine*.[27] Based on a series of speeches he gave on the Senate floor in December 1969, *The Pentagon Propaganda Machine* was a searing attack on the Defense Department's domestic public affairs programs. It focused on the ways in which a series of initiatives justified as "informational" actually served to propagandize the American people (arguably in violation of statutory law) into sustaining a permanent wartime footing and endorsing the premises of the military-industrial complex. "When the government moves from pure information to propaganda a border is crossed," Fulbright argued.[28]

Individual chapters addressed the Defense Department's general approach to domestic propaganda as well as the individual efforts of the navy, the army, and the air force before concluding with an analysis of the Pentagon's film and television initiatives and its speakers program. All in all, Fulbright noted, the executive branch spent $400 million a year on "public information." His most common criticism concerned the way in which these programs and the Pentagon leadership that presided over them aggressively advocated for a martial culture in the United States. In one representative passage—in this case regarding the air force—he wrote: "There is, of course, nothing sinister about all of these 'community relations' activities. . . . I am, however, deeply bothered by its goal—persuading the American people of the special importance of the Air Force in our society and of its need for more and more and more of the country's resources. This goal the Air Force up to now has certainly achieved. Measured in dollars, its public relations program must be termed a resounding success in obtaining and spending the taxes of the citizens of this country." In addition to denouncing the money spent on propagandizing the American people to support the military, Fulbright also decried the executive's efforts to pressure Congress into granting all the Pentagon's appropriations requests.[29]

Other complaints included the Defense Department's attempts to shape and manipulate the media, along with producing its own media for public consumption. One program included a series of elaborate junkets to fly in journalists—both foreign and domestic—to watch public displays of military prowess. Another established a liaison with Hollywood to provide moviemakers with access to US military facilities—but only if the Defense Department determined that the film would contribute to a positive portrayal of the military. In special cases, such as John Wayne's *The Green Berets*, where a film portrayed the military in a particularly favorable light, the Defense Department suspended certain regulations about the extent of the access filmmakers would receive and reduced the amount they would have to pay for it. Often, as with *The Green Berets*, these accommodations bought the Pentagon a measure of script control. As Fulbright noted, the author of the book on which the film was based believed that the movie "didn't follow the book": "In the book we showed some bad Vietnamese allies. But the movie showed only good ones. The movie should have shown the frustration with the bad Vietnamese. But that was a concession we had to make to the Defense Department. We couldn't have made the film without their approval."[30]

Most concerning to Fulbright was the way in which top military officials used the Pentagon's propaganda initiatives to demonize as unpatriotic anyone who questioned military spending or the direction of US foreign policy in general. For example, the speakers program, which sent high-profile officials around the country to address various domestic interest groups, made no bones about drumming up support for US policy in

Vietnam: "The speeches I have examined are uniformly didactic about the war in Vietnam and the President's Vietnamization program and are almost unctuously self-righteous about the role we are playing there." He then quoted several Pentagon spokespersons who argued that the antiwar movement was undermining the US effort in Vietnam. (He was particularly incensed by Marine Corps general Lewis Walt's 1969 claim: "Without dissent, I believe the war would have been over a year ago.")[31]

Yet, despite writing eight scathing chapters detailing a military-industrial complex out of control, Fulbright never examined the sources of the US military posture toward the world. In the conclusion he came close to it, denouncing the underlying imperatives of US foreign policy that had resulted in the United States becoming a practicing empire, arguing: "History did not prepare the American people for the imperial role in which we find ourselves, and we are paying a moral price for it. From the time of the framing of our Constitution to the two world wars, our experience and values—if not our uniform practice—conditioned us not for the unilateral exercise of power but for the placing of limits upon it." But he still needed to believe that "reason drawn from our history . . . and the innate common sense of Americans will prevail," that the American people would reject these new "alien values"—like a "human body reacting against a transplanted organ"—and that the United States had, essentially, become an empire by accident.[32]

Over the next two decades, Fulbright continued to push back against the globalist assumptions that drove US foreign policy. His final sustained contribution to this cause was *The Price of Empire*, which came out in 1989, near the end of his life. Published long after his political career came to an unglamorous end when he was overwhelmingly defeated in the 1974 Democratic primary, *The Price of Empire* gave the appearance—at least superficially—of being his most radical analysis of US foreign policy. Unapologetically applying the term *empire* to US domestic and foreign policy, Fulbright began with the memorable line, "If I am remembered, I suppose it will be as a dissenter," and then proceeded to outline his complaints about nearly every aspect of US foreign policy.[33]

Even here, however, Fulbright's primary objective was not to undermine the missionary role of the United States in the world but to redirect those impulses toward a more humane and less destructive path. Once again, he called for policy makers to adopt his signature blend of Wilsonian internationalism tempered with humility and a quasi-realist dose of caution. He acknowledged his preference for détente over the "philosophy of the Truman Doctrine," and he denounced Carter and Reagan for undermining détente with their decisions to confront the Soviet Union over human rights abuses, then ramping up military spending. However, he also reemphasized his commitment to international organizations to an extent that no hard-core realist could ever abide.[34]

Overall, Fulbright did not waver in his conviction that capitalism was a superior system and his belief that democratic values would triumph in the end; he just objected to Americans' relentless moralizing and their inability or unwillingness to empathize with the perspectives of others. The nation's best chance to curb these dangerous tendencies, he argued, was to promote international cultural education, whether through expanding the Fulbright program or some other means. To this end, he dismissed as "inaccurate" the charge that these sorts of exchanges could lead to "cultural imperialism."[35]

By far the most provocative chapter in the book is the one denouncing the "militarization of the economy." Continuing with the themes he first developed in *The Pentagon Propaganda Machine*, Fulbright made the case that "violence has become the nation's leading industry" and that "this militarization of the economy is undermining us internally": "Weapons are not reproductive; they are sheer non-productive assets. They do not contribute to the welfare of the country in any positive way." Citing Eisenhower's prescience in warning against the "military-industrial complex," he noted wryly: "When Eisenhower gave his speech on the military-industrial complex before he left office, I wasn't as impressed with it as I am now." Of course, that statement applied not just to Fulbright himself but to countless fellow liberal internationalists chastened by what they had wrought in Vietnam.[36]

If this chapter was the strongest evidence of an increasingly radicalized Fulbright, the chapter "Vietnam Revisited" ironically provided the strongest argument against such a proposition. Nowhere did Fulbright attempt to reckon with his own initial support for the war or, more broadly, his prior championing of the very ideology that paved the road to Southeast Asia. In a statement at once admirably candid and disturbingly oblivious, he acknowledged: "I rarely thought about Indochina before the early 1960s. The war rather crept up on us without anybody knowing anything about Vietnam." Much like the Democrats who voted in 2002 to give President George W. Bush the authorization to use force in Iraq, Fulbright argued that, in 1964, he believed the primary purpose of the Tonkin Gulf Resolution was to give Lyndon Johnson the leverage he needed to bring North Vietnam to the negotiating table. Even with twenty-five years of hindsight, he still attributed his willingness to vote for such an open-ended resolution primarily to the lies the Johnson administration told about the attack itself. It is easy to conclude in reading this chapter that his primary objective was to defend himself from the implied charge that he should have done more sooner to stop the war:

> Looking back at my role in criticizing the war in Vietnam after 1965, my only regret is that I was not more effective. I thought I was going quite far at the time. . . . [I]t is a daunting task for an individual senator to publicly challenge the president of the United States, with the aura of power that surrounds him. It is difficult to mobilize the self-confidence and to feel the degree of conviction in your own mind that will enable you to go beyond a certain limit. There's always that nagging feeling that you could be wrong. You're never quite that positive. Only fanatics are that sure of themselves.

There were those, of course, who denounced the intervention in Vietnam from the outset. But they were fanatics, so their critique could not be taken seriously. It is here, then, that we see most clearly the limits of Fulbright's dissent from empire.[37]

Fulbright's Legacy as a Critic of Empire

In *Covert Capital*, his striking recent book on the way in which northern Virginia functioned as the seat of US empire during the Cold War, Andrew Friedman notes: "The United States did not have just an empire. It had imperialists."[38] Clearly, the statement offers a provocation to ordinary Americans to consider their own role in sustaining the reality of empire and all its consequences, even if they do not endorse all—or even most—aspects of imperial practice. This is an insight that we would do well to keep in mind when considering J. William Fulbright's career as a critic of US empire.

The question that remains about Fulbright is whether—or at least how successfully—one can alter the direction of empire without challenging the existence of the empire itself. Fulbright might have answered this question in several different ways depending on when he was asked, but one possibility is this quote from *The Arrogance of Power*: "To speak persuasively one must speak in the idiom of the society in which one lives."[39] In other words, despite sharing a critique of empire with the New Left that rose to prominence alongside him—despite endorsing, for example, the general premise of William Appleman Williams's *Empire as a Way of Life*—Fulbright never really abandoned his faith in key tenets of the ideology of liberal internationalism that underwrote US empire in the first place. Instead, he sought to modify or, more accurately, delimit liberal internationalism in such a way that the empire could be maintained without the United States behaving as an imperialist power. Or, to put it in the terms preferred by some contemporary scholars of imperialism, Fulbright wanted to maintain US hegemony without the United States becoming entrapped by the burdens of empire.[40]

In attempting to transform, rather than dismantle, the defining ideology of US foreign policy in the twentieth century, Fulbright sought to speak in the idiom of the society in which he lived. And this is a noble goal. But is it really possible to sustain an empire without the violence used to acquire the material resources that provide its foundation? Is it possible to dismantle the military-industrial complex without dismantling the empire, as such? As Williams famously asked, "is the idea and reality of America even possible without empire?"[41] Or, as Congressman Adam Smith (D-WA) put it recently in reflecting upon budget cuts in military spending: "What if, all of a sudden, we don't have troops in Europe, we don't have troops in Asia, we are just, frankly, like pretty much every other country in the world."[42] J. William Fulbright surely would have disagreed with Smith's conclusion. But, if the direction of US foreign policy in the twenty-five years since Fulbright's death is any indication, we must regard his efforts to undermine imperial thinking without undermining the empire itself as a cautionary—not just a salutary—tale.

Notes

1. On the impact of the speech, see Randall Bennett Woods, *Fulbright: A Biography* (New York: Cambridge University Press, 1995), 334–39. Fulbright's three

major books of the mid-1960s were *Prospects for the West* (Cambridge, MA: Harvard University Press, 1963); *Old Myths and New Realities* (New York: Random House, 1964); and *The Arrogance of Power* (New York: Random House, 1966).

2. Fulbright, *Old Myths and New Realities*, 41–44.

3. The old debate about whether, in the post-1945 (or even post-1898) period, the United States constituted an empire has been reenergized in recent years. Among scholars who have devoted significant attention to that question, the answer more often than not depends upon how broadly the author defines the concept of empire, as well as whether the author's primary focus is upon the Global North or South. On one side are scholars who have argued that, when compared to European powers in the 19th century age of high imperialism, the United States has never qualified as an empire, since a fair amount of its dominance (particularly in Europe) was established through consent rather than coercion. Perhaps the best-known proponent of this school of thought is Geir Lundestad, who prefers to put the word *empire* in quotation marks when describing US relations with Western Europe during the Cold War. See Geir Lundestad, *The United States and Western Europe since 1945: From "Empire" by Invitation to Transatlantic Drift* (New York: Oxford University Press, 2003); and *"Empire" by Integration: The United States and European Integration, 1945–1997* (New York: Oxford University Press, 1998). Others who make similar arguments include John Ikenberry, who sees the United States as establishing a form of liberal hegemony based on mutually agreed-on rules and institutions, and Charles Maier, who treats the United States as "among empires," exhibiting "many, but not all . . . of the traits that have distinguished empires." See G. John Ikenberry, *Liberal Leviathan: The Origins, Crisis, and Transformation of the American World Order* (Princeton, NJ: Princeton University Press, 2011); and Charles S. Maier, *Among Empires: American Ascendancy and Its Predecessors* (Cambridge, MA: Harvard University Press, 2006), 3. The most demonstrative recent critique of the empire framework comes from Elizabeth Cobbs Hoffman, who explicitly argues in *American Umpire* (Cambridge, MA: Harvard University Press, 2013) that the role the United States plays in the world is better described as an *umpire* rather than an *empire*. On the other side of the question are scholars who follow in the tradition of William Appleman Williams, who treats the US adoption of Open Door trade policies in the late 19th century as an effort to develop a form of "imperial anti-colonialism." See *The Tragedy of American Diplomacy*, 50th anniversary ed. (New York: Norton, 2009). Williams and several of his most prominent students, such as Lloyd C. Gardner, Walter LaFeber, Thomas McCormick, Carl Parrini, and Martin J. Sklar, devoted much of their careers to applying this more expansive definition of *empire* to US foreign policy. If the current vogue for inserting *empire* into the title of a wide range of books on a wide range of topics in US history from the revolutionary period to the present is any indication, the importance of analyzing the United States from an imperial perspective has persuaded the majority of the American historical profession, if not perhaps a majority of historians of US foreign policy. In addition to the critical distinction Williams makes between presiding over colonies and

behaving as an empire, there is also the argument advanced by Paul Kramer in his recent overview of the historiography of US empire: "Far more is to be gained by exploring the imperial as a way of seeing than by arguing for or against the existence of a 'US empire.'" See Paul Kramer, "Power and Connection: Imperial Histories of the United States in the World," *American Historical Review* 116 (December 2011): 1348–91, 1350. My analysis here falls in line with that of Williams and Kramer in conceptualizing all that flowed from the US project to secure global hegemony in the post-1945 period—sometimes consensual and sometimes brutally coercive—as the product of an imperial "way of seeing."

4. See Sam Lebovic, "From War Junk to Educational Exchange: The World War II Origins of the Fulbright Program and the Foundations of American Cultural Globalism, 1945–1950," *Diplomatic History* 37, no. 2 (April 2013): 280–312. For other works that examine US cultural and educational exchanges as imperial practice, see Giles Scott-Smith, *Networks of Empire: The US State Department's Foreign Leader Program in the Netherlands, France and Britain, 1950–1970* (Brussels: Peter Lang, 2008); and Justin Hart, *Empire of Ideas: The Origins of Public Diplomacy and the Transformation of US Foreign Policy* (New York: Oxford University Press, 2013). Fulbright spent a great deal of time over the years protesting (too much?) that educational exchanges were not simply an extension of nationalist foreign policy imperatives or propaganda disguised in an appealing package. In addition to his comments (discussed below) in *The Price of Empire* dismissing the charge that they were a form of cultural imperialism, he makes the following argument: "Educational exchange is not a propaganda program designed to 'improve the image' of the United States as some government officials seem to conceive it." Fulbright, *The Arrogance of Power*, 177. Here, at least, he acknowledges that some officials might abuse educational exchanges for propaganda purposes, but he denies that they were intended to be used in that way.

5. See Fulbright, *The Arrogance of Power*, 19–21; J. William Fulbright, *The Pentagon Propaganda Machine* (New York: Vintage, 1970); and J. William Fulbright, *The Crippled Giant: American Foreign Policy and Its Domestic Consequences* (New York: Random House, 1972), 275–79.

6. It is notable, in this regard, that Fulbright also believed that traditional European colonialism was motivated more by security and prestige than by markets and that the world wars of the twentieth century had little to do with economics and stemmed, instead, from nationalism. See Fulbright, *Prospects for the West*, 4.

7. Fulbright, *The Arrogance of Power*, 5, 9, 4.

8. Ibid., 196, 256, 4, 21.

9. Ibid., 106–8, 14. It should be said that this quote is one of many places where Fulbright's rationale for scaling back US attempts to make the world safe for democracy embraced a racist logic premised on the assumption that many people around the world were not socially or culturally developed enough to be capable of adopting democratic values. For example, there is this much-quoted passage: "What I do question is the ability of the United States or any other Western nation to go into a

small, alien, undeveloped Asian nation and create stability where there is chaos, the will to fight where there is defeatism, democracy where there is no tradition of it, and honest government where corruption is almost a way of life." Ibid., 15.

10. Ibid., 236.

11. The most sustained analysis of the not uncommon argument that Lyndon Johnson's approach to Vietnam grew out of his commitment to imposing his vision of domestic liberalism around the world can be found in Lloyd C. Gardner, *Pay Any Price: Lyndon Johnson and the Wars for Vietnam* (Chicago: Ivan R. Dee, 1995).

12. As Fulbright wrote: "From Korea to Berlin to Cuba to Vietnam the Truman Doctrine governed America's response to the Communist world . . . based on assumptions which few really questioned. Sustained by an inert Congress, the policy makers of the forties, fifties and early sixties were never compelled to reexamine the premises of the Truman Doctrine, or even to defend them in constructive adversary proceedings. Change has come not from wisdom but from disaster. The calamitous failure of American policy in Vietnam has induced on the part of scholars, journalists and politicians a belated willingness to reexamine the basic assumptions of postwar policy." *The Crippled Giant*, 18–19.

13. On the unanticipated consequences and the limitations of Wilson's commitment to self-determination, see Erez Manela, *The Wilsonian Moment: Self-Determination and the International Origins of Anticolonial Nationalism* (New York: Oxford University Press, 2007). The most extensive explication of the Wilsonian dilemma is Lloyd C. Gardner, *Safe for Democracy: The Anglo-American Response to Revolution, 1913–1923* (New York: Oxford University Press, 1984). On the continuities of liberal internationalism as the guiding principle of US foreign policy from Wilson forward, see Lloyd C. Gardner, *Covenant with Power: America and World Order from Wilson to Reagan* (New York: Oxford University Press, 1984).

14. Fulbright made an extensive argument for empowering international organizations as early as 1966, when he called for completely overhauling existing systems for distributing foreign aid (including US foreign aid) and replacing them with a model based on the principle of progressive taxation used to fund the US government. In his vision, the United Nations would play the role of the US federal government, taxing the nations of the world progressively on the basis of GDP and then supervising the distribution of those funds to needy nations, thus eliminating the disfiguring influence of geopolitical considerations. See Fulbright, *The Arrogance of Power*, chap. 11 ("A New Concept of Foreign Aid").

15. Ibid., 245–46, 254.

16. Arthur S. Link, "The Higher Realism of Woodrow Wilson," *Journal of Presbyterian History* 41, no. 1 (March 1963): 1–13. It is important to note here that Link never gave much credence to the argument that Wilson's many interventions—in Mexico, in Russia, and in seeking to redraw the boundaries of the old colonial empires—were designed to remake those places in America's image, thus raising questions about the authenticity of his commitment to self-determination.

17. Fulbright, *The Crippled Giant*, 9.

18. The Fulbright quote is from *The Arrogance of Power*, 255. On the same point, six years later in *The Crippled Giant* (p. 15), the two quotes that Fulbright used for the epigraph to pt. 1 were John Kennedy's "pay any price, bear any burden" line from his inaugural address and John Quincy Adams's admonition against going "abroad in search of monsters to destroy" from 1821. He clearly meant to suggest that the United States needed to replace the former attitude with the latter. For the most explicit of many passages where Williams advocates for conservatism as an alternative to the liberal consensus on foreign policy, see *The Tragedy of American Diplomacy*, 311–12.

19. Fulbright, *The Crippled Giant*, 4.

20. Ibid., 11.

21. Ibid., 19–21. Fulbright particularly blames Truman's secretary of state Dean Acheson for abandoning the United Nations, noting his statement from 1970: "I never thought the United Nations was worth a damn. To a lot of people it was a Holy Grail, and those who set store by it had the misfortune to believe their own bunk." Ibid., 20.

22. Ibid., 22–23.

23. Ibid., 154–55.

24. On the role that European alliances played in the initial US intervention in Vietnam, see Lloyd C. Gardner, *Approaching Vietnam: From World War II through Dienbienphu, 1941–1954* (New York: Norton, 1988); Mark Atwood Lawrence, *Assuming the Burden: Europe and the American Commitment to War in Vietnam* (Berkeley and Los Angeles: University of California Press, 2005); Kathryn C. Statler, *Replacing France: The Origins of American Intervention in Vietnam* (Lexington: University Press of Kentucky, 2007); and Fredrik Logevall, *Embers of War: The Fall of an Empire and the Making of America's Vietnam* (New York: Random House, 2012).

25. Fulbright, *The Crippled Giant*, 155, 161.

26. Eisenhower quoted in Gardner, *Approaching Vietnam*, 294–95, 355.

27. In terms of ignored and underappreciated, it is worth pointing out that, in *Fulbright: A Biography*, Woods mentions *The Pentagon Propaganda Machine* only once—and even then in a note.

28. Fulbright, *The Pentagon Propaganda Machine*, 11–21. It is debatable, of course, whether it is even possible to draw a line between information and propaganda, since a matter of selection always arises in deciding which information to present. The least-charitable reading of Fulbright's attempt to draw such a line is that he was naive; more charitably, one might conclude that such lines are always blurry, but the Pentagon was not even trying to separate the two.

29. Ibid., 17, 101, 31.

30. Ibid., 34, 117–22.

31. Ibid., 130–32.

32. Ibid., 145–46.

33. J. William Fulbright with Seth P. Tillman, *The Price of Empire* (New York: Pantheon, 1989), vii. *The Price of Empire* was the only one of Fulbright's books

officially to assign some authorial credit to Seth P. Tillman, Fulbright's longtime speechwriter and collaborator. It is thus potentially problematic to treat this book as fully reflective of Fulbright's thinking in the same way as his previous writings. However, I think that *The Price of Empire* can—and should—be regarded as the culmination of Fulbright's public thought for two reasons. First, it is fully consistent with, if slightly more scathing than, his other public critiques of US foreign policy going back twenty-five years. Second, whenever we, as historians, are dealing with public figures who employ speechwriters, it is difficult to determine exactly how much of any public speech, article, or book came directly from the pen of the person in question. Yet historians typically use the rule of thumb that, if public figures have put their name on the document in question, they are treated as the author for purposes of historical analysis. And, after all, we do not know for sure exactly how much of *The Price of Empire*—or, for that matter, any of Fulbright's other speeches or books—was really written by Tillman.

34. Fulbright, *The Price of Empire*, 15–17, 31–33, 199–200.

35. Ibid., 33, 193–194, 215–17.

36. Ibid., 137, 140.

37. Ibid., 103–6, 123.

38. Andrew Friedman, *Covert Capital: Landscapes of Denial and the Making of US Empire in the Suburbs of Northern Virginia* (Berkeley and Los Angeles: University of California Press, 2013), 4.

39. Fulbright, *The Arrogance of Power*, 39.

40. To build on the discussion in n. 3 above, Fulbright certainly would have embraced the proposition offered by Geir Lundestad and others that, at its best, the United States sought hegemony without imperialism. Put differently, Fulbright hoped to maintain the consensual aspects of US empire while jettisoning the more coercive aspects. However, the model proposed by Lundestad has always worked better when applied to Europe and certain parts of East Asia than to the Global South. Moreover, it is difficult to imagine that, driven as it was by an unabashedly global vision in the post-1945 period, the United States could have limited itself to projecting US political and economic imperatives only into areas where they might be welcomed.

41. William Appleman Williams, *Empire as a Way of Life* (New York: Ig, 2007), vi.

42. Smith quoted in Jill Lepore, "The Force: How Much Military Is Enough?" *New Yorker*, January 28, 2013.

Part 2

The Fulbright Exchange in Historical Perspective

The Meaning of Educational Exchange

The Nationalist Exceptionalism of Fulbright's Liberal Internationalism

Sam Lebovic

Among the Cold War foreign policy elite, J. William Fulbright was an unusually moralistic and principled critic of American foreign policy. In 1943, attempting to bury interwar isolationism once and for all, he suggested that America's lack of concern with foreign affairs rendered the nation "one of the strongest psychopaths the world has ever seen."[1] Two decades later, when he had risen to chair of the Senate Foreign Relations Committee and become angered by militaristic interventions in Vietnam and the Dominican Republic, he went so far as to compare the United States in its "current imperial mode" to Nazi Germany.[2] In 1966, he gave his critique of American foreign policy a full airing in *The Arrogance of Power*, a book that was censorious in its attack on American hypocrisy. He criticized the lack of dissent in the foreign policy establishment, decried the impact of America's "missionary instinct" on the world, and bluntly pointed out American unwillingness to confront its foreign policy without ideological blinkers: "We see the Viet Cong who cut the throats of village chiefs as savage murderers but American flyers who incinerate unseen women and children with napalm as valiant fighters for freedom." And, in its title, the book provided an explanation of American imperial hubris—"the tendency of great nations to equate power with virtue and major responsibilities with a universal mission."[3] The rare senatorial book that quoted Erich Fromm and Albert Camus, *The Arrogance of Power* was a major statement of American internationalism. Hans Morgenthau called it a "moral and political document of the first rank," and it sold 400,000 copies.[4]

Fulbright's criticism of American foreign policy was balanced by his articulation of an alternative vision of liberal internationalism. Both in *The Arrogance of Power* and in his broader championing of such programs as the eponymous Fulbright educational exchange program, the Arkansan sketched a vision of an international order based not on violence and conflict but on peace, tolerance, free exchange, and mutual understanding. Particularly when juxtaposed with the hubristic militarism that Fulbright criticized as nationalist arrogance, this was an appealing and commonsensical vision of American foreign policy. But much of its appeal stemmed from the often vague and platitudinous terms in which he described this positive vision. The centerpiece of his liberal internationalism was educational exchange—a vision of a humanized and humanistic world order, one based on mutual understanding. This essay reconstructs and critically analyzes Fulbright's understanding of educational exchange from his rise to prominence in the 1940s to the publication of *The Arrogance of Power*. By drawing on his scattered and unsystematic comments on the purpose, power, and function of educational exchange, we can come to a better understanding of how this liberal internationalist actually imagined the operation of a liberal world order.

A closer examination of Fulbright's theories of cultural exchange reveals a persistent assumption that free exchanges would redound to the benefit of America—that educational exchange would promote American values and priorities and create a world compatible with American power. Fulbright's thinking about educational exchange reflected and elaborated on his thinking about American leadership, about the universal power of American values, about the causes of global conflict, and about the importance of free trade. For this reason, an assessment of his philosophy of educational exchange can illuminate his broader political assumptions and, through them, some of the central themes of American internationalism in the early Cold War. His biographer has, for understandable reasons, stated that Fulbright was "a true internationalist, committed to the notion of cultural pluralism and convinced that economic interdependence advanced the interests of all people."[5] That even such an avowed internationalist rested his theories in part on nationalist assumptions about the universalism of American values and on the mutual compatibility of American and global interests is a reminder of how ubiquitous and deep assumptions about America's global mission were during the high Cold War.

The Substance of Educational Exchange

Perhaps the most striking feature of Fulbright's theory of educational exchange is how underdeveloped it was. The actual impact of educational exchange on individuals, let alone cultures, is extraordinarily difficult to identify, measure, or predict—today, whole subfields of academe, not to mention teams of counselors and university administrators, are devoted to thinking about these questions. But Fulbright spent little time outlining how, exactly, he believed educational exchange would contribute to mutual understanding and world peace. In the 260 pages of *The Arrogance of Power*, for instance, he devoted only a few sentences to the topic, despite its importance to his vision of a more sustainable and liberal international-ism: "No part of our foreign policy does more to make international rela-tions human relations and to encourage attitudes of personal empathy. . . . [T]hus conceived, educational exchange is not a propaganda program designed to 'improve the image' of the United States as some government officials seem to conceive it, but a program for the cultivation of percep-tions and perspectives that transcend national boundaries. To put it another way, far from being a means of gaining some national advantage in the traditional game of international relations, international education purports to change the nature of the game, to civilize and humanize it in the nuclear age."[6] In 1965, in a three-page foreword to an institutional his-tory of the Fulbright program, he returned to the theme: "Civilization is what educational exchange programs are all about."[7]

Despite their brevity and abstraction, those comments are revealing. Fulbright always perceived educational exchange as a way to promote "mutual understanding" that would transcend nationalism and interna-tional division by promoting empathy and tolerance. When the Fulbright program was created in 1946, he justified it in precisely this fashion. Edu-cational exchanges, he said, "can play a major role in helping to break down mutual misunderstandings and in furthering the kind of knowledge that leads to mutual confidence."[8] By 1961, when the Fulbright-Hays Act reorganized the structure of the program, the focus on overcoming misunderstanding had become even stronger. According to the congressional statement of purpose included in the act, the program was designed "to increase mutual understanding between the people of the United States and the people of other countries by means of educational and cultural exchange" as well as to "strengthen ties" between nations and "promote international cooperation for educational and cultural advancement." Through such mechanisms, the program would "assist in the development of friendly, sympathetic, and peaceful relations between the United States and the other countries of the world."[9] The concept of mutual understanding, which implied an open-minded cultural relativism and an openness to multidirectional cultural exchanges, played a central role in the rhetorical and philosophical justification of the program.

Fulbright was always quick to distinguish this liberal vision of educational exchange from crassly utilitarian and nationalist visions of propaganda or cultural imperialism. Throughout his career, he was a principled and outspoken critic of propaganda, which he straightforwardly equated with illiberal militarism. In the 1960s, for instance, he repeatedly took on military propaganda in the domestic United States when he investigated far-right tendencies in military training programs and later published his exposé *The Pentagon Propaganda Machine*.[10] Unsurprisingly, therefore, he drew a sharp distinction between educational exchange and propaganda. In 1946, he juxtaposed the superficiality and ephemerality of propaganda with the "solid background acquired by those who can study outside of their own countries [that] can provide the basis for truer understandings of other peoples."[11] In 1953, he fought to keep the educational exchange program institutionally autonomous from propaganda agencies when the US Information Agency was created to consolidate the organs of American public diplomacy.[12] "It is not the purpose of this program," he had declared in 1948, "to indoctrinate the world with straight Americanism in its narrow sense." (That was associated with "exclusiveness, isolationism, imperialism, bigotry and intolerance.") Nevertheless, he wanted to reclaim one sense in which Americanism was more compatible with educational exchange. As he put it: "In a broader sense, and in more objective circles, [Americanism] is, of course, associated with the dignity and freedom of the individual human being and with a generosity and sympathy seldom encountered on a continental scale. The point of Americanism, even in this broad sense, is not the subject matter of education, it is rather the fruit, the end result of education."[13]

This equation of Americanism with transcendent liberal values of freedom, dignity, and sympathy was central to the logic of the Fulbright program and to Fulbright's theory of cultural exchange. Whereas his criticism of Vietnam-era foreign policy was predicated on a critique of the gap between America's actual practices and its ostensibly liberal values, his advocacy of educational exchange blurred that distinction. In the same 1948 speech in which he distinguished educational exchange from any effort to indoctrinate the world, Fulbright illustrated his vision of the power of educational exchange by referring to an elite Turkish politician who had been educated in an American university. "His mind is a channel," he declared, "open and sympathetic, through which the thoughts and purposes of the west, especially America, can be presented to his people objectively and truthfully."[14] In slipping from a metaphor of exchange to one of transmission, he revealed that his vision of cultural exchange assumed that free exchange would involve the export of American values—this was a transfer of specific cultural content, not the spread of abstractly liberal processes. In a 1944 speech, he had already indicated the subtle way in which he squared a rejection of cultural propaganda and an assumption that free exchange would spread American values: "[To give foreigners] educational opportunity does not mean that we seek to impose our own doctrines directly upon these peoples. It merely means that we have faith in the basic rightness of our Christian democratic civilization, and that if people are permitted to seek the truth through education and the free and unrestricted interchange of ideas, they naturally will develop a society compatible with our own."[15]

At the same time that Fulbright rejected any crude sense of American cultural exceptionalism, therefore, his confident advocacy of free cultural exchange was supported by a deeper assumption that America embodied universal liberal values. And intertwined with his universalizing rhetoric was always an assumption that civilizing and humanizing international relations would benefit American interests. It was not just that a more civil and humane world would benefit Americans insofar as they had to live in the world and would automatically and passively benefit from peace—though Fulbright certainly believed that to be an important justification for the program. It was also that Americans had a moral obligation to spread their liberal and peaceful culture in a confused and war-torn world. In 1946, outlining America's newly global role in an address given at the

College of William and Mary, Fulbright expressed the point this way: "It is peculiarly the responsibility of Americans to take the lead in the creation of a peaceful world. Not only is it to our selfish material interest because we have more to lose by chaos than any other people, but it is also our moral duty to give direction and strength to the bewildered people of this earth who are groping helplessly for peace and a decent life. If for no other reason it is our duty because we are the favored heirs of western Christian civilization."[16]

This conflation of Americanism and universalism meant that Fulbright saw little need to distinguish between the benefits that educational exchange would provide to the world and those that it would provide to the United States. In 1956, he argued that educational exchange was intended "to civilize this thing we call a human being, to bring us to understand one another," while also asserting: "We should rather keep in mind this program is not just to relieve the poor illiterate foreigners, but that it has a very special significance to the improvement of this country domestically."[17] In the abstract, that might have meant that Americans, too, needed civilizing—and Fulbright was always happy to argue that Americans were, indeed, less than perfect world citizens and could be improved by the experience of educational exchange.[18] But, in practice, the Fulbright program institutionalized a contradictory theory of cultural exchange, one that assumed that Americans and foreigners would draw very different benefits from study abroad.

Although Fulbright had little to do with the day-to-day operations of the program, which he generally left to the ten presidential appointees on the Board of Foreign Scholarships (BFS), his occasional criticisms reveal his conceptualization of the varied benefits of the program in its early years. In 1948, and again in 1950, he wrote to the assistant secretary of state responsible for the program to complain that Fulbright scholarships had been going primarily to students from the East Coast elite. "It is important that young people from all over the United States participate," he argued, noting: "This is probably more important to the advancement of our ultimate objective than the increase of knowledge per se."[19] To focus on academic elites was "exactly the opposite of the desirable" approach, "which is to disseminate the participants in this program as widely as possible through all the states."[20] This democratic impulse, which sought to spread the experience of foreign exchange throughout the

American population, stood in contrast to Fulbright's straightforward elitism in thinking about foreign grantees. "My original idea," he later put it, "was not a general education program for all needy people but a program designed to influence political matters through the intelligent leadership of the important countries."[21] For all Americans, foreign exchange was to be an experience, perhaps one appropriate for a democratic public at the heart of a world power. For foreigners, exchange was intended for the elite, among whom its transformative power could work the most impact through "intelligent leadership."

Fulbright rarely elaborated on this distinction, but it mirrored the assumptions about the differential impact of exchange on foreigners and Americans that permeated the program. The BFS, for instance, worried about foreign undergraduates becoming so enamored of America that they would return to their home nations as "misfits—unable to readjust to their native cultures." (For this reason, Fulbright grants were limited to graduate students who could both "absorb an understanding of our institutions" and be able to "go back and play a part in their own culture.")[22] No such concerns were raised about American students becoming overly infatuated with foreign cultures or becoming un-American. Rather, they would spread American values, develop new knowledge about the world, and come to a renewed appreciation of the American "way of life."[23]

That meant that, for all the language of mutual understanding, the implementation of the Fulbright program tended to assume not a two-way transfer of culture but an expanding sphere of American influence. "Mutual understanding and freedom are contagious," said Assistant Secretary of State Philip H. Coombs in Senate hearings on the Fulbright program in 1961, "though we might wish at times that the virus were more virulent." At the same hearings, James M. Davis, president of the National Association of Foreign Student Advisers, testified that the "United States has nothing to hide" because it benefits from the "most complete and accurate transmission": "Most of the foreign students, leaders, and specialists in this program return home to become transmitters themselves. . . . [F]oreign students and visitors who came here under it have, in fact, transmitted a more fair and a more favorable picture of the United States after they have returned to their homelands."[24] Such metaphors of contagion and transmission were revealing, and they provided the unconscious underpinnings of the theory of mutual understanding that Fulbright and the Fulbright program offered as a liberal and internationalist alternative to hegemonic militarism.

While Fulbright may have preferred a different rhetoric, these theories were more than consonant with his understanding of educational exchange, and he never criticized them. (Coombs and Davis were, after all, offering testimony in support of the program in a committee hearing chaired by Fulbright; and he had likewise been happy to let the BFS know what he thought of its overly academic implementation of his program.) And, in his own, earlier example of a Turkish politician with the mind like an open and sympathetic channel, Fulbright had adopted a similar metaphor of transmission. In that speech, he had actually gone further, revealing: "How often I have thought what a fine thing it would be if Mr. Stalin or Mr. Molotov could have gone to Robert College or Columbia in their youth." Even Stalin would be converted to Americanism by the power of education in the United States.[25] What tied this all together was not a unified theory of acculturation or cultural exchange but a faith in the power of American culture to transform without itself being transformed—American students abroad would spread American culture; foreign students in America would absorb American culture and then transmit it in their native countries.

For all the talk of mutual understanding, in other words, Fulbright imagined that educational exchange would produce a global elite that was attuned to American values and American interests and would work to remake their countries in the image of American freedom. In a revealing speech in 1962, in which he offered a "progress report" on international education, he argued that there was "clear evidence that the educational exchange program enlarges this two-way understanding among those who directly participate in it." But the evidence he presented focused on foreign participants and on a more unidirectional flow of understanding. He proclaimed that alumni had a positive image of America and contrasted this understanding with the hostile reception that Richard Nixon had recently received in Caracas from foreigners who did not truly understand America. And he boasted that among the grantees there was a "large percentage of men and women headed for positions of leadership and responsibility in their respective countries" and drew attention to many of the alumni of educational exchange who were already "active political leaders": Pierre Pflimlin and Felix Gaillard, former French prime ministers then serving in the De Gaulle cabinet; Constantine Karamanlis, prime minister of Greece; Manouchehr Eqbal, prime minister of Iran; Paolo Rossi, Italian minister of education; Phagna Bouasy, foreign minister of Laos; Sir Leslie Munro, president of the UN General Assembly. Beyond such political worthies, Fulbright also praised anonymous grantees "who have become prominent in the civil service of other countries" as well as "writers, musicians, artists, scientists, physicians, educators, labor leaders and social workers." The fact that only the political elites were worthy of mentioning by name was significant, but more significant was the cultural and political work that Fulbright imagined all the alumni of his program to be doing: "In whatever professions grantees under the exchange program may engage after returning to their homes it is obvious that they will weave into their practice of that profession some of the knowledge which they derived from the experience of living, studying, and observing in this country. Most significantly, they will transmit to others some of their acquired understanding of the United States. Whether their influence in this respect extended to one or a million of their countrymen, it is almost certain to be a constructive influence."[26]

This, then, was the theory of two-way educational exchange that was embodied in the Fulbright program. Educational exchange would redound to the benefit of America; mutual understanding presumed that the world would come to a collective understanding and appreciation of American values. Foreign program grantees would themselves become agents of an expanding liberal world order with America as its center.

The Structure of Liberal Internationalism

Fulbright's theory of educational exchange reflected several deeper assumptions of his political thought that were themselves representative of important strains of liberal internationalism in midcentury America. The first was the powerful sense of liberal exceptionalism and global leadership that permeated American politics in the wake of the victory over fascism during World War II. The historian John Fousek has dubbed this ideology *nationalist globalism*, the implication being that "the interests of the US and the rest of humanity were convergent" and that "the US was the natural, destined leader of the world—possessing values, institutions, and a 'way of life' to which all other peoples aspired."[27] This meant that there was no tension between what was good for the world and what was good for the United States—the United States was a lonely beacon of order and stability, a bastion of liberal values that had emerged unscathed from thirty years of crisis, and it was to the benefit of all that those values would now be spread around the globe. On matters ranging from UN membership to educational exchange, Fulbright was a principle advocate of American leadership of a recently devastated and newly interconnected world. "Only in the western hemisphere," he observed in 1946, "has orderly civilization remained unimpaired."[28] It now fell to the United States to take the lead in reconstructing global order, and this would benefit both the world and the United States. In 1944, Fulbright headed a US delegation to a London conference on international education at which the Allies tried to imagine the postwar reconstruction of educational facilities that had been destroyed by dictatorship and war. As a result of those meetings, he argued that "closer educational cooperation [would] be beneficial outside of this country but it would be valuable to the United States" as well.[29]

The second important assumption was a faith in the power of the American system. Fulbright's advocacy of educational exchange was untroubled by fears of foreign subversion—he seems never to have worried that reds or anarchists or malcontents would come into the United States to spread foreign ideologies. Such fears were not absent in Cold War Washington. Even as Fulbright was imagining a young Stalin converted to Americanism at Columbia University, anti-Communist congressmen were fretting about the threats that educational exchange posed to national security and national values. In 1947, debating the educational exchange provisions of the Smith-Mundt Act, Clare Hoffman thought it seemed nonsensical to "authorize the expenditure of . . . millions to bring teachers of communism here." John Rankin agreed, believing it to be "not only ridiculous but dangerous to bring into this country either students or instructors from behind that iron curtain." Another congressman was concerned that "student and communist agents, slick tongued, and smooth commentators, may come to this land for no other purpose than to propagandize and attempt to change the minds of American youth."[30] Fulbright was never concerned by such fears—in fact, he publicly defended his program from Joe McCarthy when the senator from Wisconsin tried to red-bait it.[31] More broadly, he believed that "the highly emotional attacks upon communism and Russia by some of our public orators is an indication of the weakness of their faith in our system."[32] Or, as he put it in 1965, one of the points of the Fulbright program was to "acquaint students and scholars from many lands with America as it is—not as we wish it were or as we might wish foreigners to see it, but exactly as it is—which, by my reckoning, is an 'image' of which no American need be ashamed."[33] In Fulbright's faith in American culture, in his confidence that exchange would favor American values, we can begin to reimagine the partisan politics of nationalism in the early Cold War. It was the liberals who were the ebullient nationalists; the anti-Communist conservatives were, ironically, more willing to countenance that exchange might involve a two-way flow of ideas, an idea that terrified them.

Fulbright's third important assumption was that war was a product of irrational misunderstanding. The centrality of propaganda to Nazi power led to a postwar fixation on free flows of information as a central mechanism that would produce world peace.[34] The 1945 creation of the UN Educational, Scientific, and Cultural Organization (UNESCO) was emblematic of this postwar emphasis on free exchange as the foundation of world peace. The preamble to the organization's constitution, for instance, began by declaring: "Since wars begin in the minds of men, it is in the minds of men that the defenses of peace must be constructed." It therefore announced a belief in the "free exchange of ideas and knowledge" to create "mutual understanding and a truer and more perfect knowledge of each other's lives."[35] The resonance with the themes of the Fulbright program was not coincidental. UNESCO had grown out of the Conference of Allied Ministers of Education in London, to which Fulbright had been a delegate, and it was at a UNESCO planning conference that he first broached the idea of a US-backed educational exchange program.[36] Fulbright would continue to espouse this 1940s understanding of the ideological causes of militarism into at least the 1960s. "Wars are fought over abstractions," he asserted in *The Arrogance of Power*. "If there is a root cause of human conflict and of the power drive of nations, it lies not in economic aspirations, historical forces, or the workings of the balance of power, but in the ordinary hopes and fears of the human mind."[37] Such a theory of war allowed him to avoid confronting difficult questions about exploitation and irreconcilable differences in the global economic and cultural sphere, and it legitimized American geopolitical preponderance as a natural state of affairs. It also exaggerated the potential of cultural exchange as a tool for peace—if war was about hopes and fears, if conflict was a product only of misunderstandings, then mutual understanding was a simple, pain-free solution. It was telling, for instance, that in 1962 Fulbright attributed Richard Nixon's hostile reception in Latin America to misunderstandings, not to policy disagreements—to the fact that the people who were protesting the United States had not spent time as Fulbrighters.[38]

This led easily to the final assumption of Fulbright's liberal internationalism—that free exchange in the civil sphere would produce harmony, not conflict. In this regard, his model for educational exchange seemed to be built on his theory of free economic exchange—in both instances, exchange would raise all ships and produce harmonious progress. Fulbright was long a committed free trader. In a significant passage in *The Arrogance of Power*, he bemoaned the damage the Vietnam War was doing to the potential for international trade agreements with the Soviet bloc. He hoped that liberalization of trade would transfer superpower competition from the realm of politics to that of production. "Such a challenge," he argued, "should be most welcome to the United States, for two reasons: first, because the United States, with an economy that is not only the world's greatest by far but also one of the fastest growing, has every prospect of winning an economic competition with the Russians; second, because no one can really lose a creative competition in efforts to make a better life for millions of people."[39] To hold simultaneously that the United States would win and that everyone would win, one had to bracket any question of economic exploitation—trade had to be held up as a realm of freedom and mutually advantageous competition. With no losers, there would be no conflict. Fulbright's belief that educational exchange would benefit both America and the world therefore reflected a similar set of assumptions about the potential harmonies inherent in the global civil sphere. Conflict was not a necessary part of Fulbright's vision of the civil sphere. Society was a realm of exchange that could be separated from the unnecessary conflicts of militarist propaganda and misunderstanding. Questions of inequality, of unfair distribution, of genuine cultural or political irreconcilables did not figure.

The irony, of course, was that Fulbright's liberal idealism rested on the preponderant power of the United States as both a military and an economic force in the postwar world. At the most basic level, the early years of the Fulbright program were funded by America's surplus production. At first, the program was paid for by the sale of surplus war junk—the more than $10 billion worth of trucks, jeeps, food, and tents that were left scattered throughout the global American front when the war came to a sudden halt after the dropping of the atomic bombs. These leftovers of the military economy—its literal excess—were converted into a cultural network intended to create a liberal world culture.[40] What we call the Fulbright Act to create the program was, in reality, an amendment to the Surplus Property Act of 1944 and designed as a way to salvage some return on material that was otherwise likely to be abandoned. The *Washington Post* summed up the economic logic justifying the program: "Certainly the furtherance of international understanding which the Fulbright bill would encourage is preferable to watching our property rust away and finally be abandoned."[41] In the 1950s, the Fulbright program expanded with additional funding in the form of currencies accrued through the sale of surplus agricultural commodities.[42] The economic exchanges from which the Fulbright program received its funding rested on a profoundly unequal global economy—the United States sufficiently prosperous to have a surplus of disposable goods, foreign nations sufficiently impoverished to have a need for that surplus.

Thus, for all the talk that educational exchange would transcend competition and power politics, it could not, in the end, be separated from them. It was not just that the program could be turned to instrumental, geopolitical uses, even though it certainly became enmeshed in Cold War politics. Dean Acheson, for instance, described it as part of the "Campaign of Truth," the massive international propaganda program launched in 1950 to counter Soviet propaganda.[43] Similarly, one of the considerations at play when the program was consolidated and restructured in 1961 seems to have been how to find a way to fund exchanges with the postcolonial world, which had risen in geopolitical importance but remained underserved by existing funding arrangements—Senate hearings on the bill appended a fifty-page report on Sino-Soviet cultural exchange efforts in the decolonizing world.[44]

Rather, the early philosophy and the institutional structure of the program were inseparable from assumptions about American world leadership, about the mutual compatibility of American economic and cultural expansion and world harmony, and about the inherently harmonious nature of the liberal world order that America was constructing after World War II. In a 1961 hearing on the reorganization of the program, Fulbright asked Robert G. Storey, then chairman of the BFS, to evaluate the effectiveness of educational exchange in promoting foreign relations and mutual understanding. Storey provided two examples, and neither could be fairly described as moments of two-way cultural exchange. First, he related a moment when he saw 350 Indian exchange students who were asked to reflect on their American educational experiences. Ninety-nine percent of their responses were favorable, he testified, continuing: "Those people are the leaders or the leaders to come in India, one of the critical areas of the world." His other example was perhaps more instructive. Reflecting on an exchange program for Latin American lawyers to learn the "Anglo-American theory of constitutional government," he recounted the trajectory of "one of our early graduates in Argentina, a very brilliant man who became Minister of Industry and Commerce in the Aramburu Government, and . . . made the first private contract with an American oil drilling firm to explore [his country's] natural resources."[45] At the end of the day, mutual understanding looked a lot like American expansion.

Conclusion

None of this is to suggest, of course, that the Fulbright program actually worked to spread American culture in the fashion that Fulbright himself imagined. Much research on the actual operations of the program remains to be done, but, from the scholarship that already exists, it is clear that individual scholars, students, and administrators were able to carve out far more diverse and discordant agendas than the smooth and ever-expanding liberal Americanism of Fulbright's early imaginings.

Nevertheless, Fulbright's assumptions about educational exchange are significant in their own right. They provide a window into a vision of a liberal world order that was an important strain in postwar American internationalism, and they suggest some of the deeper currents of nationalist self-confidence that underpinned America's rise to global power in the years after World War II. Fulbright apparently never entertained the notion that American values would lose out in cultural exchange, that the global exchanges he created would fundamentally transform American culture or create a global public sphere centered outside the United States. America stood to benefit by promoting a value that he held to be universal—cultural exchange—and it would do so with little cost or risk. Given his importance as an advocate of liberal internationalism and a critic of American hubris, the underlying assumptions of his theory of a liberal order are significant. Although Fulbright could speak the language of cultural relativism, at a deeper level his defense of cultural exchange assumed that any universal, harmonious culture would reflect American values and be compatible with American hegemony. That the author of *The Arrogance of Power* so comfortably assumed that free international exchanges would benefit American power is a sharp reminder that both nationalist logics and theories of American exceptionalism were pervasive during the height of the Cold War.

Notes

1. "Our Foreign Policy," Speech on Texas Radio Hour, July 15, 1943, ser. 72, box 2, folder 10, MS F956, J. William Fulbright Papers, Special Collections of University of Arkansas Libraries, Fayetteville, Arkansas (hereafter Fulbright Papers).

2. Randall Bennett Woods, *Fulbright: A Biography* (New York: Cambridge University Press, 1995), 418.

3. J. William Fulbright, *The Arrogance of Power* (New York: Vintage, 1966), 9, 107–8.

4. Hans J. Morgenthau, "Time for a Change," *New York Review of Books*, April 6, 1967, https://www-nybooks-com.mutex.gmu.edu/articles/1967/04/06/time-for-a-change-2. See also Woods, *Fulbright: A Biography*, 442.

5. Woods, *Fulbright: A Biography*, 418.

6. Fulbright, *The Arrogance of Power*, 177.

7. J. William Fulbright, foreword to Walter Johnson and Francis J. Colligan, *The Fulbright Program: A History* (Chicago: University of Chicago Press, 1965), viii.

8. "Fulbright Signed by President," *Northwest Arkansas Times* (Fayetteville), August 5, 1946, box 58, file 13, Fulbright Papers.

9. 22 US Code sec. 2451, https://www.law.cornell.edu/uscode/text/22/2451; Francis A. Young, "Educational-Exchange Act: The Fulbright Hays Act of 1961," *ACLS Newsletter*, November 1961, box 172, folder 11, Bureau of Educational and Cultural Affairs Historical Collection, Special Collections of University of Arkansas Libraries, Fayetteville, Arkansas, MC 468 (hereafter CU Collection).

10. Woods, *Fulbright: A Biography*, 278–90; J. W. Fulbright, *The Pentagon Propaganda Machine* (New York: Liveright, 1970).

11. "Use of Surplus Property Credits Abroad for the Exchange of Students: Extension of Remarks of Hon. J. William Fulbright," *Congressional Record*, 79th Cong., 2nd sess., vol. 92, pt. 12, August 2, 1946, A4766.

12. See Johnson (in this volume).

13. J. William Fulbright, "Role of Education in Foreign Affairs," November 5, 1948, ser. 72, box 7, folder 3, Fulbright Papers.

14. Ibid.

15. J. William Fulbright, "A Report on the Political Aspects of the London Conference," CBS Broadcast, May 6, 1944, ser. 72, box 3, folder 3, Fulbright Papers.

16. J. William Fulbright, Charter Day Address, College of William and Mary, February 8, 1946, ser. 72, box 4, folder 6, Fulbright Papers.

17. Address by J. William Fulbright, United States and International Educational Exchanges, 8th Annual Conference of National Association of Foreign Student Advisors, Washington, DC, April 22–25, 1956, ser. 72, box 13, folder 15, Fulbright Papers.

18. Fulbright, foreword to Johnson and Colligan, *The Fulbright Program*, vii; J. William Fulbright, "If Victory Is Not to Be in Vain," *The BBC Listener*, May 4 1944.

19. Letter from Fulbright to George V. Allen, October 4, 1948, ser. 72, box 4, file 5, Fulbright Papers.

20. Letter from Fulbright to Edward W. Barrett, September 18, 1950, box 12, file 15, Fulbright Papers.

21. Leonard R. Sussman, *The Culture of Freedom: The Small World of Fulbright Scholars* (Lanham, MD: Rowman & Littlefield, 1997), 57.

22. "Summary of Proceedings," BFS Meeting, October 8–9, 1947, 3, box 108, file 35, CU Collection.

23. For more on the early logic of the BFS, see Sam Lebovic, "From War Junk to Educational Exchange: The WWII Origins of the Fulbright Program and the Foundations of American Cultural Globalism, 1945–1950," *Diplomatic History* 37 (April 2013): 280–312, esp. 308–9.

24. Mutual Educational and Cultural Exchange Act, Hearings before the Committee on Foreign Relations, United States Senate, 87th Cong., 1st sess., March 29, April 27, 1961, 113, 48–49.

25. Fulbright, "Role of Education in Foreign Affairs."

26. J. William Fulbright, "The International Exchange Program: A Progress Report," August 13, 1962, Fulbright Papers, ser. 72, box 21, folder 37.

27. John Fousek, *To Lead the Free World: American Nationalism and the Cultural Roots of the Cold War* (Chapel Hill: University of North Carolina Press, 2000), 8.

28. J. William Fulbright, "US Asked to Lead in Peace-Making," *New York Times*, March 4, 1946, 25.

29. "Statement for OWI Overseas Broadcast," March 31, 1944, ser. 72, box 2, file 31, Fulbright Papers; Benjamin Fine, "Education in Review," *New York Times*, September 23, 1945, 77; "US Group in London for Education Talks," *New York Times*, April 4, 1944, 17.

30. *Congressional Record*, 80th Cong., 1st sess., vol. 93, pt. 5, June 6, 1947, 6566, June 13, 1947, 6965, 6967.

31. Woods, *Fulbright: A Biography*, 180–83; Johnson and Colligan, *The Fulbright Program*, 96–104.

32. Woods, *Fulbright: A Biography*, 102.

33. Fulbright, foreword to Johnson and Colligan, *The Fulbright Program*, viii.

34. Sam Lebovic, *Free Speech and Unfree News: The Paradox of Press Freedom in America* (Cambridge, MA: Harvard University Press, 2016), 148–50.

35. Unesco Constitution, November 16, 1945, http://portal.unesco.org/en/ev.php-URL_ID=15244&URL_DO=DO_TOPIC&URL_SECTION=201.html.

36. Fine, "Education in Review."

37. Fulbright, *The Arrogance of Power*, 5, 8, 16.

38. Fulbright, "The International Exchange Program: A Progress Report."

39. Fulbright, *The Arrogance of Power*, 203.

40. Lebovic, "From War Junk to Educational Exchange."

41. "Property Abroad," *Washington Post*, April 24, 1946, 6.

42. Department of State Bureau of Educational and Cultural Affairs, "The Educational Exchange Program under the Fulbright Act," May 1961, box 172, folder 12, CU Collection.

43. "Launching the Campaign of Truth: 1st Phase," in *Sixth Semiannual Report of the Secretary of State to Congress on the International Information and Education Exchange Program, July 1–December 31 1950*, Department of State Publication 4375, International Information and Cultural Series 19 (December 1951), 1–2, 18–19, box 57, file 36, Fulbright Papers.

44. Mutual Educational and Cultural Exchange Act, Hearings before the Committee on Foreign Relations, US Senate, 87th Cong., 1st sess., March 29, April 27, 1961, 20–22; Johnson and Colligan, *The Fulbright Program*, 300.

45. Ibid., 20–22, 48–49.

The Making of the Fulbright Program, 1946–1961

Architecture, Philosophy, and Narrative

Lonnie R. Johnson

Established in 1946 and boasting over 370,000 alumni in 2016, the Fulbright program was the oldest and largest academic exchange program in the world up until 1987, when the European Union established its ambitious, generously funded, multilateral exchange program Erasmus, which both was inspired by and emulated the success of the Fulbright program. However, the fact that the Erasmus program has outstripped Fulbright in numbers does not detract from the latter's novelty, importance, ingenuity, or distinction. It remains, in the words of the Department of State, the "flagship international educational exchange program sponsored by the US government."[1]

The only systematic history of the Fulbright program was written by Walter Johnson, a historian from the University of Chicago who served on the program's Board of Foreign Scholarships (BFS) from 1947 until 1954, and Francis J. Colligan, a veteran from the Department of State's Bureau for Educational and Cultural Affairs responsible for overseeing the program. In 1965, they coauthored *The Fulbright Program: A History*, an indispensable, obviously sympathetic insider view of the development of the program during its critical years between the Fulbright Act of 1946 and the Fulbright-Hays Mutual Educational and Cultural Exchange Act of 1961.[2] Outside official reporting, the history of the program from the mid-1960s to the present has received relatively little attention, with the last systematic reviews dating back to the 1990s.[3] Most of the external studies of the program have focused on the "personal and professional impacts of the Fulbright experience on grantees" and have "often overlooked the institution itself and its bureaucratic environment."⁴ The following analysis will pay special attention to the institutional environment of the Fulbright program in its foundational years by looking at its statutory basis, the philosophy inherent in its architecture, and the politics of its administration.

Rhodes and Fulbright

All Fulbright biographers identify J. William Fulbright's experience as a Rhodes scholar at Pembroke College, Oxford, from 1925 to 1928 as the formative event in his intellectual development. In his standard *Fulbright: A Biography*, Randall Bennett Woods captures in detail those influences that informed the twenty-year-old graduate of the University of Arkansas in Fayetteville. His experience at Oxford was essential in shaping his thinking on internationalism and educational exchange as well as the relationship between the two.⁵ Woods describes the Fulbright program as "a reflection, a projection, of J. William Fulbright's personal experience" as well as an "institutionalization of his own overseas odyssey" that "would do for thousands of young people what it had done for him—remove cultural blinders and instill tolerance and a sense of public service."⁶ Fulbright himself readily drew the parallels between his Rhodes experience and the program that came to bear his name:

> My experience as a Rhodes scholar was the dominant influence in the creation of the Fulbright awards. Coming as I did from an interior section of our country, quite remote and isolated from foreign association, the Rhodes scholarship probably made a more vivid impact upon me than it did upon some of my colleagues from metropolitan areas. That experience, together with the devastation of the Second World War and the existence of large uncollectible foreign credits, resulted in the bill creating the scholarships. . . . The recipients of these awards may be considered as grandchildren of Cecil Rhodes, scattered throughout the world.⁷

Fulbright understood international educational exchange as an antidote to ignorance, parochialism, isolationism, exceptionalism, and arrogance that ultimately "encourages attitudes of personal empathy, the rare and wonderful ability to perceive the world as others see it."[8] When looking back on the history of the Fulbright program, it is important to recall how exceptional it was before World War II—especially for Americans—to have an international experience or participate in the movements of students and scholars that today are called *academic mobility, international education*, or *study abroad*.[9]

The conception of the Fulbright program was far broader than the Rhodes scholarships, which brought only a handful of men from seven Commonwealth countries, Germany, and the United States to Oxford. The Fulbright program was conceived as a *global* enterprise, one based on *bilateral* educational and cultural *exchanges* of students *and* scholars and men *and* women. Although merit based, competitive, and prestigious, it had an egalitarian and democratic tenor and quickly reached a larger and more diverse audience of participants inside and outside the United States.[10] Moreover, it was conceived as a publicly sponsored and funded US *government* program, and this at a time when the US government had only rudimentary experience in facilitating educational exchange.[11]

The Fulbright Act of 1946: Short, Ingenious, and Serendipitous

The establishment of the Fulbright program linked two disparate concerns: how to dispose of revenues generated in foreign currencies by the sale of surplus property that the United States had stockpiled all over the world at the end of World War II and how to fund an international educational exchange program in a postwar budgetary environment that was restrictive and averse to new expenditures. The Surplus Property Act of 1944 prohibited the return of surplus property to the United States, and, as a result, after the end of World War II some four million items ranging from "agricultural implements and air pumps to zippers and zwieback" were rotting or rusting away overseas.[12] The two big interrelated problems were how to liquidate this "war junk" and what to do with the revenues in foreign currencies accrued abroad from the sale thereof.[13]

The atomic bombings of Hiroshima and Nagasaki in August 1945 were among those factors that "focused [Fulbright's] thoughts" on educational exchange.[14] In the course of September, the senator's seminal idea of earmarking revenues from the sales of wartime surpluses overseas for the financing of educational exchanges came to fruition. On September 27, 1946, taking the floor in the Senate, Fulbright proposed the introduction of a bill "authorizing the use of credits established through the sale of surplus properties abroad for the promotion of international good will through the exchange of students in the fields of education, culture, and science."[15] He spent the next ten months unobtrusively drafting an amendment to the Surplus Property Act of 1944, revising his proposal on the basis of consultations with the executive branch, and discreetly maneuvering it with unanimous consent through Congress with little to no debate.[16]

There were two isolated but widely cited precedents for the idea of using windfall government funding overseas to finance educational exchange. In 1908, the Theodore Roosevelt administration used indemnities the United States had received from China after the Boxer Rebellion in 1900 to establish the Boxer Indemnity Scholarship Program, which funded the studies of Chinese students in the United States. In 1920, Herbert Hoover was instrumental in the rededication of the balances of US relief funds in Belgium for educational purposes, which led to the establishment of the Belgian-American Educational Foundation.

Fulbright's amendment to the Surplus Property Act of 1944 was technical and obtuse, and it did not immediately appear to have anything to do with educational exchange. On August 1, 1946, President Harry Truman signed Fulbright's amendment into law. The act itself was exceptionally brief: not even two pages long. However, it tersely laid the foundations for the architecture of the Fulbright program in four points:

1. It made the Department of State the "sole disposal agency for surplus property" overseas.
2. It authorized the secretary of state to enter into "executive agreement or agreements with any foreign government for the use of such currencies or credits for currencies" related to the "disposal" of surplus properties to establish "by the formation of foundations or otherwise." These "executive agreements" implicitly provided the Fulbright program with its trademark philosophical and organizational agenda: the establishment of special binational commissions based on the idea of *shared sovereignty*.
3. It stated the purposes for which funds accrued by the disposal of surpluses could be used for "(A) financing studies, research,

instruction, and other educational activities of or for American citizens in schools and institutions of higher learning in such foreign countr[ies]" where surplus property and corresponding revenues were available or for "(B) furnishing transportation for citizens of such foreign countr[ies] who desire to attend American schools and institutions of higher learning." It is noteworthy that there is no statement of philosophy in the Fulbright Act and that its purpose—the financing of *bilateral academic exchanges*—is stated obliquely at best. Furthermore, the act asymmetrically defined the benefits for future US and foreign exchange program participants. Funding was comprehensive for US participants (costs for travel, study, and maintenance), whereas funding for foreign participants initially was limited to travel because the foreign currencies accrued could be used to cover only costs incurred abroad. Finally, there were no provisions in the act to cover the expenses in US dollars related to the administration and execution of the program in the United States. In order to make the program reciprocal, dollars had to be found.[17]

4. The Fulbright Act authorized the president to appoint a ten-person board (the BFS)[18] consisting of nonpartisan, expert representatives of "cultural, educational, student, and war veterans groups . . . for the purpose of selecting students and educational institutions qualified to participate in this program and to supervise the exchange program."[19]

Between the signing of the Fulbright Act on August 1, 1946, and the conclusion of the first binational exchange agreement (one with China) on November 10, 1947, the Promethean achievement of the original members of the BFS—in collaboration with a handful of cultural exchange specialists from the Department of State—was to put the policies, procedures, and nongovernment support structures together that were necessary to recruit US Fulbright students and scholars to go abroad and to host incoming Fulbrighters in the States.[20] It was also Fulbright's intention from the start to insulate the Fulbright program from partisan political influences as much as possible and to keep government involvement in the program's operations to a minimum. As noted in a retrospective on the program in

1966, the role of the BSF was a "unique requirement of the Act." The BFS was "so designed to give assurance in the United States and abroad that the program's essential character would be educational and non-political."[21]

The conception of the Fulbright program was noteworthy in many respects. At the time, no one in the Truman administration or the American academic community at large was calling for the establishment of an educational exchange program. The Fulbright Act did not originate in the executive branch like most legislation. It was a *congressional* initiative that Fulbright *personally* conceived and shrewdly guided through Congress, and it can be considered in many respects his individual achievement. Coupling the revenues associated with the disposal of US surpluses overseas with the financing of an educational exchange program was an ingenious idea but by no means apparent in the legislation. Retrospectively, Fulbright observed: "The bill was potentially controversial . . . and I decided not to take the risk of an open appeal to the idealism of my colleagues—deeply idealistic men though they may be."[22] Indeed, after it had been passed, Senator Kenneth McKellar (D-TN), the powerful chair of the Senate Appropriations Committee, complained to Fulbright that he considered it a "very dangerous bit of legislation . . . to send our fine young girls and boys abroad": "They'll be infected with those foreign 'isms.'"[23]

"Military geography"[24] also initially determined where the Fulbright program could be established because it could be funded only where the United States had revenue from the sales of wartime surpluses: predominantly in Europe, parts of Asia, and the Pacific. A list of the twenty-eight states that concluded bilateral Fulbright agreements with the United States between 1947 and 1953 included the occupied countries of Germany, Austria, and Japan but otherwise reads like a catalog of the immediate postwar European and Asian-Pacific friends and allies of the United States, great and small.[25]

Furthermore, revenue for the program was predicated on partner governments' preparedness to buy US surpluses in the first place. In light of the initial popularity and success of the program, Congress extended the idea of using revenues accrued from the sale of other overseas surpluses in 1953–1954, such as agricultural surpluses, to fund educational exchange elsewhere. This led to the establishment of a second wave of fifteen new agreements establishing binational commissions between 1955 and 1960, eight of which were in Latin America.[26]

The initial foundations of the Fulbright program were, as Richard Arndt has observed, "flimsy."[27] The foreign currency revenues available to fund the program were not only scattered in former theaters of war all over the world; they were uneven, limited, and bound to be consumed in the foreseeable future. The Fulbright Act provided for revenues in the form of foreign currencies, but it did not provide for the urgently needed dollars necessary to cover the costs associated with the program in the United States. The BFS and the State Department put together the component parts for the administration of the program in the course of 1947, but there were no funds available to pay for domestic operational costs. Under these circumstances, the Carnegie Corporation and the Rockefeller Foundation fortuitously agreed to assume the costs for stateside recruitment and selection of candidates for the first six months of 1948, which helped get the program off the ground and sustain it until funding for exchanges was secured in 1948 under the auspices of the landmark Smith-Mundt United States Information and Educational Exchange Act, which provided annual appropriations for information and exchange activities.[28]

Furthermore, the vigorous support provided by American civil society was essential in getting the program off the ground. The Fulbright Act provided support for the travel of foreign participants but not for their on-site costs after arrival. US institutions elected to waive tuition and fees for incoming grantees and provided additional support for students and scholars in the form of scholarships, grants, stipends, or salaries. Other organizations, such as fraternities, sororities, associations, and clubs, were instrumental in providing hospitality and helping cover on-site living costs. Reliance on cooperation with and the support of private institutions, agencies, foundations, universities, colleges, and individuals became one of the basic organizational principles as well as a sign of public generosity and the impressive civic spirit of the Fulbright program in its inaugural decades.[29]

The Smith-Mundt Act put the Fulbright program on a sounder basis of mixed financing: revenues in foreign currencies from the sale of surpluses—where they existed—for expenses incurred outside the United States and funding in US dollars for costs incurred inside the United States or elsewhere if revenues from the sale of surpluses were not available. This also made it possible to fund individual Fulbright awards to and from countries without foreign currency revenues, gave the program a bit broader reach in principle, and provided resources for other exchange programs, too. The Smith-Mundt Act completed a mixed funding formula for the Fulbright program: foreign currencies from the sale of surpluses overseas, where available; substantial private-sector support in the United States, which was forthcoming; and US dollars from the federal budget for expenditures inside and outside the United States, if available when necessary.

The Architecture and Philosophy of the Fulbright Program: 1947–1949

There was no statement of philosophy for the Fulbright program in the Fulbright Act. However, between 1946 and 1948, important collaboration between the predominantly academic BFS and the exchange specialists at the Division of Exchange of Persons in the State Department's Office of International Informational and Cultural Affairs put the component parts of the program together, and they implicitly articulated its philosophy in the process.

In its meetings during 1947–1948, the BFS outlined the policies of the program that informed its principles and procedures, which can be summarized as follows: "binational administration in the field, a focus on university-to-university relationships, independence from politics, high academic quality, merit selection through peer review, open competition, public-private cooperation, reciprocity, focus on individuals not institutions, and skepticism about questions of 'loyalty'": "It was a spelling out of American university values."[30] The role that academics on the BFS played in articulating the principles of the exchange program made academic freedoms one of its guiding principles from the very start.

At the same time, the State Department was actively organizing the program infrastructure. It contracted with private organizations—the so-called cooperating agencies—to manage the stateside agendas of the Fulbright program. The Institute of International Education (IIE) in New York City assumed responsibility for the recruitment and screening of outward-bound US students for the program as well as for the orientation of incoming foreign grantees and their placement at colleges and universities. The Conference Board of Associated Research Councils, an umbrella organization for leading academic and professional organizations,[31] assumed analogous roles for the outgoing American and incoming foreign Fulbright scholars.

By moving unprecedented numbers of foreign students and scholars to the United States and Americans abroad, US government–sponsored exchange programs played a major role in inventing the fields of international education and study abroad at US colleges and universities in the late 1940s. American institutions not only had little or no previous experience in dealing with the needs of the incoming foreign students and scholars they hosted; they also had to learn how to manage the opportunities of outward-bound academic mobility for their own students and faculty members, too. Representatives of the State Department, IIE, and colleges and universities founded the National Association of Foreign Student Advisors, NAFSA,[32] in 1948 to respond to the needs of incoming foreigners, and the cooperating agencies responsible for the stateside management of the program also asked US institutions to appoint Fulbright program advisers on campus to advise potential candidates. Study abroad advising at American colleges and universities was born.

While the State Department was putting the stateside pieces of the program's administration together, it simultaneously began to negotiate the first bilateral agreements with eligible countries to establish binational educational exchange commissions. The first two Fulbright agreements (with China and Burma) were concluded in November and December 1947; seven other agreements followed in 1948, six more in 1949, five in 1950, three in 1951, and five in 1952. The State Department developed a general formula for establishing binational commissions with specific governance and reporting requirements. After the initial mechanics with their many moving parts (see fig. 1) were put in place, the program grew rapidly. The number of US and foreign participants rose from eighty-four in 1948 to over four thousand in 1951.[33] The Fulbright Act's provision for the conclusion of executive agreements with participating countries allowed the State Department to create "a new type of agency." Binational commissions were one of the Fulbright program's unique structural features, and the "binational approach"[34] that informed their operation embodied the program's philosophy.

Although these commissions were unilaterally funded and named *US educational commissions*, they were characterized by a sense of joint owner-

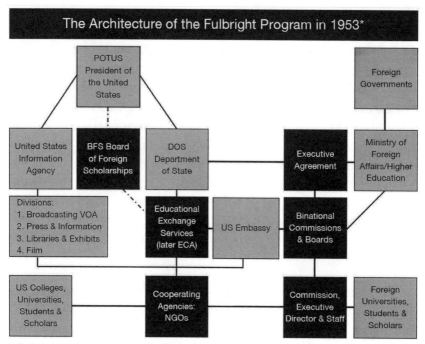

The Architecture of the Fulbright Program in 1953*

POTUS
President of
the United
States

Foreign
Governments

United States
Information
Agency

BFS Board
of Foreign
Scholarships

DOS
Department
of State

Executive
Agreement

Ministry of
Foreign
Affairs/Higher
Education

Divisions:
1. Broadcasting VOA
2. Press & Information
3. Libraries & Exhibits
4. Film

Educational
Exchange
Services
(later ECA)

US Embassy

Binational
Commissions
& Boards

US Colleges,
Universities,
Students &
Scholars

Cooperating
Agencies:
NGOs

Commission,
Executive
Director & Staff

Foreign
Universities,
Students &
Scholars

*Black boxes indicate organizations involved in the governance, administration, and execution of the Fulbright Program.

ship and shared responsibility and generally referred to in the vernacular as *Fulbright commissions*. The provisions for their governance on a country-by-country basis initially foresaw the participation of representatives from both governments—diplomats from US embassies or representatives of national ministries—and experts appointed by both governments—frequently distinguished educators or professionals—on the six- to twelve-member boards of commissions, with the US ambassadors frequently serving as honorary chairs. US influence was preponderant in the foundational years of the program,[35] but one of its unique organizational features was the buy-in required by foreign governments to participate.

These binational commissions functioned autonomously *outside* the respective bureaucratic structures of both governments. They were procedurally related to the BFS as a policy-making and oversight body as well as the State Department. They were required to submit annual program plans and budgets to the BFS and the State Department for approval and to report on the program's outcomes. However, they otherwise enjoyed substantial autonomy to articulate their own national objectives and were vested with considerable program authority. Finally, they assumed a central role in the hands-on administration of the program overseas by recruiting and nominating candidates to go to the United States and by selecting and providing for incoming US grantees.

The initial approach of the BFS and the educational exchange experts at the State Department was to trust the judgment of the commissions because it was based on the dialogue and insights of experts in the field, who understood local needs and interests better than any central body in Washington could. This predominantly hands-off and bottom-up approach acknowledged the global diversity of the countries and cultures that participated in the foundational phase of the Fulbright program, and this attitude was a part of the program's philosophy, too.

The Institutionalization of the Fulbright Program, 1948–1953: The Cold War, McCarthy, and the Establishment of the US Information Agency

A variety of pressures came to bear on the institutionalization of the Fulbright program in its initial years. In 1947, the Truman Doctrine made the containment of communism an operative US foreign policy objective, and the House Un-American Activities Committee (HUAC) started hunting for Communist sympathizers in Hollywood and elsewhere. By 1950, President Truman called for a US propaganda offensive—the Campaign of Truth—to counteract Communist anti-American propaganda. The Cold War turned hot in Korea two months later.

During this period, there were wide-ranging debates about the organization of American information and cultural exchange activities. The structure of the Smith-Mundt Act caused part of the confusion by lumping together funding for two dramatically different activities without legislating how they were to be administered: (*a*) the production of propaganda that was designed for unilateral dissemination outside the United States to influence public opinion abroad and that relied predominantly on the fast modern media of print, radio broadcasting, and film and (*b*) the promotion of mutual cultural and educational exchange that relied on slower media, such as books, libraries, and the exchange of citizens.[36]

Principal differences between the advocates of information and the advocates of cultural exchange drove organizational debates. The "unilateral informationists"[37] frequently had backgrounds in advertising, marketing, or journalism and were interested in selling or "telling America's story to the world."[38] They felt that cultural exchange activities should be ideologically and administratively subordinated to the immediate or short-term information needs and partisan policy interests of the US government. In contrast, the advocates of cultural exchange often had academic backgrounds and interests and previous experience abroad. They saw exchange as a form of communication characterized by equality and dialogue: a long-term investment based on learning from each other and giving people opportunities to find things out for themselves and form their own opinions. Finally, they believed in the administrative separation of culture and information, not the subordination of the former to the latter.

McCarthy and HUAC targeted the State Department in general and overseas libraries and exchange programs in particular as strongholds of Communist sympathy. These political pressures on the State Department made the loyalty of Fulbright grantees into national security issues that threatened the autonomy of BFS regarding its final selection of Fulbright grantees.[39]

Furthermore, funding for information and cultural exchange programming was limited, and Fulbright played the "dangerous game of pushing student and faculty exchange while denigrating the activities of [Voice of America] and [Radio Free Europe]"[40] in order to leverage more funding for exchanges. In 1951, John J. Rooney, a hard-nosed Democratic congressman from Brooklyn and the chairman of the House Appropriations Subcommittee for the Department of State, Justice, and Judiciary, seized on Fulbright's criticism of information programs as an opportunity to propose a $34 million cut to all information and cultural exchange funding. This required Fulbright to hustle to advocate in the Senate to get Congress to pull "the appropriation back up from $63 million to $85 million."[41] Rooney, an ardent anti-Communist and an outspoken critic of the State Department for its bureaucracy in general and the alleged extravagance of educational and cultural programming in particular, would take another more successful run at cutting exchange funding in the late 1960s.

Furthermore, McCarthy attacked the Fulbright program directly in a hearing on July 24, 1953. He insulted Fulbright by referring to him as

"Halfbright," grilled him about "security checks" for US participants, wanted to know whether it was BFS policy "to give Communists or Communist sympathizers scholarships," and asked that statements by Fulbright students "condemning the American way of life and praising the Communist form of government" be inserted into the congressional record. Fulbright's spirited resistance to this line of questioning has been lauded as the "first successful resistance to McCarthy,"[42] and it established the tenor of his subsequent relationship to the congressman from Wisconsin. Fulbright was the only member of the Senate to vote against appropriating more money for McCarthy's Permanent Investigations Subcommittee[43] and was among those who organized the congressional censure of McCarthy in December 1954.[44]

Less dramatic than Fulbright's encounters with McCarthy but more important for the institutional positioning of the Fulbright program was the role that Fulbright played in senatorial hearings between October 1952 and June 1953 as the chair of the special Senate Foreign Relations Subcommittee on Overseas Information Programs. The issue at stake during the so-called Fulbright-Hickenlooper hearings[45] was a global evaluation and reorganization of the State Department's information and cultural exchange programs. Fulbright argued vigorously to keep the cultural and exchange agendas (books, libraries, information centers, English-language teaching, American studies, and exchange programs) under the auspices of the State Department because he was suspicious of the propagandistic nature of information programming.

Among the many who testified to the efficacy of educational exchanges or who advocated separating their administration from the government's information activities were members of the BFS and Fulbright himself, who regularly used the term *propaganda* instead of its more benign synonym *information*. In particular, he objected to the idea of subordinating the BFS to "a governmental propaganda agency" and to assuming that the foreign members of binational Fulbright commissions overseas would want to become part of an "information organization that would coordinate them and direct them as what to do."[46] In May 1953, the Senate submitted a final resolution proposing that, if a new information agency were to be established, educational exchange programs should remain in the State Department. The reorganization plan that President Eisenhower submitted to Congress in June combined four agencies and all information programs into the new and independent US Information Agency (USIA) and left the administration of educational and cultural exchanges in a small unit in the State Department, the Office of Educational and Cultural Affairs (CU), which was the forerunner of the modern-day Bureau of Educational and Cultural Affairs (ECA), established in 1961.

The end result of Fulbright's efforts to maintain the autonomy of cultural and exchange programming by keeping it in the State Department ended with a mutually unsatisfactory compromise. When USIA came into existence on August 1, 1953, it assumed—along with its broad spectrum of information activities (print, radio broadcasting, film)—a substantial portion of the cultural agenda (books, libraries, information centers, English-language teaching, American studies, and exhibitions). Fulbright regretted losing these assets to USIA, where there was great and lasting disaffection about having to leave exchanges behind in the State Department.

The institutional antagonisms between USIA and CU attended the birth of both organizations and were reinforced by their different philosophies and missions and enhanced by their disparities in size. There were in the vicinity of ten thousand USIA employees around the world in the 1950s and 1960s, whereas the number of CU workers never exceeded many more than three hundred. At US embassies in the field, operational agreements between the State Department and USIA dictated that the staffs and the activities of USIA and CU were to be managed under the auspices of one USIA mission at each embassy. As Foreign Service officers, cultural affairs officers (CAOs) responsible for educational and cultural programming were employees of USIA. Furthermore, in terms of USIA mission hierarchies, CAOs were subordinate in rank to public affairs officers (PAOs), who had the overall responsibility for USIA mission programming. The fact that cultural and educational exchange appeared in the field to be a USIA activity and that CAOs were administratively subordinated to PAOs—who maintained information agendas of their own—was a structural and organizational peculiarity that generated ongoing friction among the practitioners of information and cultural exchange throughout the 1950s and 1960s.[47]

Despite the differences between USIA information and CU cultural exchange agendas and interests, there was one particular field where they overlapped: American studies. Before and after World War II, there was very little systematic study of the United States at schools or universities outside the United States, and one of the central tasks of USIA was to inform foreign publics about *American civilization* in the broadest sense of the term. USIA information programming included establishing overseas libraries and information centers that were open to the public, stocked with American books, periodicals, and newspapers, and enormously popular. While seeking to insulate the Fulbright program from propaganda efforts, the BFS was sympathetic to the government's interest in disseminating information about the United States and, under the auspices of the Fulbright program, encouraged the study of American literature, history, and culture as an academic enterprise at foreign universities.[48] These efforts ultimately led to the institutionalization of American studies as an academic discipline outside the United States. By providing foreign students and scholars with unprecedented opportunities to study in the United States, the Fulbright program also contributed to the development of indigenous populations of Americanists all over the world.[49]

Coming of Age: The Fulbright-Hays Act of 1961

Throughout the 1950s, the annual number of participants in the Fulbright program fluctuated between four thousand and forty-five hundred. One-third of the participants were US citizens, two-thirds came from abroad,[50] and the vast majority of bilateral Fulbright exchanges were with countries with binational commissions.[51] Although the program had become the largest and best-known academic exchange program in the world, its foundations were based on a combination of fortuitous circumstances and improvisation. It relied on a patchwork of legislation that made its administration increasingly complicated, and there was a genuine need to consolidate the existing laws into a more coherent piece of legislation. Furthermore, the revenues from the sale of government surpluses overseas began to wane, and the problem of financing became more acute.

In October 1960, Fulbright set in motion new procedures for drafting legislation by soliciting policy recommendations from a small group of "individuals with broad knowledge of, and concern for, these international programs."[52] In a departure from the established procedure for the introduction of legislation by the executive branch, Fulbright proposed that the Senate Foreign Relations Committee (SFRC) draft the legislation so that it could be introduced to Congress by the incoming Kennedy administration during its next session, and this put the task of coordinating what was to become the Mutual Educational and Cultural Exchange Act of 1961—named after its sponsors Fulbright and Hays—in the hands of Carl Macy, the legendary SFRC chief of staff. President Kennedy signed the Fulbright-Hays Act into law on September 21, 1961.

The act opened with an inspired statement of purpose that described both the objectives and the instruments of educational exchange:

> The purpose of the Act is to enable the Government of the United States to increase mutual understanding between the people of the United States and the people of other countries by means of educational and cultural exchange; to strengthen the ties which unite us with other nations by demonstrating the educational and cultural interests, developments, and achievements of the people of the United States and other nations, and the contributions being made toward a peaceful and more fruitful life for people throughout the world; to promote international cooperation for educational and cultural advancement; and thus to assist in the development of friendly, sympathetic, and peaceful relations between the United States and the other countries of the world.[53]

The absence of a reference to the traditional public diplomacy objectives of informing and influencing foreign audiences and opinion was—and remains—noteworthy.

The Fulbright-Hays Act of 1961 reiterated the core elements of the original Fulbright Act of 1946—bilateral exchanges based on executive agreements establishing unique binational commissions and the supervisory role of the BFS, which was expanded to twelve members—and reflected the manner and scope in which the Fulbright program had developed institutionally in its initial fifteen years. However, it was also conceived to provide a comprehensive framework for all educational and cultural exchanges. Although the program accounted for the lion's share of educational exchange expenditures, the act does not mention it by name; it was part of existing provisions for educational exchanges.

Funding for exchanges was now a line item in the federal budget, effectively eliminating the restrictions placed on the program by the Fulbright

Act's dependence on foreign currency revenues generated or held abroad. The new act extended the potential reach of the program, making it easier for the US government to fund Fulbright programs in countries where revenues from the sale of surpluses were not available and bilateral agreements establishing commissions did not exist, and also allowing for the acquisition of foreign currencies to execute exchanges if necessary.

The act reiterated the idea of basing exchanges on the conclusion of bilateral agreements with other governments and provided "for the creation or continuation of binational or multinational educational and cultural foundations and commissions."[54] In order to get the program onto its new statutory foundations, the United States had to renegotiate agreements with participating countries to replace the old US educational commissions with new entities that also gave participating countries equal billing in their new names. For example, the old US Educational Commission established in Austria in 1950 was reestablished as the Austrian-American Educational Commission in 1963. The hyphenated names of the reinvented Fulbright commissions reflected the spirit of parity, partnership, and joint ownership that informed the program. Inside of three years, the Fulbright-Hays Act also provided the basis for the negotiation of a third wave of nine new agreements in countries where none had previously existed.[55] (In the 1990s, nine more new commissions were established, including six in Eastern European countries following the end of Soviet hegemony.)[56] Furthermore, it replaced the initial Fulbright Act's idea of funding the program with revenues generated by the sale of US surpluses overseas with the idea of cofunding the program with the contributions of participating partners overseas and augmented that by providing opportunities for nongovernment entities to contribute to the program as well: "Foreign governments, international organizations and private individuals, firms, associations, agencies, and other groups shall be encouraged to participate to the maximum extent feasible in carrying out this Act and to make contributions of funds, property, and services, which the President is authorized to accept, to be utilized to carry out the purposes of this Act."[57]

Germany and Austria indicated that they would consider cost-sharing agreements[58] and were among the first of the ten countries that did so by 1965.[59] It would be difficult to overestimate the importance of these provisions for cost sharing. Not only were they a manifestation of the binational spirit of the program; they also proved to be critical for the stability and the growth of the Fulbright program because US government funding for it fluctuated in the future.

Finally, the Fulbright-Hays Act not only provided for bilateral cost sharing; it gave the State Department greater opportunities to establish and unilaterally fund Fulbright programs managed out of US embassies in those countries without the traditional Fulbright trademark attributes of bilateral agreements and commissions. In light of the absence of partner government participation in decision making and funding, these post- or embassy-based Fulbright programs are effectively in a category of their own, although this is not apparent. They are unilaterally funded by the State Department and managed out of US embassies in a manner that makes it easier to align them with US foreign policy priorities. At the same time, the absence of cost-sharing agreements makes them more expensive for the US government to operate.[60]

The Fulbright Program's 1968 Funding Crisis

The Fulbright-Hays Act eloquently articulated the objectives of educational and cultural exchange and put the Fulbright program on a sound administrative, fiscal, and statutory foundation, one based on its signature spirit of binationalism. It also was a sign of its times, characteristic of the optimism and innovative educational and cultural programming being promoted during those heady years of the Kennedy and the early Johnson administrations. The American allocation for mutual educational and cultural exchange activities climbed, peaking at $53 million in 1966, and the Fulbright program accounted for almost three-quarters of this: $38.8 million. Fulbright tried his best to keep educational and cultural exchange out of politics, but he was an eminently political animal himself and a dissenter, too.

The falling out between Fulbright and Lyndon Johnson in the mid-1960s was a turning point in both their political careers and a harbinger of things to come for the Fulbright program. In a speech in September 1965, Fulbright vigorously criticized the president's decision to send troops into the Dominican Republic—allegedly to address the threat of a Communist insurrection—and this dissent "destroyed his relationship with Lyndon Johnson."[61] Fulbright's *Arrogance of Power*, a scathing critique of

US foreign policy, appeared the following year, and his decision to organize televised hearings on the US engagement in Vietnam cemented the rupture. By 1968, funding for the Fulbright program had been slashed 43 percent to $20.2 million for fiscal year 1969.[62]

John J. Rooney, the long-serving chairman of the House Appropriations Subcommittee for the Department of State, Justice, and Judiciary, played no small role in the bloodbath. A supporter of the Vietnam War, Rooney was known as a fiscal hawk and a long-standing critic of educational and cultural programming. The pressures Vietnam brought to bear on the federal budget were also concerns, and the relationship between the Johnson administration and the academic world deteriorated as colleges and universities became centers of anti–Vietnam War protest. Rooney was personally and politically at odds with the liberal intellectual Charles Frankel, the assistant secretary of state in charge of education and culture (1965–1967). In the presence of Frankel and LBJ, he "angrily told the President about the opponents of the war to whom we were giving grants."[63]

The sharp cuts made a uniformly bad impression in the field because they undermined the credibility of the US government's commitment to the program shortly after it had negotiated new cost-sharing agreements with partner governments. CU saw "bad publicity, the disappointed applicants, disrupted plans and total uncertainty surrounding the future" as the immediate consequences and fretted about long-term impacts: "Moreover, in many cases the existence of the binational commission itself is in jeopardy."[64]

A cable CU sent out to the field expressed the hope that the cuts would be temporary and advised US embassies in cost-sharing countries "to explain the reasons for the drastic curtailment and to seek to convince the foreign governments to keep their own contributions at the highest possible level."[65] Given this cutback, it appeared politically expedient to reduce grants in the US part of the program. The overall number of Fulbright awards in 1969–1970 was 30 percent lower than the previous year's 4,556, with 57 percent fewer awards for Americans and 27 percent fewer for foreign grantees.[66]

The response of partner governments to the reductions was muted, which was a testimonial to their commitment to the Fulbright program and the efficacy of the new provisions for cofunding. Countries with commissions held—and in some cases increased—their levels of funding to offset some of the shortfall, and this established a funding pattern in many countries with binational commissions early on that has proved to be enduring, matching or surpassing US government funding for the program. For example, in fiscal year 1969, the fourteen countries in Western Europe with binational Fulbright commissions were collectively funding the program at a level almost 20 percent higher than the American $1.3 million.[67] This was symptomatic of a widespread preparedness to contribute to the Fulbright enterprise. By 2014, the ratios of partner government funding from countries with binational commissions in Europe to US funding varied, but the regional average was two to one.[68] Thanks to the cofunding provisions of the Fulbright-Hays Act, by 2014 the forty-nine countries with binational commissions were providing 94 percent of the $110 million of the cash and in-kind support for the Fulbright program from foreign sources (with a global US appropriation of $236 million).[69] It is an underexposed fact that the contributions of foreign countries with commissions have grown steadily in absolute and relative terms since the early 1960s.

The history of federal funding for the Fulbright program has been like a roller-coaster ride, with three peaks in 1966, 1994, and 2010 and deep valleys in between.[70] The program has not recovered from the 1968 budget cuts to date. Funding for exchanges stagnated in the 1970s but grew in the 1980s and early 1990s as a result of vigorous USIA funding during the Reagan and first Bush administrations. It began to reapproach its 1966 funding peak in real terms, but it was cut again over 20 percent in 1996 by the Clinton administration in the course of post–Cold War budget consolidation and a general reorganization of information and exchange programs (which led to the consolidation of USIA with the State Department in 1999). The 9/11 attacks precipitated renewed increases in funding for public diplomacy that started under the George W. Bush administration and peaked in 2010 at $254 million, but funding slipped again under the Obama administration. In constant 1966 dollars, the fiscal year 2016 appropriation of $236 million for the Fulbright program was 18 percent lower than the peak funding level under the Johnson administration.[71]

Shifting the Fulbright Program Narrative: "Consolidating" the Fulbright Program with USIA in 1978 and the Consolidation of USIA with the State Department in 1999

Binational commissions form the historical, philosophical, institutional, and financial core of the Fulbright program. However, these facts play no prominent role in the State Department's current narrative about the program, which emphasizes US sponsorship.[72] This circumstance merits one last observation on how the politics of the administration of the program have reframed its initial philosophy twice: in 1978 and again in 1999.

In 1953, Fulbright lobbied to keep cultural and educational exchange programs outside USIA and partially succeeded in doing so because he was concerned about the credibility of exchanges and wished to dissociate them from information. In the mid-1970s, the Carter administration advanced the idea of a major reorganization of information and exchange programs into a new agency for international communication. Individual reorganization scenarios shared the premise that CU would be incorporated into a reorganized USIA, which the administration wished to rename the US International Communication Agency (USICA). When the concrete reorganization scenarios were advanced in 1977, veterans of CU, Fulbright program management, and Senator Fulbright himself fought them tooth and nail.[73]

At the end of June 1977, 123 CU employees submitted a petition protesting the proposed reorganization and expressing their concerns that "an amalgamation of the Department of State's two-way, educational and cultural exchange programs with the essentially *one-way* activities of the USIA may take place without resolving deep conceptual and programmatic differences in the purposes of both organizations."[74] On July 12, 1977, Fulbright, whose five-term career in the Senate had ended in 1975, implored President Carter to postpone implementation of the merger pending an in-depth evaluation: "The principal point I wish to make is that the inherent difference between the cultural exchange and the information programs, especially as perceived by foreigners, raises very serious problems if they should be merged into a single agency. . . . I fear that if the cultural exchange is perceived by foreigners as a part of our information program, it may no longer be considered mutual and may not attract either their services and interest or their financial support."[75] In October 1977, Fulbright was in Bonn to commemorate the twenty-fifth anniversary of the German-American Fulbright program and continued to agitate by expressing his concerns that the program might become politicized. A USIA cable from the field reported this "incident," noting: "This shook the Germans present (Foreign Ministry officials and academics jointly responsible for the Fulbright Program) who are very sensitive about this particular point."[76] Later that month, Donald S. Lowitz, chairman of the BFS, also testified to the Senate Governmental Affairs Committee against reorganization and argued that the "separate identity" for exchanges was essential "for their future effectiveness and credibility here and abroad."[77]

All this was to no avail. On March 27, 1978, CU disappeared into USICA, an organization dominated by USIA personnel, agendas, and activities. (It reverted to the name USIA under the Reagan administration three years later.) Historians have offered two different perspectives on the consequences of the 1978 reorganization, which Fulbright considered a misfortune and resented for the rest of his life.[78] In his history of American cultural diplomacy, the Fulbright alumnus and former CU veteran Richard Arndt sees the incorporation of CU into USIA as the beginning of a twenty-year period of decline that can be attributed to CU's loss of institutional and budgetary autonomy and the sacrifice of additional control over staffing and assignments.[79] Wilson P. Dizard Jr., himself a veteran Foreign Service officer, promotes the orthodox USIA version of the story when he observes that the incorporation of CU into USIA was "a latter-day acknowledgement that information and cultural programs were complementary parts of an effective overseas ideological strategy."[80] Allen C. Hansen, another USIA veteran, acknowledges the fundamental differences between information and exchanges as well as the hard feelings that accompanied the merger but maintains that the initial fears that the merger would politicize the program, to its detriment, proved to be unwarranted.[81]

Ultimately, the merger of CU and USIA did not diminish the loyalty toward or the enthusiasm for the Fulbright program among participating countries. However, it did obfuscate the historical origins and the philosophy of the program and complicate the working environment of the autonomous binational commissions. When USIA administratively absorbed the program, it institutionally appropriated the exchange narrative to meet the needs of its own agenda.

Ulrich Littmann, the legendary director of the German-American Fulbright Commission from 1963 until 1994, criticized USIA's rechristening of the Fulbright program as the "flagship of USIA programs" at a Fulbright Association meeting in 1993. He also observed that lumping together the commission-based and the non-commission- or embassy-based Fulbright programs under one umbrella obscured the core idea of the program's binational heritage and its tradition of shared proprietorship. He asked rhetorically what interest "foreign governments or appropriation committees of the respective parliaments" could have in "contribut[ing] to another program of USIA." He acknowledged that the move into USIA put the program on "a safer financial base" but noted a number of changes in its institutional culture: "Somehow the bureaucracy as a more abstract entity has transformed the administration, and maybe even some of its directions. The free flow of ideas and personal dialogues between officers or members of Fulbright Commissions and the J. William Fulbright Scholarship Board and USIA as it has been re-named has become much more formalized and scanty. . . . The concentration of USIA upon running, planning and supervising the Fulbright Program has not only caused some open and much hidden controversy, but it has led USIA away from opportunities which CU consciously grasped."[82]

The institutional appropriation of the Fulbright program and its narrative occurred again under post–Cold War conditions in the mid-1990s, when a renewed debate about the organization of the US government's information and educational and cultural exchange agendas culminated in a politically inspired merger of USIA into the State Department, something that Nicholas Cull considers a "tragedy."[83] If CU's incorporation into USIA in 1978 increased the exposure of the Fulbright program to partisan political pressures and shifted its narrative, USIA's incorporation into the State Department, which many USIA veterans experienced as a hostile takeover,[84] enhanced those political pressures and shifted the narrative once again. The Fulbright program has weathered all these transitions exceptionally well and continues to enjoy the reputation of being—to repeat the diction of the Department of State's Web site—"the flagship international educational exchange program sponsored by the US government." On this Web site, however, references to the central historical and philosophical role of binationalism in the conception of the Fulbright program are few and far between, and it is a narrative shortcoming that the eloquent preamble to the Fulbright-Hays Act, which sums up so well what exchanges are all about, is not cited at all.

Notes

1. This is the diction on the Web site of the State Department's Bureau for Educational and Cultural Affairs. See www.eca.state.gov/fulbright.

2. Walter Johnson and Francis J. Colligan, *The Fulbright Program: A History* (Chicago: University of Chicago Press, 1965).

3. Leonard R. Sussman's *The Culture of Freedom: The Small World of Fulbright Scholars* (Lanham, MD: Rowman & Littlefield, 1992) was commissioned by the Fulbright Foreign Scholarship Board and included its 1991 white paper in an appendix. The National Humanities Center Steering Committee on the Future of the Fulbright Educational Exchange Program reexamined the Fulbright program in its golden jubilee year. See *Fulbright at Fifty* (Research Triangle Park, NC: National Humanities Center, 1997).

4. Molly Bettie, "Ambassadors Unaware: The Fulbright Program and American Public Diplomacy," *Journal of Transatlantic Studies* 13, no. 4 (2015): 358–72, 360.

5. Randall Bennett Woods, *Fulbright: A Biography* (New York: Cambridge University Press, 1995), 19–42.

6. Randall Bennett Woods, "Fulbright Internationalism," *Annals of the American Academy of Political and Social Science* 491 (May 1987): 22–35, 35.

7. Senator Fulbright in a letter to Dr. Frank Aydelotte, the longtime secretary of the Association of American Rhodes Scholars, May 6, 1955, cited in Lord Elton, ed., *The First Fifty Years of the Rhodes Trust and the Rhodes Scholarships, 1903–1953* (Oxford: Blackwell, 1955), 212.

8. J. William Fulbright, *The Arrogance of Power* (New York: Random House, 1966), 177.

9. The Institute of International Education in New York City reports annually on the number of international students studying in the United States and US students studying abroad. See www.iie.org/opendoors.

10. Between 1903 and 1953, there were only a total of twenty-nine hundred recipients of Rhodes scholarships, an average of fewer than sixty per year. Elton, *The First Fifty Years of the Rhodes Trust and the Rhodes Scholarships*, 219. By 1951, there were four thousand annual participants in the Fulbright program, which had eighty thousand alumni from over one hundred different countries by 1965. Board of Foreign Scholarships, *International Educational Exchange: The Opening Decades, 1946–1966: A Report of the Board of Foreign Scholarships* (Washington, DC: Board of Foreign Scholarships, 1967), 9. For a recent analysis, see Tamson Pietsch and Meng-Hsuan Chou, "The Politics of Scholarly Exchange: Taking the Long View on the

Rhodes Scholarships," in *Global Exchanges: Exchange Programs, Scholarships and Transnational Circulations in the Modern World*, ed. Ludovic Tournes and Giles Scott-Smith (New York: Berghahn, 2017), 33–49.

11. Richard T. Arndt, *The First Resort of Kings: American Cultural Diplomacy in the Twentieth Century* (Washington, DC: Potomac, 2005), 56–69. The State Department's Division of Cultural Relations, the primordial ancestor of today's Bureau for Educational and Cultural Affairs, was established in 1938 to improve regional relations with Latin American while simultaneously counteracting Axis propaganda.

12. Harry P. Jeffrey, "Legislative Origins of the Fulbright Program," *Annals of the American Academy of Political and Social Science* 491 (May 1987): 36–47, 41.

13. See Sam Lebovic, "From War Junk to Educational Exchange: The World War II Origins of the Fulbright Program and the Foundations of American Cultural Globalism, 1945–1950," *Diplomatic History* 37, no. 2 (2013): 280–312. Lebovic catches the unique nature of the moment the program was conceived and its peculiarities.

14. Woods, *Fulbright: A Biography*, 129.

15. Haynes Johnson and Bernard M. Gwertzman, *Fulbright: The Dissenter* (Garden City, NY: Doubleday, 1968), 107–8.

16. For details, see Jeffrey, "Legislative Origins," 40–47.

17. Johnson and Colligan, *The Fulbright Program*, 36–37.

18. Renamed by Congress in 1990 the Fulbright Foreign Scholarship Board.

19. An Act to Amend the Surplus Property Act of 1944 to Designate the Department of State as the Disposal Agency for Surplus Property outside the Continental United States, Its Territories and Possessions, and for Other Purposes, Public Law 584, 79th Cong., 2nd sess., August 1, 1946, *United States Statutes at Large*, 60: pt. 1, 754–55.

20. Ralph H. Vogel, "The Making of the Fulbright Program," *Annals of the American Academy of Political and Social Science* 491 (May 1987): 11–22; Johnson and Colligan, *The Fulbright Program*, 3–65.

21. Board of Foreign Scholarships, *International Educational Exchange*, 4.

22. Johnson and Gwertzman, *Fulbright: The Dissenter*, 109.

23. Jeffrey, "Legislative Origins," 45.

24. Lebovic, "From War Junk to Educational Exchange," 289.

25. In Europe: Norway, Sweden, Demark, Finland, the United Kingdom, France, Belgium, the Netherlands, Italy, Greece, Turkey. In Asia and the Pacific: Iran, India, Ceylon (Sri Lanka), Pakistan, Burma, Thailand, China, Korea, the Philippines, Australia, New Zealand. Africa: Egypt, South Africa. Board of Foreign Scholarships, *International Educational Exchange*, 39.

26. Argentina, Brazil, Chile, Columbia, Ecuador, Paraguay, Peru, Uruguay, Iceland, Iraq, Ireland, Israel, Portugal, Spain, and the United Arab Republic. Ibid.

27. Arndt, *First Resort of Kings*, 179.

28. Johnson and Colligan, *The Fulbright Program*, 38.

29. In the interim, the gradual monetarization of international education in the United States has made it a major industry, with 975,000 international students

contributing an estimated $30.5 billion to the US economy in 2015 and the US government playing a minor role (0.5 percent) as the primary sponsor or funder of students. See "NAFSA International Student Economic Value Tool," http://www .nafsa.org/Policy_and_Advocacy/Policy_Resources/Policy_Trends_and_Data /NAFSA_International_Student_Economic_Value_Tool; and Institute of International Education, Open Doors, 2015 "Fast Facts," https://www.iie.org/Research -and-Insights/Open-Doors/Fact-Sheets-and-Infographics/Fast-Facts.

30. Arndt, *First Resort of Kings*, 228.

31. The American Council of Learned Societies for the Humanities, the American Council on Education, the National Research Council for the Physical Sciences, and the Social Science Research Council.

32. NAFSA, which renamed itself the National Association of Foreign Student Affairs in 1964 and the National Association of International Educators in 1990 but retained its original acronym.

33. Board of Foreign Scholarships, *International Educational Exchange*, 5, 9.

34. See Donald B. Cook and J. Paul Smith, "The Philosophy of the Fulbright Program," *UNESCO: International Social Science Bulletin* 7, no. 4 (1956): 615–27, 617–18.

35. See the skeptical treatment of the binationalism in Lebovic, "From War Junk to Educational Exchange," 296–97.

36. See Frank Ninkowich, *The Diplomacy of Ideas: US Foreign Policy and Cultural Relations, 1938–1950* (Cambridge: Cambridge University Press, 1981), 118–19.

37. Arndt, *First Resort of Kings*, 180.

38. This phrase became the motto of USIA.

39. Johnson and Colligan, *The Fulbright Program*, 55–65, 68–77.

40. Woods, *Fulbright: A Biography*, 194.

41. Ibid., 195.

42. Johnson and Colligan, *The Fulbright Program*, 102.

43. Johnson and Gwertzman, *Fulbright: The Dissenter*, 136.

44. On Fulbright in the McCarthy era, see Woods, *Fulbright: A Biography*, 180–95.

45. Bourke Hickenlooper (R-IA) succeeded Fulbright as the chair of this subcommittee in 1953. For a summary of the hearings, see Arndt, *First Resort of Kings*, 258–63, 272–73.

46. Johnson and Colligan, *The Fulbright Program*, 81, 82 (see also 77–82).

47. Charles Frankel, *The Neglected Aspect of Foreign Affairs: American Educational and Cultural Policy Abroad* (Washington, DC: Brookings Institution, 1965), 9–38; Johnson and Colligan, *The Fulbright Program*, 83–85.

48. Johnson and Colligan, *The Fulbright Program*, 119–36. For a detailed analysis, see Walter Johnson, *American Studies Abroad: Progress and Difficulties in Selected Countries: A Special Report* (Washington, DC: US Government Printing Office, 1963).

49. The inverse and analogous impact of the US Fulbrighters returning from abroad on the study of foreign languages and cultures in the United States has never been adequately documented.

50. Board of Foreign Scholarships, *International Educational Exchange*, 9.

51. For country-by-country and world-region statistics for 1949–2014, see "Fulbright by Numbers and Regions" (Excel version), an online addendum to the Fulbright Foreign Scholarship Board's 2014 *Annual Report*, https://eca.state.gov/fulbright/about-fulbright/j-william-fulbright-foreign-scholarship-board-ffsb/ffsb-reports.

52. Johnson and Colligan, *The Fulbright Program*, 281–83.

53. Mutual Educational and Cultural Exchange Act of 1961, Public Law 87-265, 87th Cong., HR 8666, September 21, 1961, sec. 101, *United States Statutes at Large*, 75:527, https://www.gpo.gov/fdsys/pkg/STATUTE-75/pdf/STATUTE-75-Pg527.pdf. A facsimile appears in Johnson and Colligan, *The Fulbright Program*, 332.

54. Ibid., sec. 103.

55. Nepal, Ethiopia, Cyprus, Ghana, Malaysia, Afghanistan, Tunisia, Liberia, Yugoslavia.

56. Mexico, Canada, South Africa, Poland, the Czech Republic, the Slovak Republic, Hungary, Romania, and Bulgaria.

57. Mutual Educational and Cultural Exchange Act of 1961, Public Law 87-265, sec. 105(f).

58. Johnson and Colligan, *The Fulbright Program*, 293.

59. Board of Foreign Scholarships, *International Educational Exchange*, 39.

60. In 1965, the Fulbright program was operating in forty-eight countries with binational commissions and run more or less unilaterally in sixty-three countries without them. After the mid-1960s, the most dramatic growth in the program was in the field of these embassy-based programs. However, although over one hundred US embassy–based Fulbright programs existed in 2015 and outnumbered those in countries with binational commissions by two to one, but they accounted for only about 20 percent of the Fulbright program's 370,000 alumni. See "Fulbright by Numbers and Regions."

61. Woods, *Fulbright: A Biography*, 385. See also Brady (in this volume).

62. For a tabular representation of US government support for the Fulbright program in annual and constant dollars, see *Fulbright Fiftieth: 1946–1996*, 33rd annual report of the J. William Fulbright Scholarship Board (Washington, DC: USIA, 1996), 29. This table has been updated in constant (1971) and current dollars in J. William Fulbright Foreign Scholarship Board, *2014 Annual Report* (Washington, DC: US Department of State, 2015), 10 ("US Government Support of Fulbright, 1947–2013"). For a detailed breakdown of funding in the 1960s, see "Mutual Educational and Cultural Exchange Activities, Funds by Activity, Fiscal Years 1965–1969," CU/EX 5/31/68, box 41-1, University of Arkansas Special Collections Division, MC 468, Bureau for Educational and Cultural Affairs Historical Collection (CU).

63. Cited in Arndt, *First Resort of Kings*, 390. For the "ordeal" of Charles Frankel's tenure, see ibid., 380–97.

64. "Effects of the FY 1969 Budget Cut: Backup Budget Statement," box 41-4, CU.

65. Unclassified Cable, CA 10930, September 17, 1968, Austrian-American Educational Commission Archives, General Files, 9/67–74, Fulbright Austria, Vienna.

66. *Eighth Annual Report: Continuing the Commitment* (Washington, DC: Board of Foreign Scholarships, October 1970), 5.

67. Unclassified Cable, Department of State, CA 10930, September 17, 1968, Austrian-American Educational Commission Archives, General Files, 9/67–74. Fourteen Western European commissions provided $1,565,886, the United States only $1,318,981, with many individual country contributions substantially larger, first and foremost Germany ($500,000 as opposed to the $136,000 from the United States).

68. There is no public reporting that would facilitate analysis of the respective funding levels in each country. The two-to-one ratio is based on self-reported numbers on all cash and in-kind contributions. See Alfred Rafael P. Garcia, "European Fulbright Budgets 2012: A Comparative Study" (PowerPoint presentation at a European Fulbright program executive directors meeting in Lisbon, April 15–17, 2015). Individual countries exceeded the US contribution in bilateral terms by multiples substantially higher than two to one in many cases.

69. J. William Fulbright Foreign Scholarship Board, *2014 Annual Report*, 56. Percentages are based on foreign contributions to the student and scholar programs reported for fiscal year 2013. See ibid., 57–58.

70. For a tabular representation of US government support for the Fulbright program in annual and constant dollars, see *Fulbright Fiftieth: 1946–1996*, 29. This table has been updated in constant (1971) and current dollars as "US Government Support of Fulbright, 1947–2013" in J. William Fulbright Foreign Scholarship Board, *2014 Annual Report*.

71. Based on the Department of Labor CPI Inflation Calculator using 1966 dollars. See http://www.bls.gov/data/inflation_calculator.htm.

72. See the Web site of the State Department's Bureau for Educational and Cultural Affairs, www.eca.state.gov/fulbright.

73. See Arndt, *First Resort of Kings*, 480–98.

74. Petition Appended to a Memo by Joseph D. Duffey to the Deputy Secretary, June 28, 1977, box 310-1, MC 468, CU.

75. Fulbright to Carter, July 12, 1977, box 28-13, MC 468, CU.

76. USIA Cable, Limited Office Use, Bonn 17597, October 25, 1977, box 27-17, MC 468, CU.

77. Statement of Donald S. Lowitz, Chairman, BFS, Senate Governmental Affairs Committee on Reorganization Plan no. 2, 1977, October 26, 1977, box 27-17, MC 468, CU.

78. Interview with Hoyt Purvis, September 2, 2015, Fayetteville, AR.

79. Arndt, *First Resort of Kings*, 516–19.

80. Wilson P. Dizard Jr., *Inventing Public Diplomacy: The Story of the US Information Agency* (Boulder, CO: Lynne Rienner, 2004), 149.

81. Allen C. Hansen, *USIA: Public Diplomacy in the Computer Age*, 2nd ed. (New York: Praeger, 1989), 155–58.

82. Ulrich Littman, "The Fulbright Legacy in the 21st Century and the Future of the Program" (unpublished manuscript dated October 27, 1994, "personal comments" made in conjunction with the 1994 annual meeting of the Fulbright Association in Washington, DC), 4–5, Austrian-American Educational Commission Archive.

83. Nicholas Cull, *The Decline and Fall of the United States Information Agency: American Public Diplomacy, 1989–2001* (New York: Palgrave Macmillan, 2012), 179.

84. US Advisory Commission on Public Diplomacy, "Consolidation of USIA into the State Department: An Assessment After One Year" (executive summary, October 2000), http://www.publicdiplomacy.org/6.htm#advisory.

Fulbright Women in the Global Intellectual Elite

Molly Bettie

Of the many letters that Senator J. William Fulbright received from grateful alumni of his namesake exchange program, one of the most remarkable came from ninety-nine-year-old Mabel Lee of Nebraska. In 1985, she wrote to him about her experiences as a Fulbright scholar in Iraq during the 1952–1953 academic year. It was the first year of exchanges with that country, and the retired teacher was chosen "to answer a call for help from the government of Iraq for some woman to be sent to Iraq to help organize its program in physical education and sports for girls and women." She described her experience as "wonderful and valuable" and reported that she "became a great admirer of the Arab peoples and enjoyed splendid friendships with many of them." Reflecting on the wider purposes of the Fulbright program, she concluded: "The Arabs needed to get acquainted with us as much as we needed to get acquainted with them. It was a happy mutual exchange."[1]

Margaret Henderson, a colleague of Lee's from the same cohort of Fulbright teachers in Baghdad, shared similar sentiments in her own letter to the senator, written rather more promptly in 1954. She described a great deal of cultural mediation taking place after the grant period had ended: "While being a part of the community, I came to appreciate the purposes which inspired your bill. What I didn't realize, however, were the sharing and carry-over values that would result. . . . My correspondence with my former Iraqi students is a constant reminder of my responsibility to them—to see that 'good propaganda' is told. They so need our understanding. I'm sure all of us returned with a greater social conscience."[2] These women's accounts demonstrate their outstanding achievements and the lasting impact of their Fulbright experiences. These early participants are in many ways typical of the thousands of women who followed them over the past seventy years. Female grantees have furthered and fulfilled the public diplomacy aims of the Fulbright program as it was intended. What was not intended—but to which these letters so clearly attest—was the realization of a new arena in which globally minded women could speak, develop, and participate in myriad new ways.

Since 1946, the Fulbright program has contributed to women's achievements by offering them unique opportunities, exposing participants to alternative ideas, and bestowing academic prestige on its alumnae. Likewise, women have contributed a great deal to the Fulbright program. As participants at every level from students to senior research scholars and distinguished lecturers, they have furthered the aims of mutual understanding and international goodwill during their grant periods. As program administrators, they have helped steer the exchange program through budgetary difficulties and defend it from political attacks. On selection committees at thousands of campuses as well as in offices in Washington, DC, and around the world, they have chosen Fulbright grantees, deciding between thousands of applicants each year. Perhaps most unsung of all, they have contributed to the program as accompanying spouses of Fulbright grantees. There are many accounts of women who contributed to the so-called multiplier effect of their husbands' Fulbright grants by engaging with the host community and generating cultural learning experiences of their own.

The stories of these women and their contributions are absent from the literature on the Fulbright program—which has neglected gender as an area of research, though there have been some exploratory forays into the gendered nature of Cold War public diplomacy more generally. Helen Laville's work on women's organizations, for example, explores the range of international activities that the Association of American University Women (AAUW), the League of Women Voters, and the Young Women's Christian Association (YWCA) engaged in during the Cold War era.[3] David Snyder highlights the case of the Dutch housewife as a target of US public diplomacy in the postwar era, emphasizing the primacy of national cultural contexts in determining the efficacy of overseas information efforts.[4] Laura Belmonte's *Selling the American Way* includes a chapter on the prominence of women and family as a theme in both US and Soviet propaganda.[5] Philip Nash's work on US embassies examines the ways in which the first female chiefs of mission engaged in people's diplomacy.[6] Among the women who set precedents in the US Foreign Service was Ambassador and Congresswoman Clare Boothe Luce. Alessandro Brogi explores her role and contributions within the context of US psychological warfare in Italy during the Eisenhower administration.[7] Overall, the existing literature suggests that women were important as both tools of and targets for public diplomacy efforts during the Cold War.

Yet this growing body of literature is still far from fully accounting for the role of gender in public diplomacy. This essay explores the history of women in the Fulbright program, chronicling their achievements across each of these roles, and highlighting case studies of remarkable Fulbright women throughout the program's history.

There at the Start: 1946–1960

Unlike many other prestigious academic institutions, the Fulbright program has always been open to female participants. Women first became Rhodes scholars in 1976, for example, while the Ivy League became fully coeducational only a decade later, in 1986. The Fulbright program, on the other hand, has had female students, scholars, and administrators since its inception in 1946.

Why was the Fulbright program coeducational from the beginning? There is no specific mention of gender equality in the literature on the program's origins, but two potential explanations might be the precedent set by earlier coeducational US exchange activities and Senator Fulbright's own attitudes toward women. With regards to past precedents, the Fulbright program was not the first international educational exchange program conducted by the US government. Previous cultural and educational exchanges with Latin American countries, established by the State Department's Division of Cultural Relations during the interwar era, were also coeducational. There had also been a long history of privately run educational exchanges that had included female participants, such as those organized by the YWCA and the AAUW,[8] as well as those run by women's higher education institutions, such as Smith College.[9]

For his part, Senator Fulbright said little about the role of women, either in general or in relation to his namesake exchange program. His upbringing and private life, however, offer some indication of his respect

for women. His mother, Roberta Fulbright, was a famously strong matri-
arch, successfully managing the family businesses after her husband's
death, and encouraging her son's career in public service. Likewise, his
wife, Betty, was strong, assertive, and "a political asset of immense value,"
and the couple raised two daughters together.[10] Harriet Mayor Fulbright,
his second wife, led the Fulbright Association and continued to deliver
lectures and promote international education after his passing. Anna Fulbright Teasdale, the senator's sister, was an active member of the League
of Women Voters. She shared her brother's interests in international relations and served on the organization's Foreign Affairs Committee. In his
personal life, it is clear that Fulbright was surrounded by strong, politically aware, and globally minded women.

In his career, too, we can see evidence of his respectful attitude toward
women. His very first congressional speech was a debate on the Atlantic
Charter with Clare Boothe Luce. Eschewing the paternalistic conventions
of the time, he restricted his remarks to policy matters, on which the two
representatives respectfully but strongly disagreed.[11] There were no personal attacks and no references to her gender, nor did he dismiss her views.
In his correspondence about educational exchanges with women like
Alice Stone Ilchman, Cassie Pyle, and Caroline Matano Yang, we can dis-
cern a great deal of collegiality, appreciation, and respect.

Women were not only involved as exchange participants but also
included on the executive board of the Fulbright program from the beginning. The Board of Foreign Scholarships was established as the program's
administrative body by the original legislation passed in 1946. Members
were, and still are, appointed by the president to three-year terms and have
often been reappointed for subsequent terms, even by a president other
than the one who made the original appointment. The original intention
was to draw board members from a range of "cultural, educational, student and war veterans groups," including the US Office of Education, the
Veterans Administration, and public and private education institutions.[12]
The first female members, appointed by President Truman, represented
the interests of women's higher education. Professor Helen C. White was
a former AAUW president prior to joining the board. She reached significant milestones for academic women both before and after her years of
service to the Fulbright program. In 1936, she became the first woman to
be appointed full professor at the University of Wisconsin, and, in 1956,

she became the first female president of the American Association of University Professors.[13] She was joined by two female colleagues, Sarah Gibson Blanding and Margaret Clapp, presidents of the prestigious private women's institutions Vassar College and Wellesley College, respectively.

The Fulbright women grantees of the early years were predominantly white and middle class, often recruited from prominent women's colleges in New England. They were more likely than not to go to Western Europe, where they would study modern languages and other humanistic subjects. One well-known Fulbright alumna who fits this profile is the American poet Sylvia Plath. After graduating from Smith College, Plath spent two years studying English at Newnham College, Cambridge, on a Fulbright grant. She met the poet Ted Hughes at a party in April 1956; just two months later, the couple secretly married. In a letter to her mother, she explained her secrecy: "At first, I thought I could study better away from him [Ted] and domestic cares and that the Fulbright might cancel my grant if I were married and Newnham disown me. . . . [But then] I looked up the Fulbright lists, and they have three married women on grants." When Plath informed the US-UK Fulbright Commission of her marriage, they congratulated her. "One of the main qualifications of the grant, I discovered, is that you take back your cultural experience to America, and they were enchanted at my suggestion that I was taking back double in the form of Ted as a teacher and writer."[14] After her Fulbright experience at Cambridge, Plath and Hughes fulfilled this grant condition by spending the following academic year in the United States at Smith College, where she held her first teaching position.

In *Experiences of a Fulbright Teacher*, Effie Kaye Adams described a Fulbright experience quite different from Plath's as she encountered a number of difficulties in Pakistan as a grantee in 1952. She recounted an incident after she gave a talk on American education at the Sind Madrassah Government Boys School: "When I asked the Headmaster about the probability of the school becoming co-educational, he replied, 'Never in a thousand years.' With all his education this stern, handsome gentleman is a deadringer for the orthodox practice of secluding women." Later in the book she reflected on a conversation with a man who complained of growing resistance to the burqa among women. Despite opposition from him and others, she argued that the practice of purdah must end "if Pakistan is to take its rightful place among the free, educated, and self-sustaining nations unhampered by the presence of a backward female population."[15]

Although women were allowed to participate in the Fulbright program from the beginning, they did not do so on an equal basis. Fewer than one-third of grants were held by women in the early years of the program, and women made up only 9 percent of the board's membership during the program's first three decades.[16]

The status of women in the 1950s more broadly can help us understand, in part, why women were underrepresented in the exchange program during this period. First, women were generally not seen as future leaders, and thus they were not considered the key targets of US public diplomacy. A 1959 report on US Information Agency (USIA) women's activities, prepared at Senator Fulbright's request, cited the problem of prioritization in public diplomacy efforts. It acknowledged that, despite the gains made by women in some areas, male leaders still determined the political and economic orientations of other countries. It determined, therefore, that men must be prioritized as public diplomacy targets: "Limitations of staff . . . make it impossible for the program to reach many persons in key positions. We cannot therefore expand attention to women, unless we correspondingly decrease attention to male leaders."[17] Any efforts to reach out to women were not expected to produce a significant impact because women did not hold leadership positions. As men were seen as leaders, they were considered the more valuable public diplomacy targets.

Second, the larger social context of the Cold War years saw a reaffirmation of traditional gender divisions. The divide between the male public sphere and the female private sphere had been blurred during the Second World War, but it was swiftly reinstated at war's end. Women's activism during the Cold War often emphasized concerns that related directly to the domestic, private sphere: health care, education, and social welfare, among others.[18] The separate-spheres ideology was reflected in US public diplomacy activities during the Cold War era, as the aforementioned 1959 report shows. Women were seen as having decidedly domestic interests in this note on public diplomacy strategy: "Initially at least, they must be reached at their own level of interest, on subjects which are of great concern to them, and in terms which they can understand. In many areas the women's interests are almost exclusively in the fields of social welfare, health, nutrition and childcare."[19] The assertion that women were interested in private-sphere subjects rather than public-sphere areas such as politics or economics reinforced the gender imbalance of public diplomacy efforts.

Finally, another important contextual factor is the emphasis on development in some countries. Although the Fulbright program was never intended to be a development assistance program, some countries directed their grants to development-focused areas, such as technology, natural sciences, and engineering. The emphasis on these male-dominated academic disciplines led to a situation in which women were less likely to be selected. This phenomenon was not limited to the 1950s; it has continued throughout the history of the Fulbright program.

The Golden Era of Fulbright-Hays: 1961–1965

During the early 1960s, the Fulbright program experienced peak levels of funding and legislative success. Senator Fulbright was highly regarded and well connected with members of the Kennedy administration. In 1961, he managed to secure new funding sources and new powers for program administrators with the passage of the Fulbright-Hays Act.[20] The law had a number of important implications for the program. Section 105 authorized partner nations to contribute financially to their exchanges with the United States. Cost sharing had already taken place prior to this amendment, an arrangement with West Germany having enabled the program to exchange more participants each year with it than with any other country. It also empowered administrators to enter into contracts prior to the granting of appropriations, enabling them to plan exchange activities further in advance.

The law also had substantial effects on the administration of the program. Section 106 increased the size of the Board of Foreign Scholarships from ten members to twelve and designated the board as the authority for all programs authorized by the act, not only the Fulbright program. Fulbright-Hays also established the US Advisory Commission on International Educational and Cultural Affairs, replacing the former Commission on Educational Exchange, and required a "study of the effectiveness of past programs with emphasis on the activities of a reasonably representative cross section of past recipients of aid."[21] The resulting report to Congress, entitled *A Beacon of Hope: The Exchange-of-Persons Program*, was the first large-scale official evaluation of the Fulbright program. It involved the consultation of thousands of exchange participants, educators, ambassadors, and Foreign Service officers. It mentioned the need to increase the number of women leaders participating in the program, noting: "More emphasis, particularly in the underdeveloped countries, should be put on selecting more women, especially women leaders. In the past, although about a fifth of all foreign grantees coming to the United States have been women, very few of these have been leaders. . . . [T]he program should seize more opportunities to bring women leaders to the United States, particularly from countries where . . . women have long been under social and economic, even political handicaps."[22] The matter of increasing the number of female grantees, however, was not included in the commission's "suggestions for improvement" summary.

In the years that followed the passage of the Fulbright-Hays Act, officials gave increased attention to field and regional reports on the exchange program. Many observers looked to such reports for proof of effectiveness as they sought to determine how well the exchange-of-persons programs were operating in the field. Gordon MacGregor's detailed 1957 report, republished and distributed more widely in 1962, focused on countries in the Near East and South Asia, including Egypt, India, and Iraq. It included a section that commented on women's experiences, both as participants and as accompanying spouses. MacGregor saw the contribution of Fulbright wives as immensely valuable to the social interactions and cultural engagement of the participants: "The home of the Fulbright scholar being the scene of his most frequent informal associations with local people, his wife, as hostess, becomes a very important part of his social activity." He noted that women have a unique opportunity to interact with a range of people in the host community and argued that a Fulbright wife's sociability could be essential for successful integration: "The degree to which a grantee's wife extended a cordial welcome to visitors and revealed a genuine interest in their studies and careers largely determined the couple's ability to become integral members of the community."[23] The grantee's wife contributed to the cultural mediation process by welcoming host country nationals into the Fulbright grantee's home and extending hospitality and friendship.

MacGregor recognized the important role that accompanying families could play in the cultural learning process. Spouses and children of grantees could interact with the host community in ways that a Fulbrighter could not replicate: they were peers of schoolchildren, volunteers, hosts, and cultural mediators in their own right. Countless Fulbright grantees attested to the truth of this in their own experiences. Having one's family along was typically reported as a positive experience. As the grantee Clark Bullard reflected: "Although I regret this experience did not occur earlier in my life, it is all the more rich because I am seeing Britain through the eyes of my wife and children as well."[24] In a dispute over the State Department's reimbursement of travel costs, the wife of one Fulbright teacher argued emphatically for the value of her family's presence overseas. She felt that insufficient grants would keep scholars with families from participating in the program: "It is very important that families (*good families*) be encouraged to take these jobs. Our children were better ambassadors than any of your diplomats."[25]

The contributions of accompanying spouses were not recognized by all observers of the exchange program, however. Some critics considered the presence of families overseas an unnecessary cost. During one particularly stringent cost-cutting effort in 1965, Congress slashed $300,000 from the Fulbright program budget by refusing to allocate funding for the travel costs of grantee dependents. Representative John J. Rooney, chair of the House appropriations committee, referred to dependent travel as "a luxury the American taxpayer cannot afford."[26] The view that it was not necessary for dependents to travel with a Fulbright grantee, or at least for them to do so with public funds, was shared by the program's founder. Although Fulbright disagreed with Rooney on many occasions, this was a point on which they had the same opinion. Fulbright lamented the shift toward senior scholar grants in some country programs: "The original idea [was] . . . to take your best American graduate students, not their families. . . . Too much is spent on sending professors and their families over."[27]

Despite such concerns, grantees' spouses and families were widely recognized as one of the Fulbright program's key assets and, thus, as these stories suggest, constitute one of the many ways in which women have made a valuable contribution to the Fulbright program.

Competing Priorities: The 1970s–1990s

After the successes of the early 1960s, the Fulbright program entered a new phase in its development, one marked by both political and financial challenges. Funding was cut as the United States became ensnared in the

Vietnam War, and Fulbright's opposition to that war meant that his namesake exchange program suffered ill treatment from President Johnson and his administration. It fared no better under Johnson's Republican successors, with severe cuts that reduced funding from $24 million in 1968–1969 to $16 million in 1969–1970, cuts that it still had not recovered from by the 1975–1976 academic year, when funding levels had increased only to $23 million.[28]

While many changes occurred from the 1970s to the end of the twentieth century, the status of women in the Fulbright program remained largely static, with little progress toward gender equality in terms of leadership or grant figures. The program's evolution over these three decades can be characterized by two primary themes: bureaucratic reorganization and increased alumni involvement. These two priorities dominated the agenda for Fulbright administrators. In the annual reports of the Board of Foreign Scholarships during this era, there was little mention of gender, race, or other matters of diversity among Fulbright grant recipients. There was little growth of the program over these years as well. Most of the current binational programs were in place by the 1960s; a few more were added in the post–Cold War era. Overall, it appears that survival was prioritized over matters of enhancing program diversity and women's involvement. Program officials were too busy fighting to protect the program and secure funding for its continuation.

Bureaucratic reorganization offered a small opening for greater involvement in the program of women from an unexpected place. With the loss of Fulbright as an advocate when he left Congress in 1974, alumni became the program's constituency and strongest defenders—female alumni in particular. Throughout the program's history, its bureaucratic home in Washington, DC, shifted a number of times, from the State Department to the US International Communication Agency, then to the US Information Agency, and ultimately back to the State Department. All these shifts took place during these three decades, but there had been earlier attempts to reorganize educational and cultural exchange activities. For example, Fulbright had defended the program from being subsumed into USIA in 1953.

Two decades later, when bureaucratic reorganization of exchange activities loomed again, Fulbright was no longer in the Senate. Though he wrote persuasive letters and met with key decision makers, the program had lost its strongest advocate in Congress. The Fulbright Association, an organization for exchange program alumni, was founded in 1977, just three years after Fulbright's departure from Congress. Involving alumni at this time was seen as a means of establishing a domestic constituency for the program, a group of concerned citizens who would rescue the program in times of need.

Just four years after its founding, the Fulbright Association was faced with such a moment. Substantial cuts proposed for the 1981 budget were thwarted by the lobbying efforts of Fulbright advocates, including the alumni organization. Another crisis moment occurred with the 1999 foreign affairs restructuring and closure of USIA. Fulbright advocates lobbied against proposed plans to merge the Bureau of Educational and Cultural Affairs (ECA) with USIA. Alumni were among the advocates, along with educators, international education organizations, and some members of congressional foreign affairs committees. When Secretary of State Madeline Albright changed course and decided to keep ECA separate within the State Department, advocates applauded her choice. The Fulbright alumni proved an effective, if never anticipated, source of proexchange pressure.

There is a clear link between the bureaucratic reorganizations and the increased alumni involvement that characterizes the period from 1970 to 1999. Fulbright alumni have contributed to the survival and success of the exchange program in a number of ways, and they have been crucial advocates during times of bureaucratic restructuring. This is especially true of the female veterans of the program.

Women have played a significant role in the advocacy work of the Fulbright Association. Jane L. Anderson served as executive director for more than two decades.[29] During that time, she led alumni lobbying efforts against proposed budget cuts in the mid-1990s and sought to ensure the program's future during USIA dissolution in 1999.

Caroline Matano Yang was an early and strong supporter of the Fulbright Association.[30] Although she initially came to know the program as a Fulbrighter's spouse rather than a grantee herself, she made substantial contributions to the program and established a new model for alumni involvement. As executive secretary of the US Educational Commission in Japan for over twenty years, she launched an innovative alumni fundraising campaign, the first of its kind in the world.[31] She also chaired the Fulbright Board of Foreign Scholarships, on which she served three terms.

Alice Stone Ilchman was another vital advocate for the Fulbright program amid these changes. When establishing the International Communication Agency in 1978, President Carter appointed her as assistant director for educational and cultural affairs. Her correspondence with Fulbright demonstrated her concern for the program and his faith in her advocacy. "You are doing an excellent job in giving proper leadership," he wrote. "As you know, I was apprehensive about the reorganization. . . . [O]nly strong leadership from the Assistant Director can preserve the integrity of the program."[32] During her tenure, the program developed new fellowships for public servants, launched new cost-sharing initiatives, and secured private sponsorship in partnering countries.[33]

Fulbright Women in the Twenty-First Century

The current state of women in the Fulbright program reflects a number of important advancements that women have made in other fields throughout society. Whereas the concept of women's leadership was dismissed by USIA officials in their 1959 report,[34] today it is specifically embraced and encouraged. In recent years, Fulbright program administrators conducted enrichment activities for its visiting female scholars in a series known as Fulbright Women's Leadership and Re-Entry Enrichment Seminars.[35] These seminars took place throughout the United States and brought together women from various regions, including sub-Saharan Africa, Southeast Asia, and Latin America. They discussed issues such as the role of women in public service, and they met with female leaders drawn from a broad range of fields and backgrounds.

Another recent development has been the rise of Fulbright women in male-dominated academic disciplines. During the 2015–2016 academic year, women made up 30 percent of the grantees in science, technology, engineering, and mathematics (STEM), law, business, and medicine.[36] This figure reflects the current data on women in science more generally. The National Science Foundation reported that, in 2013, women made up 29 percent of people working in science and engineering occupations.[37] These figures stand in marked contrast to earlier profiles of typical Fulbright women, who were centered primarily in the humanities.

The increase of women in STEM subjects is best exemplified by the career of the Fulbright alumna Joy Buolamwini, a computer scientist, entrepreneur, and advocate for girls' STEM education.[38] During the 2012–2013 academic year, Buolamwini was a Fulbright scholar studying in Zambia, where she created a computer science learning project for young Zambians, the Zamrize Initiative. As a Rhodes scholar, she launched Code 4 Rights, a project aimed at empowering women and girls to develop and create technology. As a graduate student at the Massachusetts Institute of Technology, she founded the Algorithmic Justice League to highlight and fight against examples of algorithmic bias, such as the failure of facial recognition software to detect the features of people of color.[39]

The twenty-first century has seen a rise in female political leadership, and Fulbright women have been part of that development. From 2001 to 2005, the alumna Ivy Leona Dumont was the governor general of the Bahamas. In 2003, the alumna Beatriz Merino Lucero served as Peru's prime minister. From 2010 to 2012, Iveta Radičová was the prime minister of the Slovak Republic. In all three cases, these Fulbrighters were the first women to hold their offices.

More recently, in 2015, the Fulbright alumna Kolinda Grabar-Kitarović was elected the first female president of Croatia. Grabar-Kitarović was a Fulbright student at George Washington University's Elliott School of International Affairs during the 2002–2003 academic year.[40] She has also served as former assistant secretary general of NATO and as the Croatian ambassador to the United States. As of March 2017, there are just fifteen incumbent female heads of state or government, and the inclusion of a Fulbright alumna on that list is a remarkable achievement.[41]

Not only have Fulbright alumnae left a lasting mark in their post-Fulbright careers; female grantees themselves have indelibly affected the host countries to which they were assigned. Amy Biehl, an American Fulbright scholar to South Africa in 1992–1993, was one such remarkable woman.[42] An international relations graduate of Stanford University, the California native was studying the role of women in South Africa's transition to democracy. Prior to her Fulbright year, she had worked with a US nonprofit organization in Namibia during that country's democratic transition. She became interested in exploring the role of South African women in the new democracy, and her research brought her into close contact with many key figures in the African National Congress (ANC). For example, her supervisor, Dullah Omar, was an ANC executive committee member and a human rights lawyer who had represented Nelson

Mandela during his imprisonment. Biehl became fully integrated into the movement, engaging with women's groups and researching and drafting responses to government proposals on women's rights. Her friends and colleagues remarked that she had truly become one of them—an achievement that underscores the tragedy of her untimely death. A victim of political violence, Biehl was attacked and killed by a group of militant students in a black township where she was giving friends a ride home.

Amy Biehl's tragic death was a sobering, rather extreme example of the potential dangers and challenges that are inherent in doing great things. Biehl fought to secure women's legal rights and gender equality measures in the new South African Constitution. Though she did not live to see it, the Constitution included one of most comprehensive equality clauses in the world.[43] Her legacy continues today through the work of the Amy Biehl Foundation, a nonprofit organization serving the young people of Cape Town.

Conclusion

As the Fulbright program enters its eighth decade of international educational and cultural exchanges, what can we conclude regarding the status and role of Fulbright women in the global intellectual elite? In some ways, little has changed since the inception of the program. Women still hold significantly fewer Fulbright grants than do men, particularly in the senior scholar grant category. In the 2015–2016 cohort of the Fulbright core program, 41 percent of grantees were women, compared with around 30 percent during the first three years of the program's operations.[44] Although this represents a substantial increase in women's representation, it suggests that the Fulbright program fails to reflect the gender balance of higher education more generally. The proportion of US bachelor's degrees earned by women has steadily increased over the past four decades, rising from 46 percent in 1976–1977 to 57 percent in 2014–2015.[45] Although women are earning a majority of undergraduate degrees, they continue to lag behind their male counterparts in the Fulbright program.

However, in a number of important ways, the profile of women in the Fulbright program has been raised. Under President Obama, women and men were appointed to the administrative board in equal numbers for the first time. In recent years, the Bureau of Educational and Cultural Affairs has held special seminars on women's leadership for Fulbright scholars. Women have increasingly pursued Fulbright research in male-dominated fields, and special efforts have been made to increase the participation of women in STEM subjects.

The Fulbright program can offer unique opportunities for its female participants. It can expose them to new ideas and experiences that can challenge their understanding of gender roles, as we have seen in the stories of women like Effie Kaye Adams. It connects them with female colleagues and leaders around the world, fostering new connections between women within the network of the global intellectual elite. It bestows academic prestige on its recipients, helping them in a wide range of future pursuits, as we can see in the profiles of women like Croatian president Grabar-Kitarović and the Pulitzer Prize–winning author Sylvia Plath. Furthermore, female grantees have transformed political systems, as Biehl's example shows. The impacts are far-reaching, lasting many years beyond the end of the formal exchange experience.

Notes

1. Mabel Lee to J. William Fulbright, September 16, 1985, folder 6, box 23, ser. 4, Special Collections, J. William Fulbright Papers, University of Arkansas Libraries, Fayetteville (hereafter Fulbright Papers).

2. Margaret Henderson to J. William Fulbright, September 20, 1954, folder 2, box 14, subser. 4, ser. 2, Fulbright Papers.

3. Helen Laville, *Cold War Women: The International Activities of American Women's Organizations* (Manchester: Manchester University Press, 2002). See also Helen Laville, "The Importance of Being (in) Earnest: Voluntary Associations and the Irony of the State-Private Network during the Early Cold War," in *The U.S. Government, Citizen Groups and the Cold War: The State-Private Network*, ed. Helen Laville and Hugh Wilford (London: Routledge, 2006), 47–65.

4. David J. Snyder, "Domesticity, Rearmament, and the Limits of U.S. Public Diplomacy in the Netherlands during the Early Cold War," *Journal of Cold War Studies* 15, no. 3 (Summer 2013): 47–75.

5. Laura Belmonte, *Selling the American Way: U.S. Propaganda and the Cold War* (Philadelphia: University of Pennsylvania Press, 2010).

6. Philip Nash, "A Woman's Place Is in the Embassy: America's First Female Chiefs of Mission, 1933–1964," in *Women, Diplomacy and International Politics since 1500*, ed. Glenda Sluga and Carolyn James (London: Routledge, 2016), 222–39.

7. Alessandro Brogi, "Ambassador Clare Boothe Luce and the Evolution of Psychological Warfare in Italy," *Cold War History* 12, no. 2 (May 2012): 269–94.

8. Liping Bu, *Making the World Like Us: Education, Cultural Expansion and the American Century* (Westport, CT: Praeger, 2003).

9. Whitney Walton, *Internationalism, National Identities, and Study Abroad: France and the United States* (Stanford, CA: Stanford University Press, 2010).

10. Randall Bennett Woods, *Fulbright: A Biography* (Cambridge: Cambridge University Press, 1995), 53.

11. Ibid., 78–79.

12. Walter Johnson and Francis Colligan, *The Fulbright Program: A History* (Chicago: University of Chicago Press, 1965), 21–22.

13. Susan Levine, *Degrees of Equality: The American Association of University Women and the Challenge of Twentieth-Century Feminism* (Philadelphia: Temple University Press, 1995).

14. Aurelia Plath, ed., *Letters Home by Sylvia Plath* (London: Faber & Faber, 1975), 279, 282–83.

15. Effie Kaye Adams, *Experiences of a Fulbright Teacher* (Boston: Christopher, 1956), 26, 104.

16. For student figures, see Sam Lebovic, "From War Junk to Educational Exchange: The World War II Origins of the Fulbright Program and the Foundations of American Cultural Globalism, 1945–1950," *Diplomatic History* 37, no. 2 (2013): 280–312; and Board of Foreign Scholarships membership figures from annual reports, author's analysis.

17. Virginia Geiger, "USIA Women's Activities: Report for Senator Fulbright," June 19, 1959, 11, folder 14, box 104, ser. 1, group 3, Bureau of Educational and Cultural Affairs Historical Collection (MC 468), Special Collections, University of Arkansas Libraries, Fayetteville.

18. Laville, *Cold War Women*; Elaine Tyler May, *Homeward Bound: American Families in the Cold War Era* (New York: Basic Books, 1988).

19. Geiger, "USIA Women's Activities," 12.

20. Public Law 87-256, Mutual Educational and Cultural Exchange Act of 1961 (the Fulbright-Hays Act), folder 6, box 103, ser. 1, group 3, Bureau of Educational and Cultural Affairs Historical Collection (MC 468).

21. Ibid.

22. US Advisory Commission on International Educational and Cultural Affairs, *A Beacon of Hope: The Exchange-of-Persons Program* (Washington, DC: US Government Printing Office, 1963), 35–36.

23. Gordon MacGregor, *The Experiences of American Scholars in Countries of the Near East and South Asia: Report on the Problems of Selection, Planning and Personal Adjustment of Americans in the Fulbright Programs with Egypt, India and Iraq* (Ithaca, NY: Cornell University, Society for Applied Anthropology, 1962), 39, folder 6, box 103, ser. 1, group 3, Bureau of Educational and Cultural Affairs Historical Collection (MC 468).

24. Clark Bullard to J. William Fulbright, November 27, 1986, folder 5, box 27, ser. 4, J. William Fulbright Papers.

25. J. Graham to J. William Fulbright, November 1, 1960, folder 7, box 14, sub-ser. 4, ser. 2, Fulbright Papers.

26. Don Oberdorfer, "Common Noun Spelled f-u-1-b-r-i-g-h-t: Senator Fulbright," *New York Times*, April 4, 1965, 87.

27. Quoted in Leonard Sussman, *The Culture of Freedom: The Small World of Fulbright Scholars* (Lanham, MD: Rowman & Littlefield, 1992), 56.

28. Board of Foreign Scholarships, *7th Annual Report, 1969* (Washington, DC: US Government Printing Office, 1969), National Archives, College Park, MD, Group 59, box 2, Board of Foreign Scholarships, Annual Reports 1970–1975.

29. Fulbright Association, *2012 Annual Report* (Washington, DC: Fulbright Association, 2012), http://fulbright.org/annual-reports.

30. Arthur Dudden Dynes to Caroline Yang, April 3, 1980, folder 37, box 112, ser. 2, group 3, Bureau of Educational and Cultural Affairs Historical Collection (MC 468).

31. Caroline A. Matano Yang, "Multiple Cost Sharing: The Japan Experience," *Annals of the American Academy of Political and Social Science* 491 (May 1987): 85–91.

32. J. William Fulbright to Alice Stone Ilchman, November 2, 1978, folder 1, box 22, ser. 4, Fulbright Papers.

33. Board of Foreign Scholarships, *Fulbright Program Exchanges, 1980*, folder 16, box 108, ser. 2, group 3, Bureau of Educational and Cultural Affairs Historical Collection (MC 468).

34. Geiger, "USIA Women's Activities."

35. "Women Fulbright Students from Sub-Saharan Africa to Attend Leadership and Re-Entry Seminar in Austin, Texas," Press Release, US Department of State, April 11, 2012, https://2009-2017.state.gov/r/pa/prs/ps/2012/04/187716.htm.

36. Author's analysis of grantee directory, https://us.fulbrightonline.org/component/filter.

37. National Science Foundation, "Figure 3-28: Women in S&E Occupations, 1993–2013," National Center for Science and Engineering Statistics, SESTAT (1993–2013), https:nsf.gov/statistics/2016/nsb20161.

38. "Fulbright Alumna Promotes STEM Education for Girls at Clinton Global Initiative," Bureau of Educational and Cultural Affairs, October 8, 2014, https://eca.state.gov/highlight/fulbright-alumna-promotes-stem-education-girls-clinton-global-initiative.

39. "Joy Buolamwini Wins National Contest for Her Work Fighting Bias in Machine Learning," *MIT News*, January 17, 2017, http://news.mit.edu/2017/joy-buolamwini-wins-hidden-figures-contest-for-fighting-machine-learning-bias-0117.

40. "Presidential Victory for Fulbright Alumna from Croatia," Bureau of Educational and Cultural Affairs, January 16, 2015, https://eca.state.gov/highlight/presidential-victory-fulbright-alumna-croatia.

41. Abigail Geiger and Lauren Kent, "Number of Women Leaders around the World Has Grown, but They're Still a Small Group," Pew Research Center Fact Tank, March 8, 2017, http://www.pewresearch.org/fact-tank.

42. Steven Gish, "Amy Biehl and the ANC: A Scholar-Activist in South Africa, 1992–93," *African Historical Review* 45, no. 1 (2013): 1–21.

43. Ibid., 6.

44. Francis Colligan, Correspondence with J. H. Yingling, April 13, 1954, folder 1, box 14, subser. 4, ser. 2, second accession, Bureau of Educational and Cultural Affairs Historical Collection (MC 468). Figures for 2015–2016 academic year, author's analysis of grantee directory, https://us.fulbrightonline.org/component /filter.

45. US Department of Education, National Center for Education Statistics, "Table 322.20. Bachelor's Degrees Conferred by Postsecondary Institutions, by Race/Ethnicity and Sex of Student: Selected Years, 1976–77 through 2014–15," September 2016, https://nces.ed.gov/programs/digest.

Tactful Visitor, Scientific Observer, or 100 Percent Patriot?

Ambassadorship in the Australia-US Fulbright Program

Alice Garner and Diane Kirkby

The meaning of ambassadorship for scholars lies at the heart of the Fulbright program. As participants in a scheme that straddled the worlds of education and diplomacy, scholars were expected to act as unofficial ambassadors for their education systems, the program itself, and their country of origin. Yet the requirements and boundaries of this role were not always clear-cut. Unlike government representatives on foreign soil, who had strict protocols to guide their behavior in a range of social and political contexts, Fulbright scholars had to work things out for themselves, in both casual social situations and formal, public fora.

In the early years, the scheme's reputation rested on the success (or otherwise) of the participating scholars. Initial impressions were crucial at a time when there was growing suspicion around the world of the true motives of the United States in promoting educational exchange. Australia's experience as one of the first countries to participate in the global Fulbright program reveals the often fraught and haphazard nature of those early years for Fulbright scholars and program administrators. The meaning of ambassadorship for academics emerged gradually as the scheme became established. Here, we show how the political context, new understandings about gender and race, and the experiences of the scholars themselves together recast the program's ambassadorial dimension in response to changing circumstances. Through the stories of individual scholars' encounters, we trace themes of political, cultural, and social change in the particular context of the Australian Fulbright program, which began in 1950.[1]

Three years after the Australian-American exchange program had been launched, the small University of Tasmania prepared on June 21, 1953, to receive its second Fulbright scholar. This was a significant event for an institution that was considered something of a remote outpost, situated as it was on a sparsely populated island off the south coast of mainland Australia. It was also an important moment for the binational program's administrators. They selected senior American scholars on the assumption that they could play multiple roles, bringing to their host community not only their intellectual abilities and interests but also exposure to the strength of the American higher education system and, by extension, the United States itself. This was to manifest in their ability and willingness to act as informal ambassadors. Not all were prepared for what this meant.

The chosen scholar for Tasmania was Dr. Walter Krause, an American economist from Utah who planned to study the effect on the Australian wool industry of the introduction of synthetics. This was an issue of great importance to his Australian hosts, whose export economy still rested to a large degree on the sheep's back.[2] When Krause arrived in the state capital of Hobart, however, a sudden cold snap hit the island, and snow started to fall. He was greeted at the airport by the head of economics, Professor Gerald Firth, and the two men drove to the house where Krause was to live for the next nine months.[3] Krause seems to have been underwhelmed by this accommodations and his posting, for, less than forty-eight hours later, he left the island. He traveled north to the national capital, Canberra, and arrived without warning at the Fulbright Commission—then called the US Educational Foundation (USEF), at the time based in the US embassy—telling the foundation's executive officer, Geoffrey Rossiter, that he had left Tasmania because he could not bear the cold.[4]

Krause had, according to Rossiter, "tried living in a hotel in addition to the private house in which accommodations had originally been secured for him," but the heating was "hopelessly inadequate," and he found it impossible to work. Rossiter arranged for Krause to stay in Canberra for the next few months, changed his affiliation to the Australian National

University, and organized access to the centrally heated National Library in the hope that he might acclimate and decide to remain for the full term of his award. Once three months were up, however, Krause returned his ticket to the foundation, headed to Sydney, bought himself a Pan Am fare, and flew back to the United States the following day—six months earlier than agreed.[5]

The foundation had only recently faced the premature departure of *another* senior US scholar, the mechanical engineering professor Merl Creech, and it appears that Krause agreed to stay on for the three months in Canberra to avoid causing further embarrassment. Creech had left Australia about a fortnight before Krause arrived, after having spent only *four days* in Australia—in Sydney this time—and his sudden flight had been reported on the front page of the *Sydney Morning Herald*, the major daily, under the attention-grabbing headline "Mysterious Departure of US Professor."[6] Other newspapers around the nation, from Rockhampton to Adelaide, had then run with the story. The *Morning Bulletin* of Rockhampton titled its article "No Lecture, No Explanation," while the salacious *Truth* went so far as to claim that the Creech mystery "rivals any bestseller detective story," the journalist even following his trail home via Honolulu to the United States in the hope of scoring an interview.[7]

It may seem surprising to us today that the early return home of an American academic was considered worthy of national news coverage, but, in early 1950s Australia, academic exchange with a country other than the United Kingdom was still something of a novelty, and overseas visitors were often profiled by the press. A perusal of the newspapers reveals that, in this postwar period of sharpening Cold War tensions, visitors from the emerging economic and cultural powerhouse over the Pacific were of particular interest.

The Creech and Krause departures were troubling events for the US Educational Foundation, which was rolling out its first year of full-strength programming since the binational exchange program's establishment. The foundation was highly conscious of the importance of publicity for the program in this early phase. Every speck of news coverage counted, whether positive or negative. In a country with a small population and a growing fascination with (combined with suspicion of) all things American, incidents that might seem insignificant in another context could have serious effects on the reputation of the program. The exchange scheme was seeking (among other things) to foster a more positive appreciation of US educational and intellectual offerings through person-to-person contacts, and the Creech and Krause stories were not helpful. These scholars' responses to their circumstances revealed that ambassadorial skills were not guaranteed.

A New Language of Ambassadorship

The original Fulbright Act (PL 584) passed by the US Congress in 1946 made no explicit reference to an ambassadorial role for Fulbright scholars—indeed, its text did not even refer to *mutual understanding*. Senator Fulbright, who designed and cleverly shepherded the bill through to legislative approval in a difficult time, envisaged that program participants would act as interpreters of their cultures abroad and then of their host culture on return. Yet he knew that, in order to get his bill passed without adverse attention from isolationist congressional colleagues, he must avoid the language of international peace or idealism. When introducing the first version of the bill, he did refer to the proposed use of credits from the sale of surplus property abroad for educational exchange as serving the "promotion of international good will," but this was apparently vague enough not to cause concern and did not appear in the final text of the act.[8]

Once the bill was passed, however, and the newly formed US Board of Foreign Scholarships (BFS) began to set general program policy, the senator's goal of international understanding came to be articulated more fully, for example, in selection and programming guidelines. The term *mutual understanding* featured prominently in the US Information and Educational Exchange Act (or Smith-Mundt Act) of January 1948, which, though it governed other US government exchanges, had some areas of administrative crossover with the Fulbright program. It played an important part in publicly identifying educational exchange with cultural diplomacy and thus promoting the notion of scholarly ambassadorship.[9]

The Australia-US executive agreement of November 1949 adopted this language, stating clearly the two governments' common desire "to promote further mutual understanding between the peoples of their two countries, by a wider exchange of knowledge and professional talents through educational contacts."[10] Although the agreement did not mention the concept of unofficial ambassadorship specifically, its wording implied that individual scholars were expected to contribute actively to the furthering of mutual understanding.

Person-to-person interactions between scholar and hosts lay at the heart of the scheme, but, for these to have a broader reach, program administrators sought to nurture media contacts. The establishment phase of the global Fulbright program coincided with the professionalization of the public relations profession in the late 1940s and the 1950s.[11] This was driven to a large degree by US practitioners, and the early shapers of the Australian program sought to build their capacity in this unfamiliar territory.

Realizing the need to spread the gospel about visiting US scholars, the foundation's staff and, in board meetings, the binational directors discussed how they might reach a broad Australian audience.[12] Several months before the Creech and Krause departures, in February 1953, the foundation had looked into making better use of the US Information Service (USIS), whose officers, based in the US embassy and consulates, sat on the foundation board. It decided to begin trialing a "system of coordinated press releases" about its scholars' activities and movements.[13] When a group of twenty American Fulbrighters—the largest contingent to come to Australia since the program had begun—set sail for Sydney in March on the ship *Aorangi*, foundation and USIS publicity machines went into full swing.

Newspapers across the country reported the scholars' impending April arrival. The scholars even starred in a newsreel produced by the Film Division of the Australian News and Information Bureau. In "Fulbright Scholars Extend Knowledge in Australia," we see a group of mostly middle-aged, bespectacled men and women wandering around the Royal Sydney Agricultural Show patting cows. Cut to the group standing around rather awkwardly and chatting in scraggly bush land while chunks of skewered meat sizzle over a campfire, a voiceover enthusing over the low cost of Australian meat. The newsreel ends with a shot of the visitors looking out over the sweep of a Sydney beach, one scholar stripped down to a stylish one-piece bathing suit.[14] Such newsreels were usually screened at Saturday cinema sessions for the general public. These academics were surely unused to having a celebrity spotlight trained on them. It was only two months after this media campaign that Krause and Creech arrived in

Australia, which helps explain why their early departures were so widely publicized.

If comfortable obscurity in the halls of academe could not be guaranteed when on a Fulbright trip, what kind of scholars would be fit for the demands of this role? Our focus here is primarily on US scholars because the US Department of State and other bodies that were involved in Fulbright selections were all very conscious of the potential cultural diplomacy effect of American scholars' experiences. Unlike their US counterparts, the Australian Department of External Affairs and Australian universities engaged in Fulbright selection procedures did not yet seriously consider the possible ambassadorial role of Australian scholars going to the United States; this would occur sometime later.[15]

The foundation was keen from the start to attract high-caliber senior American scholars who would kick the Australian program off to a good start and generate some positive publicity. USEF executive officer Rossiter claimed in his first annual report (of 1952–1953) that, although the first American grantees who came in 1951 were "for the most part . . . excellent representatives of their country" who did "much for cordial Australian-American relations," few were "world class academically."[16] For Rossiter, the best kind of scholar-ambassador was a genuine leader in his or her intellectual field. The problem was, world-class scholars were in great demand at this time—from, for example, US universities coping with a massive postwar influx of students boosted by the GI Bill and other Fulbright partner countries around the world. All sought to snare the most impressive academics they could to head growing departments and launch new teaching and exchange programs.

Australia found itself lower down in the pecking order of desirable countries for Fulbrighters than, say, France, Italy, or the United Kingdom.[17] Although Europe was still struggling with postwar shortages and only slowly rebuilding, it had a cultural cachet and intellectual pull that Australia struggled to match. As one Australian resident in the United States put it in 1950: "Most students apply for European education, where there are centuries of culture and art to delve into. It is not easy to think of something sufficiently attractive . . . as justification for study in Australia."[18] Australia was considered something of a backwater, when anything was known about it at all. Australians themselves, in what came to be called the *cultural cringe*, often saw their country in this negative light, leading the intellectually ambitious to travel abroad for further study.[19] In some cases, senior scholars awarded early Fulbright trips to more remote and less desirable countries like Australia may not have been at the cutting edge of their discipline.

Rossiter argued that "the programme, at least in the eyes of the Australian universities, will defeat itself to some extent unless some really top ranking research scholars and lecturers are brought out."[20] As for postgraduate students, Rossiter continued, those "with no serious academic purpose" brought "discredit on the programme and on American academic institutions." It was openly acknowledged in Australian and US diplomatic circles dealing with the exchange program that Australian universities did not look on the US education system with favor, in comparison with that of the United Kingdom. The Fulbright Foundation needed to work hard to prove the value of an exchange experience—in both directions.[21] Rossiter noted: "In some academic circles here, it is a fact that the standard of American education, particularly at the college and university level, is regarded as open to question, even though this attitude may be without justifiable foundation. In view of this, the Foundation believes that it is of the utmost importance that the academic standing of visiting grantees, particularly in the lecturer and advanced research scholar categories, should be of the highest order possible."[22] Being a standard bearer for an entire higher education system was something not all academics were cut out for (or, perhaps, prepared to take on).

Some scholars were both disappointed and disappointing in this regard. They may have been experts in their field but were perhaps ill equipped to handle the intellectual and physical isolation of their Australian posts and their separation from home, and thus not in a position to represent the US university system with much success. Some early American Fulbright visitors *were* able, however, to handle the emotional test of taking up a post in this far-flung land and to promote an image of a robust US education system among their hosts. Although faced with an array of social and environmental challenges, they thrived and established strong, ongoing relationships with their Australian colleagues. The exchange experience would always be a test of individual character as well as of a scholar's intellectual (or ambassadorial) qualities, particularly as navigating the ambassadorial role was left to individuals.

Mapping Out a Role

The stories of two early scholars who helped steady the Australian program's record around the time of the Creech and Krause incidents are revealing. Kenneth Brill, a geologist from Missouri, arrived in Hobart three months before Walter Krause's short sojourn to take up a visiting professorship. Finding that the University of Tasmania "consist[ed] chiefly of a number of slab huts in a paddock," he was, unlike his compatriot, happy to live with the limitations of his host institution, perhaps in part because he spent much of his time out in the bush rather than sitting in an unheated office. He discovered, however, that he could not carry out his field research in the manner he had expected to be able to. He had intended to make "lithofacies studies of the Permian strata" in Tasmania, but it turned out that Tasmania had not yet been mapped "in sufficient detail to permit the stratigrapher to do detailed work." This meant that he had to spend much of his time "beating the bush for outcrops that were rumored to be present, mapping areas where no geological work had been done, and making structural studies in regions that had been incorrectly mapped."[23] Brill might have predicted this state of affairs, considering that the map of Australia that he received from the Australian Government Tourist Bureau before he left the United States "didn't even have Tasmania on it" (an extraordinary oversight). Instead of despairing, however, he plunged in and carried out this basic mapping work, thus contributing a resource of great value to his hosts and subsequent researchers.[24]

Brill's resourcefulness and adaptability, hidden away in the Tasmanian bush, caught none of the press attention afforded the two more troublesome American professors, but some other visiting lecturers more than made up for this lack of media coverage. A fortnight after the media jumped on Creech's premature departure, some fifteen American women came to Australia under Fulbright auspices (up from seven in 1952), including eight postgraduates, five schoolteachers, and one senior scholar, Professor Mary E. Murphy, who made a particularly big impression. Murphy, who held the chair of economics and business administration at the Los Angeles State College of Applied Arts and Science, was, according to an article in *The Argus*, not only the first woman in the United States to become a certified public accountant but also the first woman ever to address the International Congress of Accountants in London. She considered her selection as the first Fulbrighter in accounting (from the United States to any country) to be "revolutionary" and praised Australian accountants for "being willing to accept a woman in what was usually regarded as a man's sphere."[25]

A journalist writing for the Adelaide *Advertiser* claimed that Murphy was one of the two most successful Fulbright "ambassador" scholars to date, the other being Harriet Creighton, a professor of botany and the first woman to be appointed secretary of the Botanical Society of America, who had come to Australia in 1952. Murphy traveled to every Australian university (of which there were only seven at the time) giving talks guaranteed to pique interest not only among accountants and commerce students but also among women and men in the broader community. The *Advertiser* reported that, during her tour, she "studied our economic and industrial set-up at first hand," spoke to "businessmen, bankers and administrators," and, "in short," spent most of her time in "a man's world."[26] But she also talked to Australian businesswomen and made some pronouncements that seem, from our twenty-first-century perspective, quite radical for Australia in the early 1950s.

The Argus reported Murphy as saying that Australia was "approaching the stage where women will automatically receive equal pay for equal work." She claimed, somewhat controversially (and, it has to be said, inaccurately), that, in the United States, equal pay for the sexes was "taken for granted in all the professions" and that, although Australia was twenty years behind the United States, it should not take another twenty to catch up.[27] A month later, she went further with her message, proclaiming: "Equality for men and women, in job, home and national life is Australia's quickest road to peace, prosperity, and a satisfactory place in international affairs." She also quoted a UN Human Rights Report revealing that "Australian women were taking a smaller part in public and professional activities than the women of India," where, for example, the health minister was a woman. She pointed out that Australia had no female Supreme Court judges, queen's counsels, or magistrates.[28]

Murphy's criticisms and exhortations were given surprisingly positive coverage by Australian journalists. Here was an unexpected ambassadorship—a feminist voice for which the all-male Fulbright board in Canberra was, one imagines, unprepared. After all, it was not until 1973 that an amendment was made to policy documents substituting the word *family* for the word *wife* in clauses dealing with scholars' travel companions—showing a built-in assumption about scholars' expected gender. In 1983, a US Information Agency report on the programming and selection procedures of the Australian Fulbright program criticized it for being run like an "old boys' support system."[29]

The report that Murphy submitted to the foundation at the end of her seven-month stay reveals something of how she interpreted the ambassadorial role. It was a thorough and bracing account of her activities in and impressions of Australia from the perspective of a high-powered, publicity-conscious professional. Murphy thought that the foundation needed to do more groundwork to "encourage host Universities to extend a welcome hand to the visitors." She would have appreciated being given "names of people, for instance, favorable or unfavorable to the Fulbright Plan." This observation confirms a continuing level of resistance to or suspicion of the program among some Australian academics. It also indicates Murphy's willingness to act in an openly ambassadorial fashion for the program itself. In response to a question about the program's success in realizing its goal of furthering mutual understanding, Murphy reported finding a "variation of interest in the Fulbright Plan"; she thought that the foundation needed to work harder "to 'convert' certain universities or Departments . . . to the efficacy of using the Lecturers assigned to the greatest extent." This may have been a comment on the gender imbalance she was exposed to in academic circles. She also proposed that the foundation publicize the scheme more widely among the general public, informing them of the "background of the Plan, how it is used," and "what the professional qualifications are of the people brought out."[30]

Murphy's hope that the foundation might do something about the attitude "prevalent" in Australian universities that an Australian BA was superior to an MA or a PhD "granted by an English or an American university" is particularly telling. She considered this attitude "antipathetic to the advancement of scholarship here." At the same time, she recognized that this condescension went both ways. "There is still the feeling," she wrote, reflecting on her colleagues back home, "that Australia is a land far away from America cut off from the rest of the world, and rather lagging behind England, America and Canada." The Australian sense of educational superiority that she and others identified sat somewhat confusingly alongside the simultaneous antipodean impulse to pursue further studies abroad (the cultural cringe); both were surely products of physical and intellectual isolation. Murphy thought that Americans were often reluctant to accept a Fulbright appointment in Australia because they felt that "little can be learned or contributed to University life here." She had found this to be quite untrue and argued that Australia presented "a great challenge to the serious teacher or student, and the best representatives of American education should be given the privilege of coming here in the years ahead."[31] Her offer to share her new knowledge and appreciation of Australia back home was the perfect manifestation of Fulbright's vision of a two-way exchange.

The impact of women like Mary Murphy in the early years of the Fulbright program is notable. Nevertheless, in contrast to the fascinated media response to her talks in Australia, the official Fulbright records of the Australia-US program over this period display no particular consciousness of the effective ambassadorial contribution that female scholars were making. Despite the effectiveness of several female scholars in the first half of the 1950s in advancing the Fulbright vision, the language of administration reveals the usual masculine biases of this period.[32] Could it be that the reluctance among senior male academics to travel to the antipodes opened up more opportunities for female scholars from the United States? The successful ambassadorial work of these pioneers in turn probably contributed to a growing interest in Australia back in their home country. The irony is that female scholars seemed not to benefit from this success: the next two decades saw a dramatic drop in the number of women participating in the Australian program, to the point that the number of female awardees dropped three-quarters from the 1950s to the 1970s.[33] Only in the 1980s and 1990s, when steps were taken to ensure the appointment of women to the binational board and to selection committees, did a measurable improvement in the gender balance of selected scholars ensue.[34] Further analysis of the gendered dimension of ambassadorship is undoubtedly merited.

Ambassadors Navigating the Cold War

Murphy surely understood what was being asked of her at this particular moment in time—it was, after all, the height of the Cold War. In 1953, American scholars coming to the end of their Australian exchange period were instructed to outline their academic activities and findings and then asked: "During the course of your stay in your host country, how much opportunity did you have for more informal social contacts, such as visits to homes?" Did they find these contacts "important in furthering international friendship and understanding," and did they think that the Fulbright program was realizing this goal? They were then directed to list any "misconceptions" held by Americans about Australia, and vice versa, and asked "in what ways, if any," they might have "contributed to clearing up any of these misconceptions" during their award period. The importance given to this last question was highlighted by the request that they "be as specific as possible" in answering it.[35] These report form queries show the extent to which American scholars' informal social relations were considered fundamental to their contribution to Australian-American mutual understanding. Not all scholars responded with Mary Murphy's enthusiasm to these questions; some were no doubt uncomfortable with the expectation that they be so actively and obviously working at bilateral diplomacy in their social relations.

Indeed, for many Americans participating in the first years of the Australian program, their ambassadorial role required them to explain the excesses of McCarthyist anticommunism to a world looking on in horror. The final US scholar reports of 1952 and 1953 reveal the damage wrought by the red-baiting senator on the international image of the US political system and the American people. One American grantee reported that Australians regularly asked him why Americans "let McCarthy get away with it." Another noted a "common misconception . . . [that] McCarthy is the most important person in the United States." A research scholar in government and constitutional law found that "many of the more thoughtful Australians are just now more interested in and fearful of America's Internal Security program and her foreign policy," while a social worker reported that Australians were most interested in "household appliances, clothes, and book-burnings or witch-hunts."[36] In other words, scholars quite often found themselves in defensive mode, which encouraged some honest reflection on the nature and pitfalls of this ambassadorial role. Anti-American sentiment already had strong roots in the Oxbridge-oriented Australian university world, and congressional witch hunts made visiting Americans' task of explaining their country all the more challenging.[37]

Drawing on his Western Australian experience, one lecturer in education advised future American scholars in 1953: "Life will probably be happier for the future grantee if he assumes the role of 'tactful visitor' or 'scientific observer' rather than that of '100% Patriot.'" He had found that Australians reacted "quickly and sometimes violently to criticism of any sort" and warned his compatriots about the Australian press, which liked to push for troublemaking comparisons between Australia and the United States.[38] A postgraduate sociologist reported in 1954: "One of the greatest hazards to 'understanding' in the first few months of one's stay in a foreign country is the matter of when and what opinions to express." She had often been encouraged to give an opinion when she felt that she had "insufficient basis for forming one" and feared that her honest opinion might "not be well received." She came to the conclusion that "experience is the only teacher in learning how to handle this." While she liked to encourage frank discussion about the United States during question-and-answer sessions at her public talks, she had learned that it was wise "to make it plain that any opinions [she] expressed were those of one person and not Americans in general."[39]

American scholars were called on not only to explain the excesses of Joe McCarthy but also to counter damaging stereotypes about American people and life. Most scholars felt that these stereotypes and misconceptions were primarily created and perpetuated by Hollywood and the press. John Rose Faust, for example, observed in 1953 that, "while Americans and Australians already have very much in common," it was "essential for Americans traveling overseas to see their country as others see them, and also help Australians to see the United States in its true perspective rather than as pictured by *Hollywood* and *Australian newspapers*." Newspapers, he argued, were doing a "great deal of harm" by playing up "the sensational stories (crime, corruption, and vice), McCarthyism, etc.," while movies misrepresented American life. It appears that Hollywood stereotypes could have specifically gendered consequences for the independent female scholar. The social worker Georgie Travis, who was divorced, wished that she had worn her old wedding ring and packed a black hat rather than a red one to avoid social misunderstanding during her 1953 Australian trip. At the same time, she felt that her presence may have countered popular stereotypes with a dose of reality—that she was "a middle-aged social worker who still washes on the board at home and worries about the rent on the house and deplores the films, and who seems to be relatively sound professionally"—and that simply being herself "may have helped to overcome a Hollywood idea of Americans!" In a similar effort to counter the popular Australian notion that "all of America is like Hollywood and the colored pictures of American magazines," the entomologist Barbara Ann Stay "tried not to emphasize American consumption goods." She hoped that her own presence may have helped "lend variety" to her hosts' conception of "the typical [American] countryman." Charles Hartshorne, an American philosopher in Melbourne in 1952, thought that it was useful for Australians to see "that some Americans are neither soldiers, business men, nor Hollywood actors and actresses, but persons with whom they may share universal cultural interests or a love of nature."[40]

"Not a good place for an American to be"?

The nature of scholarly ambassadorship would come under much closer scrutiny during the Vietnam War period, not least by Fulbright himself. The Vietnam War and the student protests of the 1960s and 1970s brought about a particularly intense questioning of the meaning of educational and cultural diplomacy, with special relevance for Australian and American exchanges owing to their governments' controversial military collaboration in Southeast Asia.[41] While questions about the extent to which the program was truly educational rather than politically driven had preoccupied some scholars and administrators from the beginning of the program, the war would sharpen these concerns and lead to significant changes.

As campus protest movements grew in strength and breadth in the 1960s, with battles raging over political, intellectual, and personal freedoms as well as foreign policy and militarism, Fulbright administrators inevitably had to reconsider and rearticulate the ambassadorial expectations of program participants. Students and academics were questioning much more vigorously the way in which government programs were impinging on research practices and limiting academic freedom, for example. Fulbright himself contributed to public debates on this subject and was all too aware of the dilemmas facing scholars who had trouble balancing their role as ambassadors for and potential critics of their own country.[42]

For the Fulbright program's administrators and grantees, serious and sustained political protest on university campuses and on the streets threw up many challenges—as well as opportunities to question actively the significance of their exchange. What might peaceful relations and mutual understanding signify for scholars in this tumultuous period when military engagement by both countries, in alliance, faced growing criticism?

That both nations were fighting in an increasingly unpopular war put Fulbright scholars from Australia and the United States on an awkward footing when they went on exchange, and many came under security surveillance. One Australian researcher, on a Fulbright award to the United States, was an architect who was also a political cartoonist publishing work with strong political messages. He found himself under investigation by the FBI because his cartoons upset the US government. Others found it uncomfortable having to endure anti-Americanism in the antiwar protests. A postdoctoral student from Yale reported: "Melbourne in 1968 was not a good place for an American to be." Meanwhile, others had found congenial colleagues in the transnational antiwar movement. Charles McCoy was a Fulbright senior scholar in political science at Monash University in Melbourne in 1966. On his return to the United States, he became a member of a radical group formed within the American Political Science Association seeking to displace connections to the CIA and encourage members to look critically at their nation's political systems and its weaknesses, particularly at the war in Vietnam, which was "no mistake."[43]

These encounters reveal some of the challenges of participating in this exchange program during a politically tumultuous period. There were other difficulties that ambassadorship could entail. The historian John Hope Franklin felt that he had been used as a token educated black man invited to join an all-white delegation to the newly independent Nigeria in 1960.[44] He had at the same time, however, accepted the Fulbright distinguished visitor award to Australia, despite deep misgivings about the country's racist history and ongoing White Australia policy with its race-based immigration restrictions,[45] because he appreciated the real benefits and impacts of educational exchange. In his memoirs, in which he described his memorable Australian tour in some detail, he explained: "I did not want to be used merely to paper over or mislead the world regarding the state of race relations in the United States. On the other hand, if the government wished to use me as an example of what was possible, I had no objection so long as I could speak as I wished and my involvement was genuinely in the interest of improving the racial climate in America." To do that he explained: "I quickly set myself the rule that so long as there was no effort to dictate what I would say, I was amenable to any overture, and I am pleased to say that no one ever asked of me anything that would compromise my professional or scholarly integrity."[46]

Franklin was ideally placed to appreciate the complex position in which Fulbright scholars found themselves, one that would become only harder to negotiate through the 1960s and 1970s as campuses became more and more politically explosive. Not all scholars were as aware of the complexity of their ambassadorial position—at least before departure. A postgraduate plant ecologist studying in Melbourne in 1966, for example, reported that his exchange period had brought about the "revelation that quite reasonable people, even citizens of one of the United States' closest allies, may disapprove of quite a lot of American foreign policy," something that, he admitted "humbly and simply," he had not understood earlier and that had reshaped his "understanding of international relations."[47] In this context, ambassadorship became an illumination to be carried back home.

Meanwhile, a different kind of revelation awaited those US scholars who were already inclined to be critical of their own government's policies. The BFS attempted to make a clearer distinction between foreign policy and educational exchange, and Fulbright called for Americans to overcome their ingrained "fear of dissent" in his best-seller *The Arrogance of Power*.[48] Nevertheless, US scholars in this period could find that taking a critical stance was not always well received by their Australian hosts. A senior scholar in life sciences, for example, reported: "Both Australians and Europeans have told me that they are embarrassed by Americans who attempt comradeship by unduly criticizing the United States." A postgraduate in soil science advised any future scholar visiting Australia: "He should not feel that he should be so open-minded that he can deprecate his own country in casual discussions; Australians seem suspicious of anyone who is not reasonably proud of his heritage. But don't overdo it!" A delicate balance to achieve indeed. Another postgraduate, studying comparative literature at Adelaide University, explored this social challenge in more detail. "The grantee will," he said, "meet a good deal of defensiveness, especially at first, when he himself is hyper-conscious of the impression he is registering. It will be very difficult to criticize institutions and customs without incurring a good deal of resentment as a 'bloody' outsider, . . . [which] may prove to be a difficult position for anyone who is accustomed to criticizing his own country freely from within whenever he sees a wrong or an injustice." "On the other hand," he continued, "[scholars] will find many people very quick to criticize the United States, sometimes with great justice and insight and sometimes not. It is with this that most of the Americans with whom I have spoken have had the greatest difficulty. It is quite often difficult not to react against it and to be driven into a posture of defense which is not at all a natural one."[49]

Scholars, then, had to tread carefully, adjusting their critical faculties to a variety of social situations and audiences. They were not alone in expressing confusion about how to interpret the goal of mutual understanding at a time when campus and youth culture more generally were changing dramatically. At a seminar sponsored by the Institute of International Education on the Fulbright-Hays student exchange program held in September 1967 in Wingspread, Wisconsin, university, government, philanthropic, and student representatives met and thrashed out questions about the premises, existing policies, and future of the program. One session was titled "The Student Overseas as Ambassador and Interpreter of His Culture." The big question of the day was whether a "hippie" should be "selected out" on the grounds that he might "misrepresent America while abroad." The participants failed to reach a consensus on "where to draw the line between an out-and-out hippie and today's American student who affects, for instance, long hair." They did manage to agree, however, that a crew cut would not be a prerequisite for a Fulbright-Hays grant! They also discussed the changing image of the Fulbrighter, current grantees no longer seeming to fit the old template of the "all-American boy" "patterned after the Rhodes Scholar" who would "go all over the place . . . feeling that he left the world better than he found it, return to campus and re-enter with as little trouble as possible."[50] There was a sense that, in these troubled times when everything was up for questioning, the old, familiar scholar types had been superseded. What, we might ask, about women scholars as ambassadors? Of them, nothing at all was said, even though women had been active participants in and shapers of the program since day one, as we have seen. The women's movement had not yet arrived in Wingspread, Wisconsin. What impact it would have on the meaning of the ambassadorial role of Fulbright scholars is yet to be explored.

Conclusion

In the mid-1970s, there was an intense period of review of all aspects of the Fulbright program, with a series of conferences held in the United States, Malaysia, and Australia. US government funding for the program was reduced through the late 1960s and early 1970s. In the face of a dramatic increase in the number of other student exchange programs, Fulbright administrators in the United States and partner countries came together to figure out how existing funds should best be allocated and reconsider how the program should position itself in relation to other schemes. They asked what was (or could be) unique about the program? One of the outcomes of these discussions was a stronger determination to clarify exactly what the goal of mutual understanding meant for scholars. This was echoed in the Australian-American Foundation's own program review in 1982, when Executive Officer Bruce Farrer argued that the foundation should "be more active in directing the Program in ways that would benefit mutual understanding." He then acknowledged the (now familiar) problem: how to "define those ways and produce an operational definition of 'mutual understanding.'"[51]

This is a question posed by both administrators of and participants in the binational scheme. It is a question that was unlikely to find a completely satisfactory answer as the program's shape and tenor was susceptible to the changing times and people who carried it. Notions of ambassadorship shifted and changed in response to lived experience. Fulbright scholars who took up academic exchange opportunities in the early years of the program played a crucial role in establishing the reputation of the scheme in partner countries and acceptance of US government motives in promoting educational exchange. Fulbright scholars were expected to act as unofficial ambassadors, but, as their experience demonstrated, the requirements and boundaries of this role were not always clear-cut and had to be negotiated often in very personally challenging situations. The experiences, questions, and impacts of Fulbright scholars and program administrators in the Australian scheme indicate how academics shaped and at times resisted the program's ambassadorial dimension. Could it be that Mary Murphy's embrace of the ambassadorial role allowed her some room to promote ideas about women's role in society and capacity for leadership positions that may not have had such a positive reception without the imprimatur of her Fulbright grant? Acknowledging the gender dimensions of being a Fulbright ambassador opens up such new questions.

In the early days, in award-offer documents, the scholar's ambassadorial role was hardly mentioned (if at all) but fully fleshed out in report form questions. More than sixty years later, the reverse is true. Scholars in the Australia-US program are told up front, even before applying, that they are required to act as "goodwill ambassadors," but their final report forms are mute on this score. Scholars are given an open-ended invitation to write a narrative of their "Fulbright journey." There are no questions about clearing up misunderstandings or requests to report on informal conversations in people's homes. The focus has shifted to the personal transformations and career-related developments experienced by scholars during their exchange, a shift reflecting other social, economic, and educational developments in the transnational relationship. The meaning of ambassadorship continues to be an outcome of scholarly negotiation, a complex interplay of lived experience and programmed planning for transnational mutual understanding.

Notes

1. There are very few scholarly studies of the Fulbright program in countries other than the United States and none that analyze the problem of ambassadorship. For British Commonwealth countries, see N. Dawes, *A Two-Way Street: The Indo-American Fulbright Program, 1950–1960* (Bombay: Asia, 1962); Joan Druett, *Fulbright in New Zealand* (Wellington: NZ-US Educational Foundation, 1988); and Alice Garner and Diane Kirkby, *Academic Ambassadors, Pacific Allies: Australia, America and the Fulbright Program* (Manchester: Manchester University Press, 2018).

2. Wool was still Australia's major export commodity in the 1950s. See Frank Bingham, "Australia's Trade since Federation," Department of Foreign Affairs and Trade, Australian Government, June 2016, 5 (chart 7), http://dfat.gov.au/about-us/publications/Documents/australias-trade-since-federation.pdf.

3. "More Rain and Snow Expected," *Advocate* (Burnie, Tasmania), June 23, 1953, 9. Gerald Firth was an English economist who had migrated to Australia and

played an important role in Canberra in national economic planning for the post-war period. See his Trove (National Library of Australia) profile: http://trove.nla.gov.au/version/44696760.

4. USEF Annual Report 1952–53, Reports on Krause Case, A1838 250/9/8/4/2 Part 2, National Archives of Australia, Canberra (hereafter NAA).

5. Ibid. For an internal report on the Krause case, see "Report on Fulbright Research Scholar: Dr. Walter Krause," September 21, 1953, USEF Memorandum 143 to Department of State (IIA/IES), A1838 250/9/8/4/2 Part 2, NAA.

6. "Mysterious Departure of US Professor," *Sydney Morning Herald*, June 10, 1953, 1.

7. "Short Stay for US Professor," *The Advertiser* (Adelaide), June 10, 1953, 3; "No Lecture, No Explanation," *Morning Bulletin* (Rockhampton, Queensland), June 10, 1953, 4; "Puzzle of Vanishing Professor," *Truth* (Sydney), June 14, 1953, 2.

8. Randall Bennett Woods, *Fulbright: A Biography* (Cambridge: Cambridge University Press, 1995), 130. For a critical discussion of this early period, see Sam Lebovic, "From War Junk to Educational Exchange: The World War II Origins of the Fulbright Program and the Foundations of American Cultural Globalism, 1945–50," *Diplomatic History* 37, no. 2 (April 2013): 280–312.

9. Julie Reeves, *Culture and International Relations: Narratives, Natives and Tourists*, Routledge Advances in International Relations and Global Politics (London: Routledge, 2004), 53–54; Liping Bu, "Educational Exchange and Cultural Diplomacy in the Cold War," *Journal of American Studies* 33, no. 3, pt. 1, "Women in America" (December 1999): 393–415, 412.

10. The Australia-US executive agreement was signed on November 26, 1949, in Canberra and was based on the provisions of the Lend-Lease Settlement agreed on three years earlier. See "Agreement between the Government of the United States of America and the Government of Australia for the Use of Funds Made Available in Accordance with the Agreement between the Government of the United States of America and the Government of Australia on Settlement for Lend-Lease, Reciprocal Aid, Surplus War Property and Claims Signed at Washington and New York on June 7, 1946" (typescript), A13307 18/1, NAA.

11. Scott M. Cutlip, *The Unseen Power: Public Relations: A History* (London: Routledge, 2013).

12. USEF Board Minutes, March 27, 1952, Australian-American Fulbright Commission Archive, Canberra.

13. USEF Board Minutes, February 25, 1953.

14. This two-minute newsreel was one of several stories appearing in Australian Diary 071 (1953), directed by Jack S. Allan, title 67328, National Film and Sound Archive Collection, Canberra.

15. On Australians in the United States, see Sally Ninham, *A Cohort of Pioneers: Australian Postgraduate Students and American Postgraduates Degrees, 1949–1964* (Melbourne: Connor Court, 2011). By the 1960s, Australia grasped the cultural diplomacy approach through its success with the Colombo Plan. See Daniel Oakman,

"The Politics of Foreign Aid: Counter-Subversion and the Colombo Plan, 1950–1970," *Pacifica Review: Peace, Security and Global Change* 13, no. 3 (2001): 255–72. This is explored further in Garner and Kirkby, *Academic Ambassadors, Pacific Allies.*

16. USEF Annual Report 1952–53, 18.

17. Ibid.

18. Extract from Lawrence Power, New York City, to Edgar Russell, Port Pirie, South Australia, August 12, 1950, "United States of America—Relations with Australia—Requests for Information on Fulbright Agreement," A1838 250/9/8/3 Part 1, NAA.

19. On the cultural cringe, see Rollo Hesketh, "A. A. Phillips and the 'Cultural Cringe': Creating an 'Australian Tradition,'" *Meanjin* 72, no. 3 (2013), https://meanjin.com.au/essays/a-a-phillips-and-the-icultural-cringei-creating-an-iaustralian-traditioni.

20. USEF Annual Report 1952–53, 18.

21. See, e.g., [12] I. "The Situation" USIE Melbourne, I-A Local Factors Affecting USIE, in 31 Dec 1952 FSD, AMConsulate Sydney to DOS, Subj: IIA: Transmitting Combined Evaluation Report for the Period Dec 1 1951 to Nov 30 1952 (includes reports from five USIS posts in Australia), DOS 59 Central Files 511.43, box 2359, National Archives and Records Administration, Washington, DC.

22. USEF Board Minutes, October 26, 1953.

23. Kenneth Gray Brill Jr., Report, 1953, 3, in "United States of America—Relations with Australia—United States Educational Foundation—General," A1838 250/9/8/4/2 Part 2, NAA.

24. Brill published several articles based on his research in Tasmania, including "Cyclic Sedimentation in the Permian System of Tasmania," *Papers and Proceedings of the Royal Society of Tasmania* 90 (1956): 131–40, in which he thanked his hosts "for the many courtesies shown" during his stay. He returned in 1978 and published another paper in the same journal in 1982, evidence of ongoing collaboration: "Palaeoenvironment of the Darlington Limestone (Early Permian) Tasmania," *Papers and Proceedings of the Royal Society of Tasmania* 116 (1982): 67–84.

25. "Equal Pay for Sexes in Sight," *The Argus* (Melbourne, Victoria), June 30, 1953, 4. On her claim to being the first American Fulbrighter in accountancy, see "I Have Enjoyed Every Moment in Australia," *The Advertiser* (Adelaide), October 2, 1953, 15.

26. "I Have Enjoyed Every Moment."

27. "Equal Pay for Sexes in Sight." The wage gap in the 1950s between men and women was 31 percent. See June O'Neill, "The Trend in the Male-Female Wage Gap in the United States," *Journal of Labour Economics* 3, no. 1, pt. 2, "Trends in Women's Work, Education and Family Building" (January 1985): S91–S116, S91.

28. "Equality as 'Quickest Way to Prosperity,'" *The Argus* (Melbourne, Victoria), July 15, 1953, 6.

29. US Information Agency (USIA) Memorandum, August 16, 1983, quoted in AAEF Board Minutes, November 10, 1983, AAFC Archives, Canberra.

30. Mary E. Murphy, Final Report, "United States of America—Relations with Australia—United States Educational Foundation—General," A1838, 250/9/8/4/2 Part 2, NAA.

31. Ibid.

32. USEF Board Minutes, passim.

33. USIA Memorandum, August 16, 1983, quoted in AAEF Board Minutes, November 10, 1983.

34. See, e.g., minuted item "8. Gender Balance in Board Membership," AAFC Board Minutes, August 24, 1998, AAFC Archives.

35. These questions appear on Murphy, Brill, and other 1950s scholars' reports in A1838, 250/9/8/4/2 Part 2, NAA.

36. The first two reports are in A1838 250/9/8/4/2 Part 3, NAA, and the last two in A1838 250/9/8/4/2 Part 2, NAA. Only a small number of grantee reports have survived from the early 1950s and 1960s. Most were destroyed by the Australian-American Educational Foundation (AAEF, the successor to the USEF) in 1970. AAEF Board Minutes, June 5, 1970.

37. Alice Garner and Diane Kirkby, "'Never a machine for propaganda'? The Australian-American Fulbright Program and Australia's Cold War," *Australian Historical Studies* 44, no. 1 (March 2013): 117–33.

38. Scholar Report, 1953, in A1838 250/9/8/4/2 Part 2, NAA.

39. Scholar Report, 1954, in "United States of America—Relations with Australia—United States Educational Foundation—General," A1838 250/9/8/4/2 Part 3, NAA.

40. John Rose Faust and Barbara Ann Stay, Scholar Reports, A1838 250/9/8/4/2 Part 3, NAA; Georgia Travis Scholar Report, A1838 250/9/8/4/2 Part 2, NAA; Charles Hartshorne Scholar Report, A1838 250/9/8/3 PART 3, NAA.

41. Paul A. Kramer, "Is the World Our Campus? International Students and US Global Power in the Long Twentieth Century," *Diplomatic History* 33, no. 5 (2009): 775–806, 783, 796–97.

42. See, e.g., the senator's correspondence with Leo Marx, reprinted in "The Responsibility of Intellectuals by Leo Marx and J. W. Fulbright," *New York Review of Books*, November 9, 1967, 5.

43. John Playford, "Political Scientists and the CIA," *Australian Left Review*, April–May 1968, 14–28, 24.

44. Ray Arsenault and John Hope Franklin, "Pioneers of History: The Sage of Freedom: An Interview with John Hope Franklin," *Public Historian* 29, no. 2 (Spring 2007): 35–54, 42.

45. The *White Australia policy* was the term commonly used for the Immigration Restriction Act, which came into law on December 23, 1901, one of the first acts of the new Australian federal parliament. This racist law began to be dismantled in practice, quietly, only in the mid-1960s under Prime Minister Holt and finally formally in 1973, under Prime Minister Gough Whitlam. For an account of the sig-

nificance and history of the policy, see Gwenda Tavan, *The Long, Slow Death of White Australia* (Carlton: Scribe, 2005).

46. John Hope Franklin, *Mirror to America: The Autobiography of John Hope Franklin* (New York: Farrar Straus Giroux, 2005), 184–85.

47. "Reports by Visiting American Fulbright Scholars," A463 1965/2313, NAA.

48. J. William Fulbright, *The Arrogance of Power* (New York: Vintage, 1966).

49. Grantee Report in "Reports by Visiting American Fulbright Scholars," A463 1965/2313, NAA.

50. G. P. Springer, *A Report on the Fulbright-Hays Student Exchange Program Seminar, Sept. 20–22, 1967, Wingspread, Wis.* (New York: Institute of International Education, 1968).

51. AAEF Board Minutes, February 25, 1982, item on program review.

The Limits of Liberal Internationalism

The Fulbright Program in Africa

Hannah Higgin

Particularly following the horrors and brutality of the Second World War, J. William Fulbright believed that the United States had a responsibility to lead on a global scale in order to prevent future wars and that exchange programs were key to doing so. He viewed world affairs through a Western lens, however, positing that Western, liberal ideas—including the trappings of modernity, progress, and respect for civil liberties and human rights—should be spread by the exchanging of Western elites, namely top intellectuals, from different nations. He believed that these men and women should be at the forefront of this civilizing, peace-creating mission and that, on returning home, they should pass along their expanded understandings of foreign cultures to ordinary people through education. He did not believe, however, that American efforts to spread liberalism would necessarily work in areas or with people who did not have, in his view, cultural backgrounds similar enough to grasp such notions. His thinking was that a strong, common foundation in the West—not a short-term task—would provide the first critical step in eventually attracting the rest of the world to willingly follow in the West's purportedly rational and superior footsteps.

The 1960s saw greater government support for student exchange programs, but, much to Fulbright's chagrin, the Kennedy and Johnson administrations also increased related programming concerned with what was then thought of as the developing world. That region, the Global South, constituted a newly active arena for Cold War conflict, where questions about potential alignment (which Washington tended to see as binary: either West or East) arose. The attendant shift away from earlier Eurocentrism was misaligned with Fulbright's regional and cultural focus and piqued his distaste for overtures to non-Western cultures, which he saw as interventionist and therefore ineffectual.

It also forced the issue of race. Fulbright was considered a racial moderate at the time, neither supporting massive resistance nor advocating desegregation. In comparison to many of his southern peers, his approach to Jim Crow was, as the historian John Kyle Day put it, "more benign [and] more palatable" to those who did not support segregation than was that of many other southern politicians in the mid-twentieth century.[1] Still, he did not seek to dismantle systematic racism, and, in resisting exchange with the Global South, he resisted exchange with people of color. In an era when the US government's bipolar view of geopolitics meant that the preference of foreigners, including those of color, could either be "won" by the West or "lost" to the Soviet Union, and given the influence Fulbright wielded over American exchange programs, the senator's approach to race damaged America's ability to spread Western, liberal ideals to those from the Global South, particularly to Africans.

African Experiences in 1960s America

The 2 A.M. arrest of a Harvard student in May 1962 by the Cambridge police threatened to spark an international incident. The student was handled roughly and verbally abused by the arresting officers—mere "overzealousness" according to the on-duty lieutenant—and this was not the first time, according to the undergraduate. Violence against a black man, even one threatening to sue the city of Cambridge and the state of Massachusetts over discrimination and mistreatment by the police, as Chukwuma Azikiwe did, was not a reason for the State Department to step in. That Chukwuma was the son of the nationalist governor general of Nigeria, Nnamdi Azikiwe, who would become the first president of Nigeria the following year, was.[2]

This incident was one in a long line of black foreigners swept up in midcentury discrimination in the United States. Although such instances were certainly not new, they garnered increased press attention beginning in the late 1950s as decolonization accelerated. More dignitaries of color were coming to the United States, and winning the hearts and minds of nonwhites across the globe was becoming more important in the context of the Cold War. In 1957, for instance, it became international news when a Howard Johnson's in Dover, Delaware, insisted that Ghana's finance minister, Komla Gbedmah, drink the orange juice he ordered outside. Eisenhower and Nixon hosted an apology breakfast—bacon and eggs, no orange juice—at the White House to defuse the backlash over the so-called Orange Juice Incident.[3] Eisenhower did nothing beyond the gesture, however, and discrimination against nonwhite diplomats became a regular occurrence along Route 40 as they drove between the United Nations and Washington, DC.[4] Bemoaning the Chukwuma incident, the American ambassador in Nigeria cabled the State Department, noting that it was "hard enough" to explain incidents of racial discrimination in the South, the wellspring of the Southern Manifesto, which opposed the integration of public spaces and of which Fulbright was a signatory, and on Route 40. Discrimination in the North, he continued, would "immeasurably compound [the] problem" of dispelling ongoing criticisms of American racism, an easy refrain for those questioning or unsympathetic to American influence.[5]

Though discrimination continued, Kennedy did take these issues more seriously than his predecessor. As the historian Thomas Borstelmann put it, President Eisenhower had only "briefly and somewhat uncomfortably" aligned himself with anticolonialism and "African American causes" when faced with domestic and global frustration over racially tinged crises in Suez, Little Rock, and the Congo.[6] Kennedy positioned himself as a critic of colonialism and acknowledged that segregation and colonialism hindered America's Cold War aims, including the winning of hearts and minds. However, like his post–World War II predecessors, he worried that too-rapid decolonization could lead to disorder, radicalism, or a Cold War conflict. He moved beyond occasional gestures to enacting policies aimed at ameliorating discrimination against nonwhite foreigners.[7] Responding to reports like those appearing in the 1960 pamphlet *African Students in the United States: A Guide for the Sponsors of Student Exchange Programs with Africa*, he issued National Security Action Memorandum (NSAM) 66 in August 1961. The pamphlet noted: "Probably every African visiting the United States encounters discrimination in one form or another."[8] "I feel very strongly," the president wrote, "that we must not allow these students—especially the Africans and Asians—to leave this country disappointed any longer."[9] NSAM 66 extended Washington's oversight of the welfare of foreign students from only those under full or partial US government sponsorship—only about 10 percent—to all of them. "What is important," a memorandum drafted by Secretary of State Dean Rusk shortly after NSAM 66 asserted, "is not how [foreign students] got here, but what they take home."[10] Inherent in Fulbright's assumptions about exchange—that it promoted mutual understanding, thereby easing internal tensions and proclivities toward violence—was the belief that students would take home an appreciation for the virtues of American culture. He did not seem to consider, however, whether some would instead take home a reaffirmation of their worst fears about American racism.

Aligning with his desire to better support foreign students, Kennedy also created the Office of Educational and Cultural Affairs (CU) in 1961. This consolidated for the first time the oversight of exchange programs previously scattered across the State Department.[11] Even after the creation of CU, however, agencies that traditionally ran exchange programs resented attempts by CU to consolidate control. Exchange programs often continued to be co-run with other soft power agencies, including the US Information Agency (USIA) and the US Agency for International Development (USAID). Those dealing with the Chukwuma incident—including Rusk, National Security Adviser McGeorge Bundy, and the assistant secretary of state for African affairs, "Soapy" Williams—never looped in anyone in CU. Instead, they dealt directly with Chukwuma and his father, who for diplomatic reasons ultimately preferred, like the State Department, to keep the incident quiet.[12] Gridlock and the continued diffusion of exchange programs led many Washington insiders to characterize CU as the "slum area of US foreign policy," the "pasture for old horses," and "the graveyard of incompetents."[13]

If CU was weak, Senator Fulbright was not. Because it housed his eponymous program—"one of the few things in Fulbright's life," according to the biographer Randall Woods, "about which he felt passionately" and "could become emotional, irrational, [and] vindictive" in defending[14]—the senator from Arkansas held sway over the whole bureau, though his program was but one small aspect of its operations. He was not, however, particularly interested in the majority of CU undertakings—which were increasingly focused on the developing world rather than Europe. He therefore acted as something of an absent yet indomitable landlord. While his preferences sometimes buoyed and sometimes constrained CU's ability to accomplish anything, they undoubtedly shaped its scope and direction.

Following on the heels of 1960—the Year of Africa, in which seventeen nations won independence—the American foreign policy establishment became increasingly concerned over power vacuums, fearing that the continent now constituted a new theater ripe for Cold War conflict. These concerns elevated the importance of the long-neglected region of sub-Saharan Africa. Conceptualizing sub-Saharan Africa as a cohesive whole overlooks the region's geographic, linguistic, cultural, and racial diversity. But this reflected the approach taken by the US government and many Americans—including black Americans—in the 1950s and 1960s. Even when academics who considered themselves Africanists used the term *Africa*, they meant the sub-Saharan part of the continent. This practice, which truncates the northern portion of the continent, fits with terminology employed by the US State Department, which at various times considered North Africa to be a part of other regions.[15] African leaders also solicited and accepted aid from nations on both sides of the Cold War divide, given their newfound leverage and importance in the 1960s. By the end of 1963, owing to the phasing out of European programs, the growth in those in Africa, and the shift away from metropole control over the region, the Bureau of Africa and Europe became simply the Bureau of Africa.[16] By 1964, US-European exchanges formed a relatively minor part of CU programming, with thousands of African, Asian, Middle Eastern, and Latin American students flowing into the United States and a "few hundred (increasingly difficult to find and persuade) American professors" sent to developing countries.[17] As we will see, this pivot away from Western-centered exchanges was one of which Fulbright became tacitly disdainful.

In response to the growing importance of the region, the US government sought to attract the most promising African students while simultaneously staving off an uncontrolled influx of less desirable ones. Fulbright, however, remained personally invested in attracting exchangees who were culturally Western and "modern" and, by his thinking, therefore enable them to participate meaningfully in the exchange of ideas. A student

funded by the US government was one deemed a potential "multiplier"—
that is, a contributor "to the development and progress of his country
and . . . a potential leader in its international and domestic activities."[18] For
many Americans—and certainly for the policy makers of the 1960s, who,
like Kennedy, adhered to modernization theory—notions of development
and progress had a distinctly American sheen to them. In fact, modernization theory asserted that the United States was the most developed nation.
In contrast, Africa, to which modernization theorists paid scant attention,
was classified in the least- or next-to-least-developed stage of growth. The
region was either in the "preconditions" stage, which, by this logic, required
external intervention to jump-start development, or not even ready
for that yet.[19] In other words, potential black African exchangees did not
meet Fulbright's criteria for exchange. On this matter, Fulbright and
first the Kennedy administration and later the Johnson administration
found themselves at cross-purposes. All championed exchange as a powerful tool for advancing multicultural understanding, thereby heightening
the chances of creating a more peaceful world, but their areas of regional
concern and the role of exchange in waging the Cold War were increasingly divergent.

Modernization theory was explicitly anti-Communist and contradicted the Marxist-Leninist view of economic development while recognizing the Soviet Union's modernity and effectiveness.[20] From the point
of view of US policy makers, then, it was imperative for the sake of global
development and winning the Cold War that multipliers not turn to the
Communist bloc, which was also working hard to attract them, for training.[21] Such concerns elevated arguments for using propaganda and posed
a major threat to the mutual understanding approach to exchange championed by Fulbright.

Determining the promise of an African student was a process often
based on identifying presumptive leaders of new nations rather than top
scholars, as Fulbright advocated. Presumptive leaders and top scholars
were not necessarily the same thing, particularly in regions devoid of educational opportunities or in political flux. Beyond a dearth of formal education, a major traditional marker of future leadership, investing in
students from contentious factions in nascent nations was potentially
fraught: it was often unclear who would hold power in the long term, and
making the wrong choice could imperil future bilateral relations.

Becoming a Magnetic Example for the World: Who Was "Worth Bothering About"?

Fulbright wanted the educated elite to guide international affairs, but his conception of the educated elite did not extend to African multipliers. The color line hemmed in his conception of universalism at home and abroad. It also limited his conception of America's appropriate sphere of influence. Fulbright believed that deeper intercultural understanding provided the best hope for preventing future conflagrations and that the American government had a duty to foster such understanding. He sought to curtail the nationalism and isolationism that foster global wars by promoting collective security and economic interdependency, and he believed that international exchange could go a long way toward achieving those goals.[22] Africa did not play much of a role, if any, in his global calculus, however.

Fulbright learned the lessons of post–World War I isolationism, and his brand of internationalism was Wilsonian.[23] He, like Wilson before him, believed that the United States, preponderant in power after World War II, had a responsibility to lead on a global scale in order to prevent future wars. His internationalism was not nationalist, but neither was it global: the anglophile former Rhodes scholar viewed internationalism through a Western lens. His internationalist vision was one of a fraternity of nations united by a belief in a common, Western culture,[24] and in that way it was exclusionary. Representatives from areas of the world on the periphery of that culture could have a seat at decision-making tables, such as during the deliberations over the post–World War I world order or at the United Nations, but they should not be the primary targets of American efforts. Fulbright believed in international cooperation but did not believe that an American approach would necessarily work everywhere.[25] Mirroring the beliefs of modernization theorists, and surely in tune with his ideas on race and integration at home, he believed that cultural preconditions—Western, "enlightened" preconditions—were needed in order to realize a liberal vision, and the Global South did not, in his approximation, meet those requirements. Such efforts, whether in aid or exchange, then, were inefficient or, worse, futile.

Fulbright articulated his view that it was unwise to spend resources in non-Western areas in a series of lectures in 1963, eschewing efforts to win over the Global South in favor of shoring up Western nations. It was better, he asserted, to make the West "impenetrable to external ideological assault" rather than fight Khrushchev for influence over "the nationalist revolutions of Asia, Africa, and Latin America." He argued that the West should go so far as to encourage Soviet economic, technical, and cultural exchange programs in those regions because "means have a way in human affairs of consuming their ends." It would be a boon to the United States for the Soviets to overextend themselves and get swept up in their own "arrogance of power" in the Global South, weakening themselves in an area that he believed the United States should stay out of. Rather than risk misspending energy and resources in "unenlightened" areas outside the West where, in his view, modernization, with its attendant Western trappings, was unlikely to stick, the United States should redouble its efforts to strengthen the West so that it could provide "magnetic examples of social justice and material well-being for the entire world."[26] Inherent in this line of thinking and in his reasons for fighting to keep the United States out of the Dominican Republic and later Vietnam was the notion that American efforts to spread liberalism in regions outside the West would be for naught.

Whether there was wisdom in Fulbright's determination to keep the US government out of the nationalist affairs of Asian, African, and Latin American countries or not, it would be a mistake to divorce those views from his understanding of race. Though Fulbright was not openly virulent in his racism, his southern background, voting record, and allegiances led many of his contemporaries to question to what degree racism colored his approach to international affairs. Kennedy initially wanted him as his secretary of state, but, as Borstelmann put it, his "domestic segregationist voting record made him unacceptable."[27] Whether Fulbright had signed the Southern Manifesto primarily for political purposes, as Woods attests, or not ultimately did not matter.[28] Just as he cautioned that the United States should not attempt to enforce social justice or provide material well-being on a global scale, he also discouraged US government efforts to provide these things for nonwhite Americans. Rumors of his appointment elicited fervent letters of concern from civil rights leaders.[29]

More critically, Fulbright's background handicapped Kennedy with African nationalists. By the early 1960s, the racial makeup of geopolitics was changing, and the president, who had an interest in African affairs and cared more about foreign issues than domestic ones, knew it. According to

Chester Bowles, Kennedy's special representative for Asian, African, and Latin American affairs, African opinions of Fulbright were "basic to his being bypassed" for the position.[30] The president's brother Robert, who was personally against Fulbright's appointment on the grounds of his position on race, believed the same.[31]

Charges of Fulbright's racism amplified during the Johnson administration, at least in private. Given his fervent, public objections to the administration's interventions in the Dominican Republic in 1965 and in Vietnam 1966, it is difficult to ascertain the extent to which the charges of racism lodged against Fulbright by Johnson and his supporters were believed by those making them. Did Fulbright actually oppose the conflict in Vietnam only because, as Johnson put it, he thought that "the yellows, blacks, and browns of the world were just not worth bothering about"?[32] That flattened reading of Fulbright's motivations certainly made it easier for Johnson and his supporters to dismiss his concerns about the merits of what turned out to be a foolhardy, costly, and fruitless war.

To better understand his views on race, one might attempt to disentangle them from his views on foreign intervention, which, as a southerner, Fulbright detested. In a lunchtime conversation with the head of CU, Charles Frankel, in 1965, the senator invoked his Arkansas roots and recalled northern interventions after the Civil War. Discussing Johnson's actions in the Dominican Republic, and raising concerns about the course of affairs in Vietnam, he remarked on the lingering weight of Arkansas's post–Civil War occupation and the imposition of tutelage by outsiders. "No matter how smart the outsiders were," Frankel recounted Fulbright saying, "they made mistakes and were resented." Though Fulbright said that being from one of the poorest parts of the country himself made him feel for "people from poor parts of the world," to him intervention by outsiders seemed the wrong course.[33] But trying to separate his ideas on intervention from his notions of race is ultimately futile. Even his opposition to interference in Third World countries was deeply informed by his views on race.

Fulbright's Eurocentric views—or at least his conviction that the foundations for peace still lay in the most positive traits of education in Western civilization—were also apparent in his vision for educational exchange. His hope for international understanding and peace lay in the exchange of culturally Western scholars and students. Reflecting on his

Rhodes experience at Oxford and how it dramatically broadened his previously narrow worldview, Fulbright came to believe that a systematic, long-range, permanent program was the best hope for preventing future mass destruction like that wrought by the Second World War. In 1946, the year the Fulbright program came into existence, the senator wrote to a friend: "The prejudices and misconceptions which exist in every country regarding foreign people are the great barrier to any system of government." The former University of Arkansas president believed that scholars and students were best suited to breaking down such barriers, believing that, as Woods put it, in a democracy like the United States, "the knowledge and understanding of other cultures would inevitably trickle down through the educational system to those who were not privileged enough to travel abroad."[34]

Fulbright either could not or would not apply this theory to racial divides globally or in his own country. A decade after the creation of the Fulbright program, he signed the Southern Manifesto, which opposed integration. Though he felt that it was too extreme, in 1956 he did not think integration's time had come. He did not aim to integrate global leadership, either: that task belonged squarely in the hands of Western liberals, at least for the time being. Despite his insistence that education would eventually stamp out prejudice and lead to integration, his involvement in CU's Africa programming in the 1960s signaled that he was not interested in spurring a trickle down of the knowledge and understanding of African cultures in his own country.[35] The ramifications of doing so for shifting racial norms could be significant, particularly given that the federal government had already demonstrated that racial discrimination against black foreigners warranted action beyond that against American citizens.

The early 1960s saw a shoring up of student exchange. The Fulbright-Hays Act, passed in 1962, aimed to foster peaceful relations by increasing mutual understanding and cooperation through the promotion of educational and cultural exchange. CU administered the legislation's major provisions.[36] Though by mid-decade his cosponsor, Wayne Hays, championed bringing more, as he put it, "non-westerners" to America under the program,[37] Fulbright remained aloof at best from exchange programming related to the developing world and obstructionist at worst. CU's Africa programming did not benefit Fulbright's dogged fight to keep the focus of exchange on mutual understanding and free from overt Cold

War politicking and posturing. Without him acting as a bulwark, Cold Warriors wielded African programming as a blunter tool for thwarting communism than they likely would have otherwise. Rather than demonstrating the presumed superiority and logicality of liberal Western ideas through the promotion of mutual understanding, as he assumed his version of exchange would, attempts at implementing those notions by force and lacing them with politics would instead irreparably damage America's ability to promote peace through such means.

"Of course it's what bothers me": Race and the "Most Important Countries"

When CU needed a new head in 1965, Fulbright privately prevented LBJ's selection, a black expert on Africa and exchange with the developing world, for assistant secretary, handpicking a white academic in his own image instead. Johnson's selection, Robert Kitchen, was poised to amplify CU's programming in developing nations, not least those in Africa. The Morehouse- and Columbia-educated career foreign aid officer, then directing USAID's Office of International Training, served as a top aide in Liberia in 1952 and as head of the US aid mission to Sudan in 1958. Since 1962, he had been involved in USAID's participant training, which brought foreign leaders to America for development-oriented educational programming.[38]

What likely appealed most to Johnson about Kitchen and was clearly offputting to Fulbright, however, was Kitchen's race. When Carl Rowan resigned from his position as head of USIA—the highest rank ever achieved by any black citizen in the federal government at the time of his appointment in 1964—Johnson hoped to place another black American in a post with a similar rank. Though the president pleaded with Rowan not to step down, he wasted no time filling the top position at USIA with a trusted member of his inner circle, Leonard Marks, leaving his desire for a high-ranking black official unfulfilled.[39] The head of CU was not as highly ranked as the head of USIA, who also sat on the National Security Council, but, if Kitchen was appointed head of CU, there would at least be one black assistant secretary of state.

Johnson's sales pitch for Kitchen did not appeal to Fulbright's priorities. There were 120 American ambassadors, Johnson told Fulbright, and only two of them were black; there were a dozen assistant secretaries, and none of them were black. The chair of the Senate Foreign Relations Committee was at best indifferent to the number of black faces in the State Department, however. He countered that the job of assistant secretary of educational and cultural affairs was a "really important" one. The implication was clear: this was not the place for Johnson to push integration. Fulbright admitted that he feared he would "be accused of bigotry" if his objection to Kitchen went public, but he felt that the matter was too important for him to keep quiet. Beyond Kitchen's race, his credentials likely worried rather than impressed the former Rhodes scholar. "I have a rather personal interest in the program," Fulbright explained, "and it's in a bad way."[40] It was true that CU was not particularly strong or well respected. Because of that, the bureau's helm was almost perennially vacant, with six assistant secretaries filling the position between 1961 and 1969. Fulbright did not reference those issues, however. Rather, he implicitly focused his ire on the increasing focus on exchange with developing countries and on the optics of having a black man steering CU.

Johnson and Harry C. McPherson, the head of CU who was stepping down, insisted that Kitchen was "the best man" for the position. "Well of course it's what bothers me," Fulbright remarked about Kitchen's race. "I don't know how he would go down in the most important countries at all." Kitchen's high-level career experience with developing countries might have been relevant to CU's programming, not to mention rare, but it was hardly germane to achieving Fulbright's exchange goals. To Fulbright, the "most important countries" were not those in the developing world.

Touting Kitchen's qualifications—extensive government work in Cairo, in Bangkok, and on the African continent—likely further dissuaded Fulbright. The senator retained a Western, elite-centric view of the program despite how it had changed. He dismissed Kitchen's experience with USAID, though McPherson pointed out that USAID dealt directly with more foreign students than CU did. McPherson, growing frustrated, gently indicated a difference in Fulbright's concerns and the purposes of CU. "He's demonstrated he can deal with other nations, Bill," he told Fulbright of Kitchen. "He's been doing it more than anybody we've ever had in the job. . . . I'm not talking about the head of state, Bill . . . countries . . . other nationalities."[41] The orientation of CU and the students it supported had

shifted: Washington's exchange programming aimed to increase understanding among ordinary people. African multipliers, Washington hoped,
were the not yet but eventual elite.

From the outset of the conversation with Fulbright, Johnson and
McPherson promised to defer to the senator's preference, and Kitchen's
potential appointment stalled. Fulbright, himself a former university president with a penchant for academic expertise in policy making, preferred
a reform-minded academic to a black expert in exchangees from developing countries. Perhaps seeing himself in his pick, he essentially bullied the
Columbia University philosophy professor Charles Frankel, who had
written a study of US cultural policy, into the position. Meeting resistance
from Johnson, Frankel, who initially told Fulbright he needed the job
as assistant secretary like he needed "a hole in his head," tried to turn
down the position. The senator became indignant, according to Frankel,
with "flint in his voice": "It was as though I were telling him that I was
defecting." Fulbright reverted back to the "gentle and relaxed man" the
professor first met only when Frankel, who, like Fulbright, believed that
intellectuals should play a more central role in international policy making, demurred and accepted the position.[42]

From Western Elites to the Global Cold War

Though Fulbright continued to wield influence over CU, as the bureau's
emphasis on European exchanges diminished, so too did Fulbright's careful
monitoring of programming operations in areas outside his interest.
McPherson mused in his memoir that Fulbright "must have found it disappointing that a program meant to make Americans more sophisticated
world citizens had become a means for instructing Africans and Asians in
skills for which there was often little demand back home."[43] CU's largest
Africa program, the Southern African Student Program (SASP), went well
beyond diverging from Fulbright's preferred target region: its "whole raison
d'être," according to a senior CU official stationed in Africa in the 1960s,
"was to counter the Soviets."[44] Fulbright had always fervently rejected "any
suggestion" that exchange programs be used as "weapons or instruments
with which to do combat." He disavowed any program or action that would
allow exchange programming to be seen as propaganda.[45] For this reason,
he always fought to keep exchange programs separate from Washington's

propaganda arm, USIA.[46] SASP, however, was the brainchild of Edward R. Murrow, the USIA head from 1961 to 1964, and it violated Fulbright's priorities—both regional and mission based—from its inception.

The creation of SASP in the early 1960s initiated one of the biggest conflicts between CU and USIA. SASP grew out of defections of African students from Soviet universities, which Murrow saw as a ripe propaganda opportunity. The head of CU, Lucius Battle, on the other hand, already grappling with the fact that the agency could not adequately support the growing influx of African students in America, thought that Murrow's desire to "clean out Lumumba University" was reckless.[47] Battle, who declared that the government would bring thousands of Africans—some with no passports, some with poor language skills—to America with "no assurance of being able to finance them on a continuing basis [only] over [his] dead body," was weak compared to Murrow. Amid rapid decolonization and Cold War pressures, Kennedy intervened, coming down on Murrow's side.[48] Cold War concerns forced CU to take a more propagandistic approach and overshadowed the mutual understanding view of exchange. SASP stretched the bounds of Fulbright-Hays funding, favoring political payoffs over carefully selecting qualified students with the potential to return home and utilize their education.[49] It bore little resemblance to the aspects of the program that Fulbright fervently defended. Believing that efforts in non-Western areas were futile, Fulbright seemed either to have little awareness of or to care little about whether exchange was really the purpose of CU operations in the Global South. If he had cared about Africa programming, perhaps a more effective trickle down of knowledge about the region and maybe also people of color would have eased racial tensions at home to some extent. It may also have ameliorated foreign policy missteps in Africa, particularly those of the mid-1970s, which saw a rise in clandestine US involvement in the region.[50]

Fulbright is nowhere to be found in the records surrounding the program, which brought more than half of CU's total African students to America and to which CU at times allocated more than half of its Africa program funding throughout the 1960s.[51] The resulting program highlighted not only the weakness of the CU apparatus, which in the case of SASP and other African exchange programming involved covert CIA operations,[52] but also Fulbright's distaste for African affairs and aloofness even when programs violated his exchange goals.

Fulbright's liberal internationalism was not global in scope. For Fulbright, the idea that nations should be more open to one another to aid in mutual understanding never extended to developing nations, even as the program that he began and loved moved in that direction. In 1946, he asserted that exchange would ameliorate "prejudice and misconceptions [about] foreign people."[53] Perhaps he believed that genuine, apolitical real exchange with Africans—untainted by propaganda and politicking—would ease the prejudice that had accrued around the color line, something for which Fulbright was apparently not ready. Perhaps he believed that the cultural chasm between those of different races—even those at home—was too wide to bridge. Whereas misconceptions about people from other nations was "the great barrier to any system of government," his outlook on race seems to have convinced him that racial integration and greater racial equality and attempts in that direction would likely create obstacles for the government. For Fulbright, the time to contend with the issue of race—whether on a national or an international scale—had still not come. This hobbled CU's ability to keep its programming in Africa about mutual understanding and dragged the United States further away from focusing on "social justice and material well-being for the entire world" and further into Cold War posturing and politicking.

Fulbright's ideas about race may have started to soften by the end of the 1960s, but his disengagement from African exchange programs demonstrates clear limits. Though in 1968 he voted for a five-year extension of the Voting Rights Act—"the first time since Reconstruction," Woods points out, "that an Arkansas senator had voted for a civil rights bill"[54]—Fulbright remained, at best, aloof from the issue as it affected his exchange program. It seems that what he treasured was a specific, culturally Western-centered program, rather than real global exchange. It was still international, but it had serious limitations.

Aligning with Fulbright's conception of exchange as a facilitator of understanding, what mattered to the Kennedy administration in 1961 was not how foreign students arrived in the United States but what they took home with them.[55] By the end of the decade, as at the beginning, race relations remained African exchangees' biggest concern.[56] Given that African multipliers were selected on the basis of their leadership potential, discrimination perpetrated against one had the potential to reverberate exponentially for decades to come.[57]

Fulbright's culturally and racially exclusionary approach to creating a West that would inspire other regions to remake themselves in its image willfully neglected to address the West's shortcomings meaningfully, particularly those related to social, economic, and racial inequality. The example set by the US government did not, like exchange as Fulbright envisioned it, fully grapple with issues of race. Domestically, the shortcomings of liberalism became apparent during the civil rights movement as white liberals failed to live up to the promises of equality that they espoused.[58] Abroad, as the power of the Global South continued to amplify through the 1960s and into the 1970s, liberalism showed its cracks also in its international dimension, whether by way of its Cold War priorities or because of the limiting beliefs of its main proponent in the US Senate.[59] Promises of equality and opportunity could not fully exercise their magnetic pull if America continued to fail even to attempt to deliver social justice and material well-being for every American, let alone everyone globally.

Notes

1. John Kyle Day, *The Southern Manifesto: Massive Resistance and the Fight to Preserve Segregation* (Jackson: University Press of Mississippi, 2014), 98.

2. "Chukwuma Azikiwe," June 8, 1962, 1, and Ambassador Joseph Palmer II, "Telegram to Secretary of State," Lagos, Nigeria, May 22, 1962, folder Nigeria, General, Azikiwe Case 5/24/62–6/30/62, NSF, Countries, box 144, John F. Kennedy Library, Boston (hereafter JFKL).

3. W. H. Lawrence, "Ghanan [*sic*] Served White House Meal," *New York Times*, October 11, 1957; "Mr. Gbedemah," *New York Times*, October 13, 1957.

4. For more on how the Kennedy administration dealt with discrimination along Route 40, see Renee Romano, "No Diplomatic Immunity: African Diplomats, the State Department, and Civil Rights, 1961–1964," *Journal of American History* 87, no. 2 (September 2000): 546–79.

5. Palmer, "Telegram to Secretary of State."

6. Thomas Borstelmann, *The Cold War and the Color Line* (Cambridge, MA: Harvard University Press, 2003), 133. For more on Eisenhower and Africa, see Thomas J. Noer, *Cold War and Black Liberation* (Columbia: University of Missouri Press, 1985), chap. 3 ("Premature Independence: Eisenhower, Dulles, and African Liberation"); James P. Hubbard, *The United States and the End of British Colonial Rule in Africa, 1941–1968* (Jefferson, NC: McFarland, 2010), 146–68; Philip E. Muehlenbeck, *Betting on the Africans: John F. Kennedy's Courting of African Nationalist Leaders* (Oxford: Oxford University Press, 2013), 3–33; and James H. Meriwether, "'A Torrent Overrunning Everything': Africa and the Eisenhower Administration,"

in *The Eisenhower Administration, the Third World, and the Globalization of the Cold War*, ed. Kathryn C. Andrew L. Statler and Johns (New York: Rowman & Littlefield, 2006), 175–96.

7. Odd Arne Westad, *The Global Cold War* (Cambridge: Cambridge University Press, 2007), 27. For more on Kennedy and Africa, see Thomas J. Noer, "New Frontiers and Old Priorities in Africa," in *Kennedy's Quest for Victory: American Foreign Policy, 1961–1963*, ed. Thomas G. Paterson (Oxford: Oxford University Press, 1989), 253–83; Richard D. Mahoney, *JFK: Ordeal in Africa* (Oxford: Oxford University Press, 1983); Muehlenbeck, *Betting on the Africans*; Waldemar A. Nielsen, *The Great Powers and Africa* (Westport, CT: Praeger, 1969), 288–302; Ryan Irwin, *Gordian Knot: Apartheid and the Unmaking of the Liberal World Order* (Oxford: Oxford University Press, 2012), esp. chap. 3; and Romano, "No Diplomatic Immunity."

8. *African Students in the United States: A Guide for the Sponsors of Student Exchange Programs with Africa* (New York: Committee on Educational Interchange Policy, December 1960), 15, folder Scholarships 1958–1960, Educational and Cultural Exchange, 1954–1961, State Department, box 14, James William Fulbright Papers, University of Arkansas.

9. John F. Kennedy, "Memorandum to the Secretary of State," August 8, 1961, folder NSAM 66 Foreign Students in the United States, NSF box 133, JFKL.

10. Dean Rusk, "Memorandum for the President: Foreign Students in the United States," September 2, 1961, and "Foreign Students in the United States," both folder NSAM 66 Foreign Students in the United States, NSF box 133, JFKL.

11. Eisenhower established CU in 1960, and Kennedy created the position of assistant secretary of state for educational and cultural affairs in 1961. The assistant secretary had no control over the bureau, however, until after the passage of the Fulbright-Hays Act in August 1961 and Kennedy's subsequent executive order, signed in September 1961. J. Manuel Espinosa, *Landmark Events in the History of CU—1938–1973* (Washington, DC: US Bureau of Educational and Cultural Affairs, 1973); Randolph Wieck, *Ignorance Abroad: American Educational and Cultural Foreign Policy and the Office of Assistant Secretary of State* (Westport, CT: Praeger, 1992), 124. For more on Eisenhower's support of and approach to psychological warfare, see Kenneth Osgood, *Total Cold War: Eisenhower's Secret Propaganda Battle at Home and Abroad* (Lawrence: University Press of Kansas, 2008).

12. Folder Nigeria, General, Azikiwe Case 5/24/62–6/30/62, NSF, Countries, box 144, JFKL.

13. Wieck, *Ignorance Abroad*, 1.

14. Randall Bennett Woods, *Fulbright: A Biography* (Cambridge: Cambridge University Press, 1995), 136.

15. For more on this phenomenon, see Larry Grubbs, *Secular Missionaries* (Amherst: University of Massachusetts Press, 2009), 42–45, 52.

16. "African Bureau Changes Name, Shifts Personnel," *Front Lines II*, no. 4 (December 30, 1963): 8, folder 1963 December, box 19, David E. Bell Papers, JFKL.

17. Harry McPherson, *A Political Education: A Washington Memoir* (Austin: University of Texas Press, 1995), 229.

18. "The Agency for International Development during the Administration of Lyndon B Johnson, November 1963–January 1969," vol. I, p. 628, folder Part III, Chapters XIV thru XVII, Administrative History, box 1, LBJ Library, Austin, TX (hereafter LBJL).

19. Hannah Higgin, "Disseminating American Ideals in Africa, 1949–1969" (PhD diss., Cambridge University, 2015), 47.

20. Nils Gilman, *Mandarins of the Future* (Baltimore: Johns Hopkins University Press, 2007), 156.

21. Hannah Higgin, "US Exchange Programs with Africa during the Civil Rights Era," in *Global Exchanges*, ed. Ludovic Tournes and Giles Scott-Smith (New York: Berghahn, 2017): 216–30.

22. Randall Bennett Woods, "Fulbright Internationalism," *Annals of the American Academy of Political and Social Science* 49, no. 1 (May 1987): 22–35, 23.

23. Ibid., 27.

24. Ibid., 27–29. On this point, see Lebovic (in this volume).

25. Ibid., 29–31.

26. "Help Reds Thaw, Fulbright Urges," *New York Times*, April 30, 1963.

27. Borstelmann, *The Cold War and the Color Line*, 140.

28. Woods, *Fulbright: A Biography*, 211.

29. Bowles Oral History, February 2, 1965, p. 13, folder Fulbright, J William, December 6, 1960, box 3, Wofford Papers, JFKL.

30. Ibid.; Wofford Oral History, February 3, 1969, p. 99, Oral History Collection, JFKL. For more on Kennedy and Africa, see Muehlenbeck, *Betting on the Africans*.

31. Harris Wofford, *Of Kennedys and Kings* (Pittsburgh: University of Pittsburgh Press, 1992), 82.

32. Woods, *Fulbright: A Biography*, 427.

33. Charles Frankel, *High on Foggy Bottom* (New York: Harper & Row, 1968), 44.

34. Woods, *Fulbright: A Biography*, 129, 131.

35. Ibid., 211.

36. For more on the Fulbright-Hays Act, see Philip H. Coombs, *The Fourth Dimension of Foreign Policy: Educational and Cultural Affairs* (New York: Harper & Row, 1964), 50–53.

37. Robert Calvert Jr., "Letter to Henry B. Ollendorff," Peace Corps, July 29, 1966, folder PC 5 Peace Corps Program 5/23/65–8/26/66, EX PC 5 Peace Corps Programs 11/23/63, box 8, LBJL.

38. "Name Robert Kitchen to Head Sudan Mission," *Jet*, April 17, 1958; "Kitchen and Nelson in High AID Jobs," *Washington Afro-American*, November 5, 1963, folder 1963 November, box 19, Bell Papers; "Recent Appointments," *Front Lines II*, no. 1 (November 15, 1963), folder 1963 November, box 19, Bell Papers.

39. Higgin, "Disseminating American Ideals in Africa," 168.

40. Lyndon B Johnson, "Phone Conversation with William Fulbright (8324), (8325)," July 2, 1965, Lyndon B. Johnson—Presidential Recordings, Miller Center, University of Virginia.

41. Ibid.

42. Frankel, *High on Foggy Bottom*, 1–2, 7–17.

43. McPherson, *A Political Education*, 229.

44. William B. Jones Oral History, June 24, 2010, Foreign Affairs Oral History Project, Association for Diplomatic Studies and Training, Arlington, VA.

45. Coombs, *The Fourth Dimension of Foreign Policy*, 52.

46. Nicholas Cull, *The Cold War and the United States Information Agency* (Cambridge: Cambridge University Press, 2008), 195.

47. Lucius Battle Oral History, August 27, 1968, pp. 71–72, and October 31, 1968, pp. 124–125, JFKL.

48. Battle Oral History, August 27, 1968, pp. 71–72, and October 31, 1968, pp. 124–25, JFKL.

49. Evelyn Rich Jones, "United States Government Sponsored Higher Educational Programs for Africans: 1957–1970, with Special Attention to the Role of the African-American Institute" (PhD diss., Columbia University, 1978), 240.

50. For more on clandestine US involvement in Africa, see Piero Gleijeses, *Conflicting Missions: Havana, Washington, and Africa, 1959–1976* (Chapel Hill: University of North Carolina Press, 2003); and Westad, *The Global Cold War*.

51. "XII. Educational and Cultural Affairs," p. 87, folder Chapter 12 (Educational and Cultural Affairs): Sections A–G, Administrative History, Dept. of State, Vol. I, Vh. 10–13, box 4, LBJL.

52. Higgin, "Disseminating American Ideals in Africa," 225.

53. Woods, *Fulbright: A Biography*, 129.

54. Ibid., 555.

55. Dean Rusk, "Memorandum for the President: Foreign Students in the United States," September 2, 1961, and "Foreign Students in the United States," both folder NSAM 66 Foreign Students in the United States, NSF box 133, JFKL.

56. Excerpt from *Changes in Attitudes and Impressions concerning the United States by Selected Groups of Short-Term African Grantees* (Washington, DC: US Information Agency, Office of Research and Assessment, 1971), in Seth Spaulding and Michael Flack, *The World's Students in the United States* (Westport, CT: Praeger, 1976), 491; Brendan Jones, "Job Program Aids African Students," *New York Times*, February 26, 1967.

57. "The Agency for International Development during the Administration of Lyndon B Johnson, November 1963–January 1969," vol. I, p. 628.

58. For more on the shortcomings of liberalism according to civil rights activists, see David L. Chappell, *A Stone of Hope: Prophetic Religion and the Death of Jim Crow* (Chapel Hill: University of North Carolina Press, 2004).

59. For more on this issue as it played out in the United Nations, see Irwin, *Gordian Knot*.

Nice to meet you, President Tito . . .

Senator Fulbright and the Yugoslav Lesson for Vietnam

Carla Konta

> Important as the Yugoslav experiment in itself, the major impor-
> tance of Yugoslavia from the viewpoint of American interest is in its
> role as a bridge between East and West. As a model and a magnet for
> less audacious Communist regimes, Yugoslavia contributed to the
> advancement of American interests by encouraging the trend toward
> both national independence and internal liberalization in Eastern
> Europe. As a nation with reasonably good connections in both Mos-
> cow and Washington, Yugoslavia is well qualified to help alleviate
> tensions by interpreting and sometimes commending the positions
> of each of the two great antagonists to the other.
> J. William Fulbright, *Yugoslavia 1964*[1]

The 1964 elections exceeded all of Lyndon Johnson's expectations. Running against the Republican Barry Goldwater, the Democratic candidate
swept up 486 electoral votes, prevailed in forty-four states, and snagged
the largest popular vote margin in American history (43,129,484 against
27,178,188).[2] The bloodbath was on the side of the Grand Old Party, the
Republicans losing more than five hundred seats in state legislatures across
the country, thirty-seven in the US House, and two in the US Senate.
LBJ's victory served as a backdrop for J. William Fulbright's political
euphoria in the moment. For the first time since taking over the Senate
Foreign Relations Committee (SFRC), Arkansas's junior senator felt that
such overwhelming Democratic control would offer a real chance to

accomplish his liberal internationalist goals. With his Senate seat assured, Fulbright departed for Yugoslavia on November 5, 1964, on a very personal trip: to chair the signing of the agreement that would inaugurate Yugoslavia's participation in the Fulbright program. For the first time in his life, he would meet Josip Broz Tito, the president of Yugoslavia, and the other main Communist Party leaders.[3] After a presidential campaign underscored by Goldwater's fierce anticommunism, Fulbright's meeting with a famed Communist renegade seemed quite provocative.

The moment could not have been more imposing. As Yugoslav state secretary Koča Popović emphasized, Fulbright departed only two days after the American elections. As a truly "progressive personality of the American public and political life" and an early friend of Yugoslavia, he arrived in Belgrade to attend the first-ever signing of a Fulbright agreement with a Communist country.[4] The visit would profoundly shape his attitude toward communism and what he considered the correct US foreign policy strategy toward regimes in Eastern Europe, Cuba, Vietnam, and the Soviet Union itself. The trip marked a watershed in his thinking about communism and the role the United States should play in the world. Yugoslavia was a Communist nation that, after the 1948 Tito-Stalin rupture, turned toward the United States and accepted an unexpected partnership that was the fruit of financial, military, and agricultural aid from and cultural cooperation with the US government during the 1950s and 1960s.[5] As a Cold War case, Yugoslavia helped inform Fulbright about approaches to independent nationalist communism.

Although there has been some scholarly interest in the political and ideological outcome of Fulbright's visit to Yugoslavia, it has been neither extensive nor comprehensive. Lee Powell suggests that Tito favorably impressed Fulbright during their Brdo appointment, to the extent that the senator "began to speculate that a communist but independent and nationalistic Vietnam would serve American interests . . . better than a corrupt, unstable regime dependent on American manpower and financial aid."[6] But Powell overlooks the logic that induced Fulbright to embrace the Yugoslav solution. This logic led him to a fine-grained conceptualization of US policy toward the Communist world precisely when Vietnam was leading other policy makers to oversimplify the approach to Communist expansionism. The initial political connotations of that 1964 visit and its later implications have, in other words, not been fully explored.

The Political Background of US-Yugoslav Relations before the Visit

During Koča Popović's period as the state secretary (1953–1965), Yugoslavia's foreign policy strategy first adopted a neutralist policy toward the Soviet Union, one that permitted Yugoslav independence in internal and foreign affairs while maintaining cordial bilateral relations with the Soviet Union. Following the Hungarian crisis, Belgrade muted its 1955–1956 rapprochement with Moscow, and Tito turned to new partners (by the late 1950s Egypt, India, and Indonesia) with whom he founded the Non-Aligned Movement.[7] Through nonalignment, as Robert Rakove explains, Tito aimed to accomplish several foreign policy objectives: to widen the breach between China and the Soviet Union, to take advantage of Khrushchev's apparent interest in good relations with Yugoslavia, and to exploit anticolonialist and nationalist movements in Africa and Asia.[8] In early September 1961, just two weeks after the Bay of Pigs invasion and the Soviet cosmonaut Yuri Gagarin's successful space flight, he gathered Indian prime minister Jawaharlal Nehru, Indonesian president Sukarno, Egyptian president Gamal Abdel Nasser, Gahanian president Kwame Nkrumah, and twenty other state delegations in the First Non-Aligned Conference in Belgrade. The conference confirmed Washington's suspicions about the Non-Aligned Movement.[9] Tito's diatribe against the United States and the West came as a shock to Ambassador George F. Kennan, who cabled Washington: "Tito's statements on Berlin and on Soviet resumption of tests came as a deep disappointment. . . . Passage on Berlin contains no word that could not have been written by Khrushchev; and that on [Soviet resumption of nuclear testing] . . . is weaker and more pro-Soviet than even those of Nasser and Nkrumah." Kennan noted: "Neither I nor any of my Western colleagues were prepared for so one-sided an attitude on Tito's part as this." And he advised Washington to reflect carefully "on its implications for our treatment of conference and, in more long-term, our attitude towards role of Yugoslavs."[10]

Several days after the conference, Kennedy ordered a halt to export licenses for products destined for Yugoslavia, while, a week later, the House of Representatives authorized an investigation into jet sales to the country.[11] A meeting on October 19 between Secretary Rusk and Yugoslav ambassador Marko Nikezić aimed to reduce the tensions,[12] but the congressional offensive against Kennedy's foreign aid program continued to grow throughout 1962 and 1963. Although this offensive derived from conservative disaffection with the president's foreign policy, it also received support from moderate and liberal Democrats.[13] On June 6, 1962, during the aid act voting, the US Senate adopted the Frank Lausche (D-OH) amendment, which restricted US economic aid to all Communist-dominated countries, including Poland and Yugoslavia. The following week, while considering the Kennedy administration's request for widened authority to negotiate trade agreements, the House Ways and Means Committee introduced legislation (HR 1818) that included a provision withdrawing most-favored-nation (MFN) status from Poland and Yugoslavia. Specifically aimed at Cuba, the amendment denied trade concessions to any Communist government, regardless of its relations with the Soviet Union.[14] The bill passed the House on June 28 by a vote of 298–125.[15] State Secretary Popović and Ambassador Marko Nikezić rushed to meet with Dean Rusk, whom the vote surprised since the MFN retraction "was contrary to the wishes of the Administration."[16] Relations between Belgrade and Washington deteriorated still further. In a meeting with Rusk in October 1962, Veljko Mićunović, the Yugoslav ambassador in Washington, underlined "Yugoslavia's sense of bewilderment and consternation" since "great political damage had been done to Yugoslavia's international reputation and prestige."[17]

Somehow, both parties overcame the crisis, first as a result of Rusk's meeting with Tito in Belgrade in May (he afterward intervened with Kennedy over the sale of military spare parts to the Yugoslav army, the interruption of which was expected that year),[18] then thanks to Tito's first official visit to the United States on October 17, 1963 (Kennedy's last meeting with a foreign statesman).[19] According to Walter Roberts, the US Information Service public affairs officer in Belgrade from 1960 to 1966, on his return home Tito asked his staff whether there was "anything in the American-Yugoslav relations that he could do to further them," to which the American desk officer at the Yugoslav Foreign Office replied: "Maybe we can sign a Fulbright agreement."[20] As was Dean Rusk in May 1963, Fulbright was invited to Belgrade because, as the Yugoslav Federal Executive Council acknowledged in a meeting in July 1964: "[Our] long-lasting successful relations with the United States are one of the components of Yugoslavia's independent international position and its prestige and influence on other countries, including the socialist world."[21]

Senator Fulbright from Belgrade to Brdo Kranj

The signing of the Fulbright agreement with Yugoslavia was the result of more than six years of tough negotiations. Congress had originally voted to include Yugoslavia in the Fulbright program in 1959, hoping to set a precedent with a Communist country.[22] Informal talks commenced when Krsto Crvenkovski, the secretary for education and culture of the Federal Executive Council, who was visiting the United States as a participant in the Foreign Leader Exchange Program, encountered State Department officials in Washington, DC, in 1960.[23] A memorandum of exchange gave formal shape to the negotiations,[24] although the talks brought to the table several unsettled difficulties: the impossibility of using Yugoslav dinars for international travel, deciding on an acceptable system of candidate selection, and the nationality of the executive director and secretary of the proposed Fulbright binational commission. Both parties resolved the conversion issue quickly. After all, the "excess" currencies owned by the US government in Yugoslavia through Public Law 480[25] and based on the Agreement of the Surplus Agricultural Supplies would be easy to use for Yugoslav travel expenses (the State Department and the American host institutions would supply the rest) and American full grants (i.e., tuition plus living expenses).[26] The second sore point complicated negotiations throughout 1962 and into 1963. As Walter Roberts underlined, the free choice of candidates was the chief barrier in a country where no open competition existed for the candidate selection in exchange programs and where foreign organizations were permitted only to screen the preselection list.[27] Not surprisingly, the Yugoslav authorities strongly lobbied to obtain preselection rights in the Fulbright program as well.[28] Quite pragmatically, both parties agreed on a double-process solution. Such an agreement reveals the realism that Fulbright discovered in Communist "revisionism" as well as the US ability to show the pluralist nature of its democracy right at the time when that pluralism became most evident but was still doubted by foreign observers. After a first-glance selection by the binational commission, the proposed candidates would be submitted to the Yugoslav Commission for Cooperation with the American and other Foundations.[29] This final list was then returned to the commission and, subsequently, forwarded to the Board of Foreign Scholarship in Washington.[30] On the commission, the American side reluctantly conceded to the appointment of a Yugoslav executive director and secretary, a concession compensated for by the appointment of an American chairperson.[31] The Fulbright agreement, envisioned "to promote further mutual understanding between the peoples of the United States of America and the Socialist Federal Republics of Yugoslavia by a wider exchange of knowledge and professional talents through educational activities," was signed in Belgrade on November 9, 1964.[32]

Apparently, 1964 was not Fulbright's first time in Belgrade. While on his Rhodes scholarship at Oxford University in the 1920s, Fulbright, like many of his fellows, undertook extended study trips to continental Europe. His travels included Paris, the usual Grand European Tour stops in Italy, Germany, and Austria but also Central and Eastern Europe. While visiting Budapest, Bucharest, Belgrade, and Sofia in spring 1929 with new local friends, a Polish count and a Hungarian journalist, he became "absorbed," as he recalled, "by the thought of how apparently limited is the capacity of leaders to transcend the elemental, centuries-old divisions among peoples and forge through reason a basis for lasting peace."[33]

Accompanied in 1964 by his wife, Elizabeth, Seth Tillman of the SFRC staff, and Assistant Secretary of State for European Affairs William Tyler, Fulbright was "received cordially and hospitably" during his nine-day-long tour of Yugoslavia.[34] Above all, what impressed him were the conversations he enjoyed with Yugoslav leaders. His meeting with Tito at Brdo Kranj (Slovenia) passed in "good humor"; the Yugoslav president highly appreciated Fulbright's pro-Yugoslav campaigns in the Senate. He met with Edvard Kardelj, the president of the Federal Assembly and a leading theoretician of the Yugoslav Communist Party; pro-Western politicians such as Koča Popović and Marko Nikezić; Jože Brilej, the president of the Federal Executive Council's Committee for Economic Relations with Foreign Countries; and Janez Vipotnik, the federal secretary for education and culture.[35]

The visit substantially alleviated deadlocked Yugoslav-American relations. That Fulbright had lobbied for the restoration of MFN status to Yugoslavia proved to Tito that the Arkansas senator was a "unique friend of Yugoslavia." As a matter of fact, by restoring MFN status, Congress backed a new agricultural surplus agreement and liberalized Yugoslav exports in the United States.[36] During the talks, Tito stressed Yugoslav opposition to US policies in Latin America, Congo, and Cyprus, although he very much appreciated Fulbright's efforts toward détente with the Soviet Union. He was impressed by Fulbright's flexibility on Cuba (as compared to Kennedy's anti-Castro interventions),[37] Panama (as opposed to the rigid application of the 1903 treaty),[38] and China (as compared with the general US impatience with Beijing).[39] He also appreciated Fulbright's call for negotiations on atomic weaponry and nuclear nonproliferation, and he already shared the senator's belief that international exchanges promoted a peaceful internationalist order.[40] As he acknowledged to Foreign Minister Koča Popović, Fulbright considered Yugoslavia and its nonaligned policy an example of "pragmatic adjustment," "an experiment of worldwide impact," and a "bridge between the capitalist and socialist world."[41] While he disagreed with the Yugoslav position on German rearmament, NATO multilateralism, and the Berlin question, both he and Tito actually concurred in criticizing the US strategy toward Cuba and the necessity of a "peaceful coexistence" rapprochement with the Soviet Union.[42] Speaking to his Yugoslav audience, he remarked that, while pursuing the battle against communism domestically, the US government often conducted socialist-like state programs internationally, the Fulbright program being just one of them.[43]

After his return to Washington, Fulbright wrote to his friend Ronald B. McCallum, a historian and the master of Pembroke College, Oxford, about what would become his core idea regarding Tito's regime: "If I am any judge, the Yugoslavs are revisionists, as the Chinese allege. They appeared to me experimental and open-minded . . . and quite pragmatic, especially in the field of economics. They have many problems, of course, but I believe they are moving in the right direction, and are worthy of our encouragement."[44]

Old Nationalism and New Communism: The "Old Myths" and the "New Realities" Reconsidered

Clearly, Yugoslavia represents a turning point in Fulbright's conception of America's role in the world. The decision to preside personally over the agreement ceremony came just on the heels of one of his most celebrated public foreign policy statements: the "Old Myths and New Realities" speech.[45] Months before, on March 25, 1964, in an almost empty Senate hall,

Fulbright delivered one of his most famous and influential foreign policy speeches, declaring that the United States had to abandon its long-held myths about the Communist world and adapt to new realities. He emphasized that aggression involved unacceptable risks, as the Cuban Missile Crisis proved; no "total victory" was possible. Since Khrushchev had apparently retreated from his expansionist intentions and signed the test ban treaty, a more flexible and sophisticated response to the Communist threat to the free world was, he argued, required.[46] The gap between "fact and perception" and "the realities of foreign policy and our ideas about it," he noted, indicated that the American policies were "handicapped" and "based on old myths, rather than current realities," thus creating "dangerous and unnecessary" divergences. Disagreements about reality, he continued, arose partially because of radical changes in the relations between Communist and free countries and to some extent because of the general American trend of confusing "means with ends" and, accordingly, "adher[ing] to prevailing practices with a fervor befitting immutable principles."[47]

Expressing the political courage that would mark his later political career, Fulbright challenged "self-evident truths" such as the presumption "that, just as the President resides in Washington and the Pope in Rome, the Devil resides immutably in Moscow." Now that "the Devil" had escaped Moscow and reached China, Vietnam, and Cuba ("turning up now here, now there, and in many places at once"), Americans must confront and adapt to "a complex and fluid world situation" by surmounting the permissible bounds of public discussion and by embracing the "unthinkable thoughts": about the Cold War, East-West relations generally, the underdeveloped countries of Latin America, the changing nature of the Chinese Communist threat in Asia, and, certainly, "the festering war in Vietnam."

Communism was not a monolithic bloc of organized conspiracies, Fulbright argued. Rather, it ranged from a threatening China, on the one hand, to Poland and Yugoslavia, which posed no immediate threat to the United States, on the other. Although he believed communism to be hostile to the free world in principle, Fulbright nevertheless assessed that general and long-term intentions were far less important "than the variations in . . . intensity and character." Finally, it was not "communist dogma as espoused within Russia but Communist imperialism" that threatened the United States and the rest of the non-Communist world.[48] This latter view informed Fulbright's position on Yugoslavia: in March 1965, three months before he delivered a comprehensive report on Yugoslavia to the Senate, he wrote to Johnson on that country's potential for influencing American relations with the Communist world, adding: "Tito is an unusually attractive and intelligent leader."[49] Fulbright's experience in Yugoslavia was a clear reflection of the changed circumstances of the Cold War in the mid-1960s.

In the senator's view, the Yugoslav experiment consisted in the synthesis of communism and nationalism: Yugoslav internal political, social, and economic order, even though "basically authoritarian,"[50] was "pragmatic, experimental, and largely free of dogma, combining elements of Marxian communism with elements of Western syndicalism, Fabian socialism, and welfare state democracy." The Yugoslav system was Communist more because of pragmatic ideological identification than real practice. From the American foreign policy viewpoint, the Yugoslav experiment in national communism brought it to a "position approximating neutrality in the Cold War." Tito's government practiced neither aggression nor subversion against free nations, and, while it pursued to some extent policies and views disagreeable to the United States, these were usually "within the spectrum of what must be considered normal international relations." Yugoslav criticism of American policy in Vietnam was no harsher than that of other non-Communist countries generally friendly with the United States. Instead of challenging vital American interests, as other Communist countries did, the Yugoslav government held responsible and reliable foreign policies toward its American partners. More importantly, because of its unique position and its tempering of Communist ideology, Yugoslavia gained influence "beyond its size and resources," becoming a model and a magnet for other Soviet bloc countries and, to some extent, the nonaligned countries. Certainly, the country's international prestige and visibility, together with its revisionist communism imbued with pragmatic virtues, constituted the prime motive for establishing this Fulbright precedent with a Communist regime.[51]

US aid policy regarding Yugoslavia, aiming at its independence from the Soviets, was, Fulbright underlined, successful and worthy of being further sustained. In addition, the Communist regime arose from a legitimate war of liberation and was not imposed by Moscow.[52] In 1966, Fulbright criticized Johnson's obstinacy in Vietnam by arguing that there was no way of preventing the legitimacy of "an independent, nationalist, and united Vietnam." In fact: "By strengthening its ties to the Soviet Union, this Yugoslav-style entity could serve as a counterweight to China."[53]

Fulbright admired the process of Yugoslav decentralization implemented with the 1963 constitution, the "offensive of reform forces."[54] Adopted on April 7, 1963, that constitution renamed the federation the Socialist Federal Republic of Yugoslavia and, focusing on self-management, defined the republic's governing structures. The preamble mentioned the sovereign rights of the working people and the nationalities that "denied sovereignty to the republics as territorial entities, whilst opening the door to a degree of polycentrism in the governance of the federation."[55] Above all, the system of the management by workers of autonomous enterprises that allowed them "to play an important, though by no means unregulated, role in determining how the enterprises in which they work will be run, including how profits will be allocated as between wages and reinvestment," caught Fulbright's attention.[56]

The Yugoslav leadership comprised an unusually open network of elites, a "polycentric polyarchy" that was scattered through an "impressive number of autonomously organized and institutionally legalized forces, representing divergent interests and values, most, if not all, social strata," as Dennison Rusinow put it.[57] Analyzing the Yugoslav context, Fulbright commented: "The typical Yugoslav leader is an atypical man . . . relatively young, well-educated and multilingual."[58] What he failed to understand was that he met a selected group of Yugoslav leaders, not by coincidence pro-Western, without encountering any leader of the centralizing faction that sponsored a strong federal government and was less devoted to Yugoslav alliances with the United States, like the writer Dobrica Ćosić or the secret services chief Aleksandar Ranković.[59]

Returning to Washington, Fulbright brought home a basic conclusion: Yugoslavia was, from the US viewpoint, a "friendly country," even when it criticized, "sometimes harshly," the United States, even when it aligned with the Soviet Union, and even when it voted against an American proposal at the United Nations. It illustrated a flexible strategy toward communism that proved to be "an effective military and political barrier to the expansion of Soviet power in southeastern Europe," and, as a prominent nonaligned power, it led African and Asian countries in the March 1965 appeal for Vietnam, signed in Belgrade by seventeen nations.[60]

In *The Arrogance of Power*, Fulbright wrote:

> We have tended—and now more than ever are tending—to give our opposition to communism priority over our support for nationalism. The result has been that, with certain exceptions, we have strongly, and for the most part unsuccessfully, opposed those genuinely nationalist movements which have been controlled or influenced by communists. The most notable—and rewarding—exception has been Yugoslavia, whose national independence we have supported since 1948. . . . Whatever wisdom, or lack of it, our emphasis on communism has had in the past, the realities of the present require a reversal of priorities as between opposing communism and supporting nationalism. . . . American interests are better served by supporting nationalism than by opposing communism, and . . . it is in our interest to accept a communist government rather than to undertake the cruel and all but impossible task of suppressing a genuinely national movement.[61]

That is to say, the Yugoslav government's Communist revisionism, its desire to remain independent of and find an ally to counterbalance the influence of the Soviet bloc, and its clear foundation on nationalist principles offered a model that could better serve US interests in Southeast Asia than the current attitude toward Vietnam.

Fulbright was convinced that recent US history had shaped three generations of foreign policy makers. The first came out of World War II, its experiences catalyzing a vision for peace. However: "When these hopes were shattered by Stalin's expansionist policies, . . . a new generation emerged, a generation dedicated to relentless conflict against communist imperialism." The second generation, which arose after the Czech coup, the collapse of Chiang Kai-shek, and the Korean War, "prided itself on being hard-boiled and devised policies on the assumption that anything that was bad for the Russians was good for us." Yet it was the third generation that finally grasped the changed character of the Cold War. "The communist world," Fulbright announced, "has ceased to be a unified bloc and now consists of diverse nations, ranging from China, which is hostile to the West, to the Soviet Union, whose unfriendliness is much less virulent, to Yugoslavia, which is friendly to the West." Thanks to the advent of limited cooperation and tacit understanding among nuclear powers, "a new and constructive kind of competition between the communist countries and the West has emerged." Indeed, Fulbright believed that there was a new generation of politicians certain that only creative competition could build "a stronger and more prosperous society at home" and "effectively help the world's less developed nations." Or, "in Khrushchev's colorful phrase, . . . provide more and better goulash."[62]

Conclusion

Proud of the first agreement signed with a Communist country, Fulbright doubled down on the notion that the exchanges of intellectuals and leaders would end up being more powerful than diplomatic foreign policy actions in creating lasting ties and good relationships, and, in the Yugoslav case, he turned out to be right. Many midlevel Yugoslav leaders who visited the United States under the auspices of cultural exchange programs in the 1950s and 1960s contributed in the decades to come to reform movements in their home country.[63] In 1964, Fulbright wrote to Tito reemphasizing the core of his philosophy and ideology: knowledge tears apart barriers between nations and relieves the excesses of nationalism. Yugoslavia itself, he confided, was "in a position of enlightening other nations to . . . overcome the ideologies that divide them."[64] Fulbright's 1964 mission to Yugoslavia tackled two issues. As a politician, he corrected misunderstandings that had damaged bilateral relations. As an intellectual, he confirmed his support of a Yugoslavia independent of the Soviet Union and ultimately left the country even more convinced that the United States should take a different approach to the situation in Vietnam.

The Second Non-Aligned Conference—held in Cairo in October 1964, coinciding with a much relaxed Yugoslav mood toward the United States[65]—definitely paved the way for the establishment of better bilateral relations. Fulbright's visit in early November only improved the congenial mood. The senator had for the moment proved to be right about Yugoslavia, the 1968 student protests that prompted an oppressive Party response being at that point four years away.

As far as foreign relations were concerned, the Yugoslav leaders proved so enthusiastic about the Fulbright program that they agreed to participate in cost sharing from 1970 on, becoming the first Communist country to do so.[66] The Fulbright scholarships were a matter of Cold War strategy for both the United States and Yugoslavia. The Yugoslav government strongly favored the program because it internationalized higher education, developed long-term research projects, empowered specialized (American, social, and Slavic) studies, and assisted technological advancement and economic reforms.[67] But it prioritized science and technology over the humanities and the social sciences.[68] For their part, the US policy makers deemed the program an unmitigated success: Yugoslav Fulbright alumni were, as one official noted, "now to be found in all of the Yugoslav Republics, in every Yugoslav city, in every Yugoslav university and at most of the university faculties." The Yugoslav leadership, "prepared to gamble that the desired technical advances can be made without a total dislocation of socialist ideology," was eagerly implementing many US-inspired moderate policy reforms and liberalization practices.[69] Yugoslavs were becoming more and more friendly and open to cooperative relationships.[70] Finally, the cultural exchange programs had the generally positive effect of prompting anti–Vietnam War sentiments that were manifested in both politics and popular culture.[71]

For Fulbright himself, as this essay has shown, the Yugoslav experiment with national communism and its possible bridge function between East and West framed his "politics of dissent": his assumption that Communist movements were not as monolithic as most US policy makers considered them to be. Fulbright, along with Robert and Edward Kennedy, George McGovern, and others, thought that the National Liberation Front (NLF) must participate in any provisional government in Vietnam "if there was to be a compromising settlement." The Johnson administration disagreed, convinced that the NLF would manipulate any coalition government to subvert the regime, control elections, and impose communism. There was no difference for LBJ "between Hungary in 1946, Czechoslovakia in 1948, and South Vietnam in 1966."[72] By contrast, Fulbright argued that the Johnson administration could not win Vietnam; to do so the US forces would need to intervene on a scale vast enough to impose American values, institutions, and culture.[73]

The US "soft" approach toward Yugoslavian national communism only corroborated Fulbright's convictions. The Fulbright-Tito talks at Brdo Kranj, as well as several meetings that Fulbright held with the highest-ranking Party and Foreign Office officials, convinced the Arkansas senator that Yugoslavia did, in fact, demonstrate that the Cold War ideological divide was less profound and less relevant to achieving mutually beneficial binational relations than were practical cooperation and understanding, toward which the cultural exchange program was the initial step.

Notes

I am grateful to Randall Woods for his suggestions on the implicit Cold War frames of Fulbright's visit to Yugoslavia in 1964. Special thanks go to Misti Nicole Harper, from the University of Arkansas, for her generous help in sending me reference materials when I was already back in Europe, to Vera Ekechukwu, from the University of Arkansas Library Special Collections, who provided me with a copy of Senator Fulbright's *Yugoslavia 1964: Report to the Committee on Foreign Relations, United States Senate*, and to Lara Hall, archives specialist from the LBJ Presidential Library, for her indications on archival resources held there. While the Yugoslav archival records are reported in their original language, they nonetheless follow the US National Archives citation guidelines.

1. James W. Fulbright, *Yugoslavia 1964: Report to the Committee on Foreign Relations, United States Senate* (Washington, DC: US Government Printing Office, 1965), 22.

2. Randall B. Woods, *LBJ: Architect of American Ambition* (Cambridge, MA: Harvard University Press, 2007), 553.

3. "Fulbright on Way to Yugoslavia," *New York Times*, November 6, 1964; Lee R. Powell, *J. William Fulbright and His Time: A Political Biography* (Memphis: Guild Bindery Press, 1996), 223.

4. Koča Popović, Secretary of State, to the General Secretary of the President, October 22, 1964, 441257, box I-3-a/107-132, Prijemi stranih ličnosti i delegacija, Kabinet Predsednika Republike (Cabinet of the President of the Republic; hereafter KPR), Record Group 837 (hereafter RG 837), Arhiv Josipa Broza Tita (Archives of Josip Broz Tito; hereafter AJBT).

5. First the Truman administration and then the Eisenhower administration adopted a policy of "keeping Tito afloat." The State Department policy makers coined the term *wedge strategy* to characterize its foreign relations approach to Yugoslavia. The strategy involved supporting Yugoslav nationalism and thus instigating divisions between the Soviet Union and other Communist countries and showing that socialism was possible outside the Soviet sphere. Nevertheless, as Lorraine Lees argues, using Yugoslav nationalism as an example for other, Soviet-dominated Communist states, the American government jeopardized its strategy by futile attempts to change Tito's regime. Lorraine M. Lees, *Keeping Tito Afloat: The United States, Yugoslavia, and the Cold War* (University Park: Pennsylvania State University Press,

2005). See also Beatrice Heuser, *Western "Containment" Policies in the Cold War: The Yugoslav Case, 1948–53* (London: Routledge, 1989).
6. Powell, *J. William Fulbright and His Time*, 223–24. Other scholarly assessments of the Yugoslav example in Fulbright's political thought are briefly noted in Lee R. Powell, *J. William Fulbright and America's Lost Crusade: Fulbright, the Cold War and the Vietnam War* (Little Rock, AR: Rose, 1984), 87, 103–4; and Randall Bennett Woods, *J. William Fulbright, Vietnam, and the Search for a Cold War Foreign Policy* (Cambridge: Cambridge University Press, 1998), 58. On the other hand, the Serbian historian Dragan Bogetić tackled Fulbright's visit to Tito within the general framework of the Yugoslav-US bilateral relations crises in the early 1960s. Dragan Bogetić, *Jugoslavensko-američki odnosi 1961.–1971.* (Belgrade: Institut za savremenu istoriju, 2012), 128–32, 174–77.
7. The Yugoslav geostrategic approach toward the Soviet Union after the 1948 Tito-Stalin split is explored, in a comparative Yugoslav-Finish perspective, in Rinna Kullaa, *Non-Alignment and Its Origins in Cold War Europe: Yugoslavia, Finland and the Soviet Challenge* (London: I. B.Tauris, 2012).
8. Robert B. Rakove, *Kennedy, Johnson, and the Nonaligned World* (New York: Cambridge University Press, 2013), 181.
9. Tvrtko Jakovina, *Treća Strana Hladnog Rata* (Zagreb: Fraktura, 2011), 50–61; Bogetić, *Jugoslavensko-američki odnosi 1961.–1971.*, 30–34.
10. Telegram from the Embassy in Yugoslavia to the Department of State, September 3, 1961, *Foreign Relations of the United States [FRUS], 1961–1963*, vol. 16, *Berlin Crisis, 1961–1962* (Washington, DC: US Government Printing Office, 1988), doc. 93. See also "Text of the Final Declaration of the Belgrade Conference of Non-Aligned Nations," *New York Times*, September 7, 1961.
11. Rakove, *Kennedy, Johnson, and the Nonaligned World*, 182. As Rakove underlines: "These concerns meshed with growing conservative doubt over the administration's handling of the Berlin crisis and anger at the perceived pro-Moscow cast of the Belgrade Conference, the Republican opposition argued, had exposed the 'utter bankruptcy' of Kennedy's foreign policy." Ibid. For more on the significance of Yugoslav aviation policy, see Phil Tiemeyer, "Launching a Nonaligned Airline: JAT Yugoslav Airways between East, West, and South, 1947–1962," *Diplomatic History* 41, no. 1 (2017): 78–103.
12. Assistant Secretary of State for European Affairs (Kohler) to the Ambassador to Yugoslavia (Kennan), October 19, 1961, *FRUS, 1961–1963*, vol. 16, doc. 102; Telegram from the Department of State to the Embassy in Yugoslavia, October 20, 1961, *FRUS, 1961–1963*, vol. 16, doc. 105; David L. Larson, *United States Foreign Policy toward Yugoslavia: 1943–1963* (Washington, DC: University Press of America, 1979), 292–302. Smooth bilateral relations were interrupted even before the Non-Aligned Conference by the Yugoslav government trade agreement with the Soviet Union, which projected a continuing two-way trade increase (July 1961). For the Yugoslavs, the agreement was the outcome of their economic pragmatism, while their anti-US rhetoric was "a way of profiling the Yugoslav voice and leadership

among the non-aligned movement." John R. Lampe, Russell O. Prickett, and Ljubiša S. Adamović, *Yugoslav-American Economic Relations since World War II* (Durham, NC: Duke University Press, 1990), 66.

13. Rakove, *Kennedy, Johnson, and the Nonaligned World*, 180.

14. Lampe, Prickett, and Adamović, *Yugoslav-American Economic Relations since World War II*, 68.

15. MFN status is an economic position that allows a country, regardless of size, to enjoy the best terms offered by its trading partner. For Yugoslavia in 1962, the retraction of MFN meant a doubling or trebling of tariffs on its exports.

16. Memorandum of Conversation, June 12, 1962, *FRUS, 1961–1963*, vol. 16, doc. 129; Bogetić, *Jugoslavensko-američki odnosi 1961.–1971*, 74–76.

17. Memorandum of Conversation, October 23, 1962, *FRUS, 1961–1963*, vol. 16, doc. 139.

18. Telegram from Secretary of State Rusk to the Department of State, May 5, 1963, *FRUS, 1961–1963*, vol. 16, doc. 160.

19. Bogetić, *Jugoslavensko-američki odnosi 1961.–1971.*, 139–62. In the aftermath of the Kennedy-Tito meeting, Congress withdrew the MFN restrictions on Yugoslavia. Ibid., 152. See also Lampe, Prickett, and Adamović, *Yugoslav-American Economic Relations since World War II*, 68–69.

20. Mark Taplin, "Global Publicks: Walter Roberts: The Fulbright Program in Yugoslavia—'Tito Thought It Was an Excellent Idea,'" February 22, 2016, http://globalpublicks.blogspot.hr/2015/02/walter-roberts-fulbright-program-in.html.

21. Informacija o stanju odnosa SFRJ i SAD i zaključcima SIV-a, 18 July 1964, Str. Pov. 01/-23/64, box 640, Međunarodni odnosi 1953–1970, Savezno Izvršno Veće 1953–1990 (hereafter SIV), RG 130, Archives of Yugoslavia (hereafter AY), 3.

22. DSIP to SIV, 11 June 1959, 91842, box 640, Međunarodni odnosi 1953–1970, SIV 1953–1990, RG 130, AY.

23. Telegram 038335 from the Department of State to American Embassy Belgrade, June 7, 1960, 511.68/6-760, box 1074, Central Decimal Files 1960–1963 (hereafter CDF), RG 59, National Archives at College Park (hereafter NARA).

24. Pro Memoria Sent from US Government to the Government of Yugoslavia, July 7, 1960, 511.683/6-2660, box 1074, CDF 1960–1963, RG 59, NARA; Telegram 038335 from the Department of State to American Embassy Belgrade, June 7, 1960, 511.68/6-760, box 1074, CDF 1960–1963, RG 59, NARA; DSIP to SIV, December 19, 1963, 91430/3, box 640, Međunarodni odnosi 1953–1970, SIV 1953–1990, RG 130, AY.

25. The Need for a Policy Decision re the Conversion of "Excess" Currencies, February 27, 1961, folder 3, box 46, Bureau of Educational and Cultural Affairs, Manuscript Collection 468, Special Collections, University of Arkansas Library (hereafter UAL).

26. Zabeleška o Fulbrajtovom programu, August 21, 1967, box 61, Kulturno-prosvetne veze sa inostranstvom 1967–1971, Savezni savet za obrazovanje i kulturu 1960–1971, RG 319, AY.

27. Dispatch 173 from American Embassy Belgrade to Department of State, September 27, 1961, box 2, Eastern Europe, Bureau of Educational and Cultural Affairs, Department of State, Roosevelt Study Center Microfilm Collection, Middelburg, The Netherlands.

28. Many reports and memos testify to such lobbying negotiations. See, e.g., Airgram 13 from the Department of State to the American Embassy in Belgrade, July 16, 1962, 511.003/7-1662, box 1050, CDF 1960–1963, RG 59, NARA; Telegram 09151 from the Department of State to the American Embassy in Belgrade, March 19, 1963, EDX 4/48-4460, box 3254, Central Foreign Policy Files 1963, RG 59, NARA; Godišnji izvještaj Jugoslovensko-americke komisije za Fulbrajtov program, May 12, 1967, box 61, Kulturno-prosvetne veze sa inostranstvom 1967–1971, Savezni savet za obrazovanje i kulturu 1960–1971, RG 319, AY: 8; and Elaborati o međunarodnim vezama, May 1968, box 34, Sednice Saveznog saveta 1968, Savezni savet za obrazovanje i kulturu 1960–1971, RG 319, AY: 72.

29. This twenty-two-member commission, appointed by the Yugoslav federal secretary of education and usually referred to as the "Ford Commission" or the "Academic Committee," was created in 1958 by Yugoslav authorities to guide the selection process both for Ford foundation and Fulbright program candidates.

30. Zabeleška o sprovodjenju i produženju ugovora o Fulbrajtovom programu, 1968, box 61, Kulturno-prosvetne veze sa inostranstvom 1967–1971, Savezni savet za obrazovanje i kulturu 1960–1971, RG 319, AY; Saradnja SFRJ-SAD u oblasti obrazovanje (Fulbrajtov program), November 1970, 021/1, box 61, Kulturno-prosvetne veze sa inostranstvom 1967–1971, Savezni savet za obrazovanje i kulturu 1960–1971, RG 319, AY: 20–21.

31. Branislav Grbić, Chief of the Federal Secretary of Finance, to Paul Wheeler, PAO, 1963, box 240, SAD, Kanada i Latinska Amerika 1953–1967, Savezni sekretarijat za obrazovanje i kulturu, RG 318, AY; and Janez Vipotnik, Federal Secretary for Education and Culture, to C. Burke Elbrick, American Ambassador, November 9, 1964, box 1, Komisija za prosvetnu razmenu između SFRJ i SAD, RG 472, AY.

32. Agreement between the Government of the United States of America and the Government of the Federal Socialist Republic of Yugoslavia, November 9, 1964, box 1, Komisija za prosvetnu razmenu između SFRJ i SAD, RG 472, AY. It established a binational commission composed of eight members, four of Yugoslav and four of American nationality.

33. Eugene Brown, *J. William Fulbright: Advice and Dissent* (Iowa City: University of Iowa Press, 1985), 11; Randall Bennett Woods, *Fulbright: A Biography* (Cambridge: Cambridge University Press, 1995), 37.

34. Senator Fulbright visited the Yugoslav capital, Belgrade, the Serbian university town of Novi Sad, the town of Dubrovnik on the Dalmatian coast, the city of Pula and the island of Brioni at the southern tip of the Istrian Peninsula, and the two major cities of northern Yugoslavia—Ljubljana, the capital of Slovenia, and Zagreb, the capital of Croatia. The official host of Fulbright's delegation was Vladimir Popović, former ambassador to the United States and Fulbright's counterpart in

the Yugoslav Federal Chamber. James W. Fulbright, *Yugoslavia 1964: Report to the Committee on Foreign Relations, United States Senate* (Washington, DC: US Government Printing Office, 1965), 1.

35. See Reports to Josip Broz Tito from October 24 and November 3, 1964, box I-3-a/107-132, Prijemi stranih ličnosti i delegacija, KPR, RG 837, AJBT.

36. Informacija povodom prijema senatora Fulbrighta, November 14, 1964, 611/8, Box I-3-a/107-132, Prijemi stranih ličnosti i delegacija, KPR, RG 837, AJBT.

37. Woods, *Fulbright: A Biography*, 261–75.

38. William J. Jorden, *Panama Odyssey*, 2nd ed. (Austin: University of Texas Press, 2014), 74–76.

39. Woods, *Fulbright: A Biography*, 336.

40. Informacija povodom prijema senatora Fulbrighta, November 14, 1964, 611/8, box I-3-a/107-132, Prijemi stranih ličnosti i delegacija, KPR, RG 837, AJBT.

41. Zabilješka o razgovorima dr. Vladimira Popovića, predsjednika Odbora za spoljne poslove i međunarodne odnose SIV i James William Fulbrighta, November 7, 1964, 611/5, box I-3-a/107-132, Prijemi stranih ličnosti i delegacija, KPR, RG 837, AJBT.

42. Zabeleška o izlaganju Predsednika SFRJ Josipa Broza Tita u razgovoru sa predsednikom Spoljnopolitičkog komiteta Senata SAD, James William Fulbrightom, November 14, 1964, box I-3-a/107-132, Prijemi stranih ličnosti i delegacija, KPR, RG 837, AJBT; Zabeleška o razgovoru Predsednika SFRJ Josipa Broza Tita sa predsednikom Spoljnopolitičkog komiteta Senata SAD, James William Fulbrightom, November 14, 1964, box I-3-a/107-132, Prijemi stranih ličnosti i delegacija, KPR, RG 837, AJBT.

43. Zabeleška iz neformalnih razgovora druga V. Popovića i sa Senatorom W. J. Fulbrightom, November 11, 1964, 611/3, box I-3-a/107-132, Prijemi stranih ličnosti i delegacija, KPR, RG 837, AJBT.

44. J. W. Fulbright to Ronald B. McCallum, November 27, 1964, box 19, ser. 88, Personal and Business Correspondence, James William Fulbright Papers 1960–1974, MS F956, Special Collections, UAL.

45. No archival evidence in the Fulbright Papers at the University of Arkansas Library and Johnson's presidential library evinces that his trip was imputed to any LBJ recommendation.

46. Woods, *J. William Fulbright, Vietnam, and the Search for a Cold War Foreign Policy*, 59–61.

47. Sen. Fulbright (Ar.), "Foreign Policy—Old Myths and New Realities," *Congressional Record—Senate 133*, 25 March 1964, file 17, box 20, ser. 71, MS F956 144, J. William Fulbright Papers, Digital Collection, UAL, http://digitalcollections.uark.edu/cdm/ref/collection/Fulbright/id/312.

48. Ibid.

49. Powell, *J. William Fulbright and His Time*, 231.

50. Despite its dictatorial system, Fulbright argued, Yugoslavia's rule was quite "benign" by Communist standards. Indeed: "As long as the legitimacy of Commu-

nist rule is not questioned, people at every level, including the highest levels of government, are more or less free to criticize and even ridicule the way in which the sacred ideology is practiced." Fulbright, *Yugoslavia 1964*, 14.

51. Ibid., 3.

52. Ibid., 4–6.

53. Woods, *Fulbright: A Biography*, 367. See also Woods, J. *William Fulbright, Vietnam, and the Search for a Cold War Foreign Policy.*

54. Dušan Bilandžić, *Hrvatska moderna povijest* (Zagreb: Golden Marketing, 1999); John R. Lampe, *Yugoslavia as History: Twice There Was a Country*, 2nd ed. (Cambridge: Cambridge University Press, 2000), 276–98.

55. L. Benson, *Yugoslavia: A Concise History*, 2nd ed. (Houndmills, Basingstoke: Palgrave Macmillan, 2003), 108. While, in Communist doctrine, polycentrism signifies different paths to socialism, in the Yugoslav case it also coincides with federalization, at the ideological and practical levels, where state power or governance is delegated to republican and local centers. For more, see Dejan Jović, *Yugoslavia: A State That Withered Away* (West Lafayette, IN: Purdue University Press, 2008).

56. Fulbright, *Yugoslavia 1964*, 11.

57. Dennison I. Rusinow, *The Yugoslav Experiment, 1948–1974* (Berkeley and Los Angeles: University of California Press, 1978), 346.

58. Fulbright, *Yugoslavia 1964*, 7–9.

59. Latinka Perović, *Dominantna i neželjena elita: Beleške o intelektualnoj i političkoj eliti u Srbiji (XX–XXI)* (Belgrade: Dan Graf, 2015).

60. Though endorsing the idea of peaceful coexistence within foreign ideologies, Yugoslavia retained an adversarial attitude toward Communist China and its satellites and Albania. See Fulbright, *Yugoslavia 1964*, 15.

61. J. William Fulbright, *The Arrogance of Power*, 3rd ed. (New York: Random House, 2011), Kindle Locations 1220–31.

62. Ibid., Kindle Locations 3333–50.

63. Carla Konta, "Waging Public Diplomacy: The United States and the Yugoslav Experiment (1950–1972)" (PhD diss., University of Trieste, 2016).

64. Izjava senator J. W. Fulbrighta povodom potpisivanja sporazuma o razmeni u oblasti obrazovanje između Jugoslavije i SAD, November 9, 1964, box 1, Komisija za prosvetnu razmenu između SFRJ i SAD, RG 472, AY.

65. Jakovina, *Treća Strana Hladnog Rata*, 61–68.

66. Yugoslavia agreed to contribute 20 percent of the country's annual Fulbright budget. See John Richardson Jr. to the Department of State, October 3, 1969, folder 5, box 21, Bureau of Educational and Cultural Affairs, UAL; Yugoslav-American Commission for Educational Exchange to Federal Council on Education and Culture, January 11, 1971, 4/021-2, box 61, Kulturno-prosvetne veze sa inostranstvom 1967–1971, Savezni savet za obrazovanje i kulturu 1960–1971, RG 319, AY.

67. Saradnja SFRJ-SAD u oblasti obrazovanje (Fulbrajtov program), November 1970, 021/1, box 61, Kulturno-prosvetne veze sa inostranstvom 1967–1971, Savezni savet za obrazovanje i kulturu 1960–1971, RG 319, AY: 23.

68. Prilog 1: Informacija o sprovođenju zadataka iz programa razmene u oblasti prosvete između SFR Jugoslavije i Sjedinjenih Američkih Država, June 2, 1969, enclosed in Predlog za učešće u finansiranju programa razmene u oblasti prosvete između SFRJ i SAD (Fulbright programa), June 11, 1969, 01.1092, box 640, SIV 1953–1990, RG 130, AY.

69. Airgram 366 from the American Embassy Belgrade to the Department of State, October 8, 1970, box 2, Eastern Europe, Bureau of Educational and Cultural Affairs, Microfilm Collection, Roosevelt Study Center, The Netherlands (hereafter RSC).

70. Airgram 969 from the American Embassy Belgrade to the Department of State, August 15, 1968, box 2, Eastern Europe, Bureau of Educational and Cultural Affairs, Microfilm Collection, RSC.

71. Airgram 969 from the American Embassy Belgrade to the Department of State, August 15, 1968, box 2, Eastern Europe, Bureau of Educational and Cultural Affairs, Microfilm Collection, RSC; Airgram 366 from the American Embassy Belgrade to the Department of State, October 8, 1970, box 2, Eastern Europe, Bureau of Educational and Cultural Affairs, Microfilm Collection, RSC. For Yugoslav reactions to the Vietnam War, see James Mark, Péter Apor, Radina Vučetić, and Piotr Osęka, "'We Are with You, Vietnam': Transnational Solidarities in Socialist Hungary, Poland and Yugoslavia," *Journal of Contemporary History* 50, no. 3 (2015): 439–64; and Radina Vučetić, "Violence against the Antiwar Demonstrations of 1965–1968 in Yugoslavia: Political Balancing between East and West," *European History Quarterly* 45, no. 2 (2015): 255–74.

72. Woods, *Fulbright: A Biography*, 421.

73. Woods, *J. William Fulbright, Vietnam, and the Search for a Cold War Foreign Policy*, 128.

The Fulbright Program in China

Guangqiu Xu

After Deng Xiaoping came to power in 1976, the Chinese leaders realized that their country had to open its education system to developments in the outside world so as to help their people learn Western science and technology and thus attain the Four Modernizations in science and technology, industry, agriculture, and defense. To speed up the Four Modernizations drive, in 1979 China opened its doors to foreigners, especially teachers from the West, for the first time since 1949. Many of the nation's universities and colleges were inviting American and Canadian as well as British, French, German, and other European teachers into their classrooms, mostly to teach basic foreign-language courses. Since 1979, these cohorts have included many American Fulbrighters conducting research and attaining teaching experience in the previously secluded nation.

Do American Fulbrighters have a noticeable impact on the Chinese campus? If so, how? What is the significance of the China Fulbright program? What are Beijing's reactions to Fulbrighters' influence in this respect? What are the implications of the Chinese government policy toward Western ideology? This essay explores and seeks to answer these questions.[1]

Educational exchanges have been among the most significant developments in US-China relations. The study of this subject, using a previously underutilized archive, undoubtedly helps readers better understand US-China relations in terms of not just bilateral educational exchanges but also the broader bilateral relationship and its ups and downs since the late 1970s. This is a story of how the interaction between China and the West has evolved.

As early as in the aftermath of the Opium War of 1842, some Chinese leaders advocated learning from the West because they realized that, while their country was vast, it was also militarily weak and could not withstand invasion by the powerful Western countries. When the Western powers posed a threat to China in the latter half of the nineteenth century, the Chinese government started to invite Western educators— advisers, administrators, and teachers—to impart Western science, technology, and other applicable knowledge. After the fall of the last Chinese emperor in 1911, national leaders invited Westerners to introduce advanced technology to the country and, in general, promote modernization. For over five decades, thousands of Western teachers took this opportunity to teach in Chinese universities, and their influence continued until 1949.

Westerners brought to China not only their technology but also their ideology. Many Chinese believed that acceptance of Western ideology meant submission and that that ideology posed a threat to the hierarchical and authoritarian political system in China. They therefore tried to reject Western ideas while adopting Western technology. To them, maintaining traditional Confucian virtue was paramount. The Communist takeover of mainland China put a halt to this ambivalent process, ending both its technical and, more understandably from the regime's ideological standpoint, its political influence.

Scholars differ over the impact Westerners have had on Chinese society. Some historians believe that the Westerners who labored in China had great influence. For example, after studying sixteen Western advisers in China from 1620 to 1960, Jonathan Spence concluded: "If their wider goals were not realized, the Western advisers nevertheless left their imprint firmly on Chinese society by compelling some form of confrontation with the most advanced levels of Western technique."[2] According to Spence, the Chinese adhered steadfastly to their own religious and cultural traditions, but they eagerly accepted Western technical advice.

Other scholars argue that Westerners in China have had little impact. Edgar Porter, for example, found that foreigners have had limited roles in Chinese education. After studying foreign teachers in China from 1979 to 1989, he concluded: "I can . . . attest that no foreigner lives long in China without realizing that he or she makes little or no impact on the Chinese people without permission to do so from those same people."[3]

The issue of cultural encounter, with its political implications, can best be assessed by framing this focus on ideology and the younger generations of Chinese students within a general overview of the Fulbright program in both China and the United States. The study of the impact of American Fulbrighters on China will illuminate the influence of Westerners in general and Americans in particular on the Chinese.

Origins of the Fulbright Program in China

China was the first country to establish educational exchange programs with the United States after the Second World War. The postwar period was not the first time Americans had instituted an international educational exchange program there. At the beginning of the twentieth century, following the failed Boxer Rebellion of 1898–1900, Americans established the Boxer Indemnity Scholarship Program. The weak Chinese government was forced to sign a final settlement to various foreign powers agreeing to pay about $330 million in damages in 1901. In 1906, President Theodore Roosevelt became interested in a plan to establish a scholarship program to send Chinese students to the United States. After conferring with Chinese authorities, he suggested the plan to Congress, which in 1908 passed a bill authorizing the president to modify the Boxer indemnity so that the balance would be returned to China and be used for Chinese students' education in the United States.[4]

The Boxer Indemnity Scholarship Program was set up in 1909, and part of the first remission of money included the establishment in 1911 of a preparatory school in Beijing for the Chinese graduates pursuing further studies at American universities. In 1911, the first eighteen American teachers arrived in Beijing. About fifty or more students chosen from among the graduates were sent to the United States for higher education annually in the following years. The school was later expanded to offer four-year undergraduate and postgraduate programs and renamed Qinghua University, which has become the number one university in China today. A second remission in 1924 provided for the establishment of the China Foundation, which would in turn fund the China Institute in New York City in 1926. Approximately thirteen hundred students were able to study at the institute from 1909 to 1929. A total of five groups of scholars were educated in the United States before the Japanese invasion of China in 1937.[5] This program was the most important scheme for educating Chinese students in America and arguably the most consequential and successful in the entire foreign study movement of twentieth-century China.

For the first time, Americans instituted an educational exchange program with a foreign country, creating a precedent for international educational exchange programs in the following years.

The Boxer Indemnity Scholarship Program had an impact on freshman senator J. William Fulbright from Arkansas. On September 27, 1945, Fulbright introduced to Congress a new bill to amend the Surplus Property Act of 1944. This bill "authoriz[ed] use of credits established through the sale of surplus properties abroad for the promotion of international good will through the exchange of students in the fields of education, culture and science."[6] As the main initiator of this debate, Fulbright reminded members of Congress of the Boxer Indemnity Scholarship and the importance of the international educational exchange advocated. Before the debate, he frequently mentioned that technology and science had made the world smaller and more mutually dependent. On April 26, 1943, delivering a speech at Gettysburg College, he proclaimed: "In this modern world of instantaneous communication and swift transportation, isolation is a figment of the imagination."[7] He also believed not only that Americans had a moral obligation to engage in international affairs but also that the postwar realities of power required it. Three years later, in another academic address, he stated: "It is peculiarly the responsibility of Americans to take the lead in the creation of a peaceful world. Not only is it to our selfish material interest because we have more to lose by chaos than any other people, but it is also our moral duty to give direction and strength to the bewildered people of this earth who are groping helplessly for peace and a decent life. If for no other reason it is our duty because we are the favored heirs of western Christian civilization."[8] On August 1, 1946, President Truman signed Fulbright's amendment into law because, as he noted: "If we do not want to die together in war, we must learn to live together in peace."[9] After Congress passed legislation proposed by the Arkansas senator in 1946 to advance international understanding through educational exchange, the US government established the Fulbright program to promote mutual understanding between American people and the other peoples of the world.

The Fulbright Bill was passed through the ingenious reworking of wartime debts and loans to foreign countries, which helped sell surplus war material abroad quickly.[10] Since the new Fulbright program was not funded, the US government negotiated executive agreements with foreign governments to sell surplus war materials to other countries to carry out exchanges in countries with minimal surplus property sales.[11] In September, 1946, 1.5 tons of material were sold to China in return for the cancellation of American war debts to China, including $20 million for cultural and educational exchange, which benefited the devastated country enormously.[12]

The surplus sale to China proceeded slowly until US administrators hit on the idea of a bulk sale, and Americans became "optimistic that the Chinese will buy a lot of the stuff that is unsaleable."[13] Progress toward this end was being made, and American army officials in Beijing successfully offloaded surplus candy, a deal suggesting the extent to which all surplus was considered salable in China. However, in July 1947, almost a year after the bulk sale to China, Tillman Durdin reported in the *New York Times* that negotiations had "hit a snag over the question of who is to control expenditure of the money involved." The Chinese Foreign Office wanted a Chinese majority on the board controlling such sales, "but the U.S. [was] unwilling to concede this, since the Chinese then would have the deciding voice in the allocation of the funds."[14]

A separate board was established to administer the Chinese exchange program, chaired by US ambassador to China John Leighton Stuart. Its members included the second secretary of the embassy, the cultural relations officer of the embassy, the chief US Information Service cultural officer, a representative of the Rockefeller Foundation, and a representative of the National City Bank of New York in Shanghai.[15] As the board wrapped up proceedings on the final day of its meeting in October 1947, news arrived that a Fulbright agreement had been finalized with China.[16] By that time the US government had established academic links with twenty nations, as the *New York Times* declared: "The United States has embarked on the most comprehensive program of student exchange ever undertaken by any nation."[17]

China was the first country to join the new Fulbright program. An official Fulbright accord was not signed by both Nationalist Chinese foreign minister Wang Shiqie and American ambassador Stuart until November 10, 1947. This accord was significant in the history of US international educational exchange, as a persuasive brochure for the program commented later: "[It is] obvious that the Fulbright Act makes possible a program of educational exchange on a scale without precedence in modern times."[18]

The academic exchange program was in business. The first participants—47 Americans and 36 foreign nationals in exchanges with China, Burma, and the Philippines—started their travel in the fall of 1948. The pace of binational negotiations soon quickened. Within a year, agreements had been signed with New Zealand, the United Kingdom, Belgium (including Luxembourg), France, Italy, the Netherlands, and Norway. In all, 823 Americans and 967 foreign citizens were selected to participate in the exchange program in academic year 1949–1950.[19]

The geographic distribution of the surplus material determined the geographic distribution of Fulbright grantees. Since China bought the second largest amount of surplus material in the first two years of the Fulbright program, 148 of 1,934 grants were made for exchange between it and the United States. But, by August 1949, only 27 American scholars and students and 24 Chinese students and scholars had taken part in the exchange.[20] And, while the Fulbright program was expanding rapidly in other countries, it came to an abrupt halt in China when the People's Republic was established in October 1949.

A Soviet Model for Chinese Universities, 1950–1978

After 1949, the Chinese government tried to achieve two goals for its higher education system: first, that system should have the right political nature and belong to the new government led by the Chinese Communist Party; second, it should directly serve the needs of the rapid economic development taking place in the new country. The major focus was on building a national education system.[21] Since the Communist Soviet Union already had over thirty years of construction and development under its belt, the Chinese government adopted not only the Soviet model of economic development but also the Soviet model of educational development because it lacked experience regarding education reform.[22]

More importantly, the Chinese leaders tried to learn from the Soviet Union how to impose on Chinese students the ideological orthodoxy of Marxism-Leninism and thus protect them against the penetration of Western ideologies and values. In 1952, a countrywide adjustment of colleges and of university departments took place that followed the Soviet concept of remodeling education, leading to the restructuring of the higher education system itself.[23] Much depended on Soviet assistance. In the 1950s, 861 education experts from the Soviet Union were sent to China to participate in the reform of higher education and the establishment of new universities. Russian became the major foreign language taught at the universities.[24]

However, from the late 1950s to the mid-1960s, China established a mixed Confucian-Western style of higher education. The reasons for this change were more political than scientific. China was on less than friendly terms with the Soviet Union by the end of the 1950s, and, therefore, it might not have seemed politically expedient to follow the educational model of a state that was out of favor with the Chinese government. Thus, the Western-style model came back, although for only a short time. The blossoming of Western-style higher education came to an abrupt end in 1966 with the Cultural Revolution and the subsequent eradication of all formal education. A decade of deterioration set in, leaving an entire generation largely uneducated. This was a great disaster for the Chinese education system, and its repercussions were felt for a long time.[25]

With the passing of Mao and the downfall of the radical Gang of Four in 1976, China ushered in a new era, one that saw the pragmatist faction in command. The national emphasis shifted to the Four Modernizations. The Chinese referred to this endeavor as the New Long March, which was meant to take China to the front rank of nations by the end of the century. Again, higher education was asked to play a significant role, but it was not up to the task, the years of political upheaval having taken their toll, especially on the social and behavioral sciences, but on science and technology as well. Therefore, an adjustment was needed if the higher education system was to rise to contemporary international standards.[26]

To strengthen its science and technology programs as well as international scientific exchanges, the Beijing government in 1978 decided to send ten thousand students to various countries. An initial five hundred were to come to the United States. This trend was given formal recognition by the scientific and cultural agreement signed between the US and the Chinese governments during Vice Premier Deng Xiaoping's historic visit to the United States in January 1979.

With Chinese-American relations reestablished, the Fulbright program made a reappearance, and exchanges of Chinese and American scholars began anew. The US government remained interested in sending teachers to China. Using educational exchange as a tool of its China policy, it had been trying to influence a generation of young Chinese since the Communists came to power. The Fulbright program having been created to promote mutual understanding and contribute to scholarly intercultural knowledge, it encouraged the Chinese government to participate. Washington hoped that the China Fulbright program with its emphasis on theoretical work in the social sciences would help promote an understanding of US scholarship and the American way of life as well as developing the skills of the Chinese students. It also hoped that the program would offset the strong focus on the sciences and technology of the Chinese students and scholars who were sent by Beijing to American campuses.[27]

The Return of the China Fulbright Program

In the fall of 1979, the Chinese government agreed to join the Fulbright program, but it required the US government to send only English teachers at first because it was still concerned about the ideological impact of Fulbright exchanges on the social sciences and humanities, formally requesting American assistance in the recruitment and support of about twenty specialists in English-language teaching over a three-year period. The Council for International Exchange of Scholars, a private agency cooperating with the US government in the administration of Fulbright scholar grants for advanced research and university teaching, selected four specialists in teaching English as a second language and assigned them to Beijing University. For the first time since 1949, American scholars selected solely on the basis of their academic qualifications taught regularly enrolled Chinese university students. In March 1980, four Fulbrighters, led by Richard Light of the State University of New York at Albany, taught English at Beijing University. Because of the enthusiastic support of the Chinese government, the Americans encountered great responsiveness and hospitality from the Chinese. Their students were experienced university English teachers, selected by competitive examination from twenty-six universities all over China. The Americans were successful in providing information on American literature, history, and culture as enrichment and background in their program.

That first American group returned to the United States in time to orient a second group of eleven who were assigned to three different cities in China—Beijing, Shanghai, and Tianjin. The first year's program was limited to lectureships in the teaching of English as a second language; the second year included lecturing appointments in American literature, history, economics, and law. After 1980, the number of American Fulbrighters teaching in China increased substantially.

By 1989, the China Fulbright program had grown into one of the largest in the world, with twenty-four American professors teaching on Chinese campuses and a like number of Chinese graduate students and scholars studying at US universities. Following the Tiananmen Square uprising in June 1989, however, the Chinese government put the whole program on hold. After the suppression of the student movement for democracy, Beijing announced in July that it would withdraw its invitation to Fulbright professors to teach at Chinese universities for at least one year because of their late opening.

It is not surprising that, after Tiananmen, the Chinese government immediately suspended the China Fulbright program. Delivering a speech before a national higher education meeting in July 1989, Li Tieying, commissioner of the State Education Commission, connected bourgeois liberalism with courses in the social sciences and humanities, which, he asserted, uncritically introduced bourgeois social theories. He implied that American social science and humanities professors were responsible for the flood of bourgeois ideas onto Chinese university campuses.[28]

The social sciences and the humanities were once again subject to tight control; Chinese professors and graduate students had to strive hard for professional survival—their own and that of their departments. Americans also took action. In July 1989, the trustees of the Yale-China Association (established in 1909) voted to cancel the English-language teaching program at three colleges in China for the 1989–1990 academic year, given that the Chinese government would not ensure the safety of American teachers in such an unstable situation. Some American institutions and organizations, however, continued to send teachers to China—for example, Johns Hopkins University, which continued to operate its Nanjing center, and the Christian-oriented English Language Institute.[29]

At the same time, official attacks on US educational exchange policy toward China began. On August 24, 1989, the official *Renmin ribao* (People's daily) published an editorial welcoming the early returning students back to China, criticizing the 1989 student demonstrators for understanding little of China's "essence," and claiming that bourgeois liberal ideology from the American-led West had poured into Chinese universities in recent years to fill an ideological vacuum created by the lack of study of Marxist-Leninist thought.[30] The Beijing government saw the far-reaching Western influence on Chinese university campuses in the 1980s as a clear consequence of conscious cultural imperialism and an effort to bring about "peaceful evolution."[31] The official attack on US cultural and educational policy toward China also indicated the impact of Americans, including Fulbrighters, on the Chinese campus.

Washington was not happy with Beijing's policy toward the China Fulbright program. The US Information Agency reported in a news release on August 16, 1989, that Beijing had informed Washington that no American Fulbright professors would be permitted to teach in China. The US government deeply regretted this decision to suspend the program; the mutual benefits of the academic exchanges, Washington reiterated, should have been apparent to both nations. China canceled exchanges in reaction to America's criticism of its military suppression of the student movement, but, in March 1990, the China Fulbright program was restored on a limited basis. In the following years, the number of Americans sent to China increased annually, their numbers ranging from thirteen to thirty every year.[32]

Originally, the US research scholar and graduate student components of the program were conducted under a grant given to the Committee on Scholarly Communication with China. A new formal US-China educational exchange accord was signed in Beijing in March 2000, according to the terms of which the US Department of State and China's Ministry of Education were named as executive agents. Beginning with the 2000–2001 academic year, these two programs were placed under the Fulbright umbrella and included grants for senior scholars and doctoral students. Five recent American graduates were included in the 1999–2000 program and were the first graduating senior Fulbrighters sent to China since the reestablishment of the program in 1979. Since then, graduating seniors have come to form the largest group of US Fulbrighters going to China each year.[33]

Today, the Fulbright program has expanded to include many of the major higher education institutions and research academies in China. Many of them are universities under the direct jurisdiction of the Ministry of Education, which is responsible for formulating and implementing educational policy at all levels. In addition to higher education, the China Fulbright program serves the institutions directly under the Ministry of Education, which are authorized to send and receive Fulbright grantees. Other institutions that are under provincial, autonomous, regional, or municipal authorities or other central ministries take part in the Fulbright program as well.

Significance of the China Fulbright Program

Today, the China Fulbright program consists of three parts: American lecturers and research scholars in China, American graduate students in China, and Chinese visiting research scholars and graduate students in the United States. Currently, approximately ten to twenty US lecturers, five to ten US research scholars, and fifty to seventy American graduate students and recent graduates come to China each year. In the academic year 2012–2013, thirty American Fulbrighters were teaching and conducting research in China. The teaching locations have increased, expanding beyond Beijing to Shanghai and cities in Fujian, Jiangsu, Liaoning, Guangdong, Hunan, Sichuan, Shaanxi, Gansu, and Zhejiang Provinces. The number of American professors' teaching disciplines has also been increased to include American history, literature, law, journalism, business, economics, political science, sociology, philosophy, international relations, music, anthropology, library science, environmental sciences, agriculture, public health, public administration, urban planning, and the humanities. From 1979 to 2014, more than seven hundred American scholars taught and conducted research in China.

Mutual Understanding

The Fulbright exchange program was developed to ensure cultural immersion and interaction. Approximately one hundred Chinese visiting research scholars, professional associates, and foreign-language teaching assistants are in the United States each year under the program's auspices. Their studies and research in the United States help them not only uncover new knowledge in their fields of study but also familiarize themselves with American culture and society.

Most Chinese scholars and students were shockingly ignorant about the United States when China opened its doors to Western society in 1979. They lacked basic knowledge of the American political and legal systems, federalism, the US Constitution, the structure of the American welfare state's working and living conditions, and the social reality of a multiracial, multiethnic society. Under the influence of powerful official propaganda, many Chinese scholars and students still had negative perceptions of the United States when they first entered the gates of American campuses. Their stereotypes of Americans were often of a hedonistic, violence-prone, and restless people who indulged themselves in all their desires and neglected their family responsibilities. American professors promoted a better understanding of American society and culture and the country's political and economic system among the Chinese students and professors. And most of those Fulbrighters were eager to learn and remained fully capable of absorbing virtually all ideas that American professors aired in their classrooms. They heartily welcomed the courses. The American teachers noted their Chinese students' and scholars' eagerness to learn, despite the problems involved in attending classes taught in English and conducted in a very different teaching style. Such enthusiasm impressed the Americans, and some professors reported that the Chinese students and professors were the best they had ever encountered.[34]

Professor Li Guo, of Sun Yet-sen University in Guangzhou, was one such example. He was a Fulbright visiting professor at Harvard University during the academic year 1994–1995. He remembered that, before coming to the United States, he was taught that Americans were haunted by the specter of joblessness and enjoyed no social security and that the white people had carried out the genocide of Native Americans and discriminated against black people. He also said that "the Chinese textbooks often identify American women's liberation with divorce and sexual license" but that "after several months in the U.S. he no longer believe[d] such stories about American society."[35] It is clear that many Chinese Fulbrighters in the United States began to appreciate and value American customs and gradually took responsibility for creating a constructive image of Americans.

American Fulbrighters' experience in China also helped them understand Chinese culture better. A case in point is that of Amy Werbel, a professor of art history at the State University of New York—Fashion Institute of Technology. Werbel was a Fulbright scholar teaching at the Guangdong University of Foreign Studies (GDUFS) in the city of Guangzhou, the capital of Guangdong Province. From August 2011 to July 2012, she taught such courses as "Culture in the United States from the Civil War to World War I" and "America in the 1960s" to graduate students at GDUFS. She and her students discussed subjects such as race relations, the counterculture of the 1960s, censorship, the undercurrents of reform, and the Vietnam War. She introduced them to the practice and skills of dialogue, critical thinking, and the use of primary sources, which, in turn, raised important questions about the nature and future of both Chinese society and American society. She traveled throughout China as a guest lecturer, mentored and befriended several graduate students, learned the ins and outs of negotiating ethnic and linguistic divisions and barriers within China; and absorbed much else about contemporary China's cultural, intellectual, and political environment.[36]

Enrichment of Americans' Education Experiences

American professors in China have been very welcomed by Chinese students. Many universities adopt liberal policies, and thus the Americans are free to teach their subject matter. As a result, most American professors enjoy their time in China. The main merit of their educational experience in China, however, lies with their learning experience. The benefit that American Fulbrighters bring to Chinese students is mirrored by their own opportunity to explore their disciplines in a new environment and a different culture. In 2002, for example, a team of American Fulbrighters visited China under the leadership of Professor Zheng Zhou, the project director, of St. John's University. The twelve Fulbright participants included six psychology faculty members from five universities, two clinical psychologists affiliated with universities in New York, and three teachers from New York City public schools. For more than a century, Western philosophers and psychologists have based their discussions of mental conditions on a fundamental theory that the same basic processes underlie all human thought. By examining China, whose culture is profoundly different from that of the United States, the team identified essential differences in the psychological processes of Chinese and American children. Such information is key to acquiring a theoretical framework on which models of assessment and intervention in the reasoning, behavioral, and personality domains can be constructed. As Zhou wrote: "The Fulbright seminar provided us with the opportunity to examine Chinese children's educational and psychological functioning in a variety of environmental and social contexts. This enabled us to develop a deeper understanding of Chinese children and of our own assumptions and past experiences."[37]

China's Higher Education Reform

American professors have played a key role in Chinese higher education reform. First, they have developed new disciplines. From 1949 to 1979, disciplines in the social sciences and the humanities, such as political science, law, sociology, and psychology, were criticized or ignored in the Chinese classroom for political and ideological reasons. Initially, in 1980, priority was given to lecturers in English, American literature, and history to help China in its move toward the Four Modernizations. In 1983, the Chinese Ministry of Education decided to focus Fulbright exchanges in areas related to American studies, including American history, American literature, law, journalism, business, economics, political science, sociology, philosophy, and international relations. Now many universities in China have developed more courses in more disciplines than were available in the 1980s, courses that have become increasingly popular.

Second, American lecturers offer new courses to Chinese students, although many courses contradicted official Chinese ideology. During the 1980 academic year, Anthony G. Trimarchi, teaching the history of early American political thought at the Beijing Institute of Foreign Languages, said that the course was "the first of this kind in China since 1949."[38] Henry Rosemont noted: "I am the first Western philosopher to offer a year-long course in the history of Western philosophy in China since Liberation."[39] Teaching courses in political science and American foreign policy for both undergraduate and graduate students at the Zhongshan University in Guangzhou, Kent Morrison wrote in 1983: "Only those students who had taken my classes last semester had any previous exposure to courses in political science. There has been no political science in this country for 30 years."[40] Peter Chang, teaching economic management at Shangdong University in 1984, wrote: "My mission also calls for an introduction of new courses: Quantitative Analysis in Economics and Management Science, which Chinese scholars have lacked for three decades."[41] After offering a two-semester graduate seminar in literary theory, Bruce Wilson, a 1984–1985 Fulbright lecturer in Fudan University's Department of Foreign Languages and Literature, learned that "the department leaders were obviously proud that Fudan was the first university in China to offer such a course."[42] Americans thus played a crucial role in filling the gaps in knowledge in these and other areas that had been off-limits in China for many years.

Third, American scholars have introduced novel teaching methods, methods that usually stress the kind of individual-centered learning discouraged by the Chinese government, which promoted action by the collective in line with traditional Confucianism. These new methods have helped students develop independent thinking, which was far removed from the traditional Chinese education methods of rote memorization of classical texts. When teaching American literature, Mary Louis Buley-Meissener encouraged students to participate in the learning process: "I resisted assuming that kind of authority over the students and stories. Instead I depended on the students to assume new roles as leaders. Rather than studying their texts in traditional ways, they were encouraged to be active in questioning their texts, their teacher, and each other about possible ways to put meaning together."[43] Some American professors have their students make comparisons between East and West. When Thad Barnowe taught business administration at Zhongshan University, he tried to make comparisons between the American and the Chinese economic systems while noting that both China and the United States were facing some common basic problems. He presented facts about and possible solutions to the management problems American organizations faced, and he told the Chinese students that American enterprises' success resulted not only from their management techniques but also from their treatment of employees and their socially responsible policies. He concluded that China needed to learn not only the technologies of the West but also its economic theories.[44]

Establishment of Academic Links

Both American and Chinese Fulbrighters have helped establish academic links between universities in China and the United States. In fall 2006, for example, Professor Li Benxian of Xi'an International Studies University in

Xi'an had the honor to teach Chinese literature as a Fulbright scholar at the University of Cincinnati. After returning home, he helped establish academic links between these two universities. Since 2006, both Xi'an International Studies University and the University of Cincinnati have exchanged professors and students every year. As Li noted: "Great opportunities are there for increasing academic cooperation between Chinese literature programs in the United States and China."[45] In fall 2007, Professor Donna Infeld of George Washington University had the privilege of teaching public administration as a Fulbright scholar at Renmin University of China in Beijing. After returning home, she started exploring several jointly sponsored research projects related to master's of public administration programs in both countries.[46] Today, with Fulbrighters' help, many universities in China have established durable academic links with universities in the United States.

Ideological Impact on Chinese Students

American professors not only play a role in higher education reform but also import into broader Chinese culture Western values and ideology. American professors in China see the importance of teaching Western culture in addition to their academic subjects. Learning US technology, they often suggest, cannot be separated from learning US values and ideology. However, the overwhelming majority confirm that they have no intention of imposing Western notions on Chinese students. Since American Fulbrighters create an environment of academic freedom in their classrooms, that environment helps Chinese students question their own values and political system. Eugenia Kaledin, who was teaching "Themes in American Life: Individualism and Dissent," received in 1986 a final paper called "Twenty Years at Hull House," by a third-year student at Beijing University, "that seem[ed] to make all the hardships of a teacher's life worthwhile." The student argued that both the great men and the masses were shaping history, challenging the Marxist opinion that the masses and only the masses did so.[47] In such an environment, Chinese students began to reject blind acceptance of customs and tradition and question and challenge official ideology—both Marxism and traditional Confucianism and the Chinese political and economic systems. Some students became dissatisfied with their own country and began to demand Western political and social values. The American Fulbrighters' ideological impact on the Chinese students is clear. Anthony G. Trimarchi remarked: "The Chinese are not interested in any strong anti-American views of America. They had their stomachs filled with this before. Now they are interested in a less biased approach."[48] William Whiteside, teaching at Beijing University for the academic year 1982–1983, noted that the students' "view of Americans is not that of the purveyors of anti-American propaganda."[49]

To complement the existing records, I conducted interviews at several universities in China, interviews that indicate that Americans played a significant role in introducing Western ideology to those Chinese students who were taking their courses.[50] For example, after taking a course taught by Kent Morrison, Liang Xiaofan, an undergraduate student in the History Department at Zhongshan University, said: "We learned a lot of new political concepts and ideas that changed our opinions of our political and economic systems."[51]

It seems that some courses taught by Americans have offset some of the official Chinese rhetoric about capitalist decadence, the demise of the Western economic system, the oppressive exploitation of workers in Western companies, and so on. Western values and ideas seem to be gaining strength on Chinese campuses. Still, however open Chinese students, academics, and universities are to American influence, the official ideology still casts a jaundiced eye on the Fulbright program, and the official attack on US educational exchange policy with regard to China continues. In 2015, China's education authorities still pledged to redouble efforts to limit the use of foreign textbooks in universities to stem the infiltration of Western values. In January 2015, Education Minister Yuan Guiren urged tighter control over the use of imported textbooks "that spread Western values." Universities in China have been told to step up propaganda efforts and the teaching of Marxism and Chinese socialism to ensure that such values "get into the students' heads." The institutes would be assessed on their use of standard textbooks on Marxism.[52]

Conclusion

China was the first country to establish an educational exchange program with the United States and the first country to join the Fulbright program. The Beijing government restored the China Fulbright program in 1979 to speed up its Four Modernizations drive. Since 1989, the China Fulbright program has become one of the largest Fulbright programs in the world. It offers an opportunity for American and Chinese academics to explore both their countries and their disciplines in new environments and establish academic exchange programs between Chinese and American universities. Americans are able to learn to work together with Chinese scholars on shared global problems, and a Fulbright experience is one small step in that direction.

The China Fulbright program emphasizes dialogue and exchange and the promotion of mutual understanding between the Chinese and the American participants. It helps the Chinese students and professors understand American society better and US foreign and domestic policy more deeply, thereby developing a more positive image of the United States. Thus, it helps strengthen and expand contacts between Americans and Chinese and encourages more extensive and durable educational links between these two countries, links that contribute to the improvement of the US-China relationship.

When Chinese come into contact with Western ideas, cultures, practices, and institutions, having no critical perspective, they are willing to absorb whatever they regard as useful, expecting Western knowledge and methods to be useful in handling the practical problems of China. The China Fulbright program, however, brings to the Chinese scholars and students not only Western technology but also Western ideology and values. This intellectual influence plays a role in helping shape the perspectives of the rising generation of Chinese. It created increasing discontent among Chinese students, culminating in the growth of Western values on Chinese campuses. That unavoidable and unexpected side effect of inviting American lecturers to China and the return of the Chinese Fulbright scholars from the United States is especially significant there. The Chinese leaders see Western ideology as posing a threat to the existing hierarchical and authoritarian political system; they are therefore faced with the dilemma of rejecting that ideology (in order to maintain traditional Confucian virtue) at the same time as Western technology is being embraced.

The China Fulbright program seems to aggravate political and cultural contradictions within China and may help transform China in the future. Despite the long hiatus between exposure to Western values and the serious concerns about those values harbored by some officials, the

China Fulbright program is functioning exactly as its primary architect intended when establishing it seven decades ago.

Notes

1. For a comprehensive study of the China Fulbright program from 1979 to 1989, see Guangqiu Xu, "The Ideological and Political Impact of U.S. Fulbrighters on the Chinese Students, 1979–1989," *Asian Affairs* (Contemporary US-Asia Research Institute, New York) 26, no. 3 (2000): 139–59.

2. Jonathan Spence, *To Change China: Western Advisers in China, 1620–1960* (Boston: Little, Brown, 1969), 291.

3. Edgar Porter, *Foreign Teachers in China: Old Problems for a New Generation, 1979–1989* (New York: Greenwood, 1990), 92.

4. See Weili Ye, *Seeking Modernity in China's Name: Chinese Students in United States* (Stanford, CA: Stanford University Press, 2001).

5. Larry Clinton Thompson, *William Scott Ament and the Boxer Rebellion: Heroism, Hubris and the "Ideal Missionary"* (Jefferson, NC: McFarland, 2009), 219.

6. "Statement by J. William Fulbright of Arkansas," Washington, DC, September 1945, file 6, box 8, J. William Fulbright Papers, Special Collections Division, University of Arkansas Library, Fayetteville. I would like to thank the Special Collections Division of the University of Arkansas Library for allowing me to use the Fulbright Papers and the records of the Council for the International Exchange of Scholars, from which most of the professors' comments on the Fulbright program have come.

7. J. William Fulbright, "Isolation and Foreign Policy: Commencement Address at Gettysburg College," Gettysburg, PA, April 26, 1943, 5, file 1, box 2, ser. 72, Fulbright Papers.

8. J. William Fulbright, "Charter Day Address," College of William and Mary, Williamsburg, VA, February 8,1946, 2, file 6, box 4, ser. 72, Fulbright Papers.

9. Harry Truman, "Address to the United Nations Conference in San Francisco," August 25, 1945, https://www.trumanlibrary.org/publicpapers/index.php?pid=17.

10. Department of State, Office of the Foreign Liquidation Commissioner, *Report to Congress on Foreign Surplus Disposal*, State Department Publication 2571 (Washington, DC: US Government Printing Office, July 1946), 8.

11. For a study of the sale of war materials and the origins of the Fulbright program after World War II, see Sam Lebovic, "From War Junk to Educational Exchange: The World War II Origins of the Fulbright Program and the Foundations of American Cultural Globalism, 1945–1950," *Diplomatic History* 37, no. 2 (2013): 280–312.

12. Wilma Fairbank, *America's Cultural Experiment in China, 1942–1949* (Washington, DC: US Department of State, Bureau of Educational and Cultural Affairs, 1976), 154.

13. Notes from Staff Meeting, Tuesday, May 7, 1946, File: Pacific Area Reports of Conference, box 10, National Archives and Record Administration, Record Group 59; General Records of the Department of State, Office of the Foreign Liquidation Commissioner, Miscellaneous Files, 1945–49.

14. Tillman Durdin, "U.S., China at Odds on Cultural Fund," *New York Times*, July 10, 1947, 11; Fairbank, *America's Cultural Experiment in China*, 155–56.

15. Tillman Durdin, "Educational Aid to China Mapped," *New York Times*, December 18, 1947, 16.

16. Kenneth Holland to Senator Fulbright, October 20, 1947, file 13, box 12, Fulbright Papers.

17. "Student Exchange Enlists 22 Nations," *New York Times*, October 10, 1947, 27.

18. "Current Information Regarding the Fulbright Educational Program of Interest to University Professors and Scholars," December 20, 1949, 1, file 2, box 94, MC 703, Council for International Exchange of Scholars Records, Special Collections of University of Arkansas Libraries, Fayetteville (hereafter CIES Records).

19. See Jack Nac-Chyi Hwang, "Internationalism with Different Face: The Evolution of J. William Fulbright's Beliefs in China Policy (1943–1974)" (PhD diss., Tammang University, 1999).

20. "The Fulbright Program in China Is Stalled," *New York Times*, September 7, 1949, 19.

21. Kang Ouyang, "Higher Education Reform in China Today," *Policy Futures in Education* 2, no. 1 (2004): 141–49.

22. Mingyuan Gu, "Influence of Soviet Union's Educational Theory on Chinese Education," *Journal of Beijing Normal University (Social Sciences)* 181, no. 1 (2004): 5–13, 6.

23. Kathryn Mohrman, *Higher Education Reform in Mainland Chinese Universities: An American's Perspective* (Hong Kong: Chinese University Hong Kong, 2003), https://www.bpastudies.org/bpastudies/article/view/2/9.

24. Hui Chen, "Adjustment of Colleges and Departments of Universities in 1952" (in Chinese), *Modern China Studies*, vol. 82, no. 3 (2003); *China Education Newspaper*, June 7, 2007, http://www.jyb.com.cn/zs/gxzs/ptgxzs/zszx/t20070607_89340.htm.

25. See Ruth Hayhoe, *China's Universities, 1895–1998: A Century of Cultural Conflict* (New York: Garland, 1996), 71–110 ("The Socialist Story, 1949–1976").

26. Ibid.

27. For the goals of the China Fulbright program, see Committee on Scholarly Communication with the People's Republic of China, *American Studies in China: Report of a Delegation Visit, October 1984* (Washington, DC: National Academy Press, 1985).

28. *Zhongguo jiaoyu bao* (China's education newspaper), August 30, 1989, 6.

29. See Xiao Cai, "Higher Education in China: Outward Conformity, Inner Despair," *Education Digest* 56, no. 6 (1991): 8–11.

30. *Renmin ribao* (People's daily), August 24, 1989.

31. See Sun Renjian and Bai Zhongkao, "Xifang zhexue sichao shentao gaoxiao sixiang jiaoyu" (Western ideology penetrated into political education of universities), *Jiangsu gaojiao* (Jaingsu higher education), no. 4 (1990): 7–9; Guo Xiaocong, "Cong Xifang sichau dui daxuesheng de yingxiang fansi gaoxiao sixiang zhengzhi gongzuo" (To reexamine the political ideological work in universities with regard to the Western influence among university students), *Caojiao tansuo* (Higher education study) (Guangzhou), no. 1 (1990): 34–39.

32. "U.S. and China Resume Fulbright Program," *New York Times*, March 6, 1990.

33. See "The Committee on Scholarly Communication with the People's Republic of China," https://library.gwu.edu/sites/default/files/grc/CSCPRC.pdf.

34. For the comments on American society and culture by the Chinese visiting research scholars under the China Fulbright program, see *Zhongguo Fubulaite xueyouhui lunwenji* (A collection of the Chinese Fulbright alumni's articles), ed. Chinese Fulbright Alumni (Beijing: Zhongguo renmin daxue chubanshe, 2014).

35. Li Guo, interview with the author, Boston, June 6, 1995.

36. See Amy Werbel, *Lessons from China: America in the Hearts and Minds of the World's Most Important Rising Generation* (self-published, 2013). Werbel's book is an engaging, thoughtful, and stimulating account of her experiences in and out of the classroom in China. See also David Caragliano, "What Do Chinese Students Think of American History?" *The Atlantic*, July 2, 2013, http://www.theatlantic.com/china/archive/2013/07/what-do-chinese-students-think-of-american-history/277480.

37. https://www.researchgate.net/publication/229664689_Academic_achievement_of_children_in_China_The_2002_Fulbright_experience.

38. Anthony G. Trimarchi to CIES, March 1981, box 153, CIES Records.

39. Henry Rosemont Jr. to CIES, July 1983, box 154, CIES Records.

40. Kent Morrison to CIES, August 1984, box 154, CIES Records.

41. Peter Chang to CIES, August 1985, box 154, CIES Records.

42. Bruce Wilson, "Thoughts on Teaching at Fudan University," *China Exchange News* 13, no. 3 (1985): 13–15.

43. Mary Louis Buley-Meissener, "Teaching American Literature in China," *English Education* 22, no. 3 (October 1990): 192–99.

44. Thad Barnowe to CIES, July 1983, box 153, CIES Records.

45. Li Benxian, interview with the author, June 6, 2011, at Xi'an International Studies University.

46. Donna Lind Infeld and Li Wenzhao, "Teaching Public Administration as a Fulbright Scholar in China: Analysis and Reflections," *Journal of Public Affairs Information* 15, no. 3 (2018): 333–47, http://www.naspaa.org/jpaemessenger/Article/jpae-v15n3-05Infe.pdf.

47. Eugenia Kaledin to CIES, July 1986, box 154, CIES Records.

48. Anthony G. Trimarchi to CIES, March 1981, box 153, CIES Records.

49. William B. Whiteside to CIES, July 1983, box 153, CIES Records.

50. Yang Dong, interview with the author, August 10, 1986, Beijing University; Hong Yu, interview with the author, August 27, 1986, Fudan University; Song Yao,

June 1, 2012, Xi'an International Studies University; Wang Nan, interview with the author, July 10, 2013, Jinan University; Deng Wu, interview with the author, June 10, 2014, East China Normal University.

51. Liang Xiaofan, interview with the author, July 4, 1986, Zhongshan University.

52. Andrea Chen and Zhuang Pinghui, "Chinese Universities Ordered to Ban Textbooks That Promote Western Values: Universities Told to Clamp Down on Use of Foreign Textbooks and Criticism of the Party," September 27, 2015, *South China Post*, http://www.scmp.com/news/china/article/1695524/chinese-universities -instructed-ban-textbooks-promote-western-values?page=all.

Acknowledgments

This volume attempts to follow the spirit of Senator J. William Fulbright's dual commitment to serious, unbiased scholarship and to the critical examination of crucial, timely international issues. Gathering the opinions, expertise, and insights of scholars based in cities worldwide would not have been possible without the generous support and academic sponsorship of the Diane D. Blair Center of Southern Politics and Society, housed in the J. William Fulbright College of Arts and Sciences of the University of Arkansas. We particularly wish to thank the center's director, Professor Angie Maxwell, and the dean of the Fulbright College, Todd Shields, for their unwavering commitment to this project, the most ambitious, to date, among the already prolific series of events arranged by the Blair Center. We also wish to thank Professor Calvin White Jr., chair of the History Department of the Fulbright College, for joining in this endeavor with additional funding and always wise suggestions. As this was an interdisciplinary project, we knocked on several other doors for additional funding. And we were pleased to find enthusiastic support from the King Fahd Center for Middle East Studies (thanks to its former director, Professor Joel Gordon) and from the African and African American Studies Program of the University of Arkansas (directed by Professor White).

Since 2002, the Blair Center has sponsored forums and symposia that have contributed to an impressive book series. This is the sixth volume of that series, the purpose of which is to assess the regional, national, and international impact of southern politicians, intellectuals, and social leaders. No other post–World War II southern leader, outside of President Bill Clinton—who, not by accident, was the subject of the inaugural Blair Center conference in 2002—matched the international importance, influence, and legacy of Senator J. William Fulbright.

This volume is the result of the center's 2015 symposium, J. William Fulbright in International Perspective, and it combines contributions from that conference with additional essays from experts in the fields of southern politics, international history, and, specifically, the Fulbright Exchange Program.

Contributors

Neal Allen is associate professor of politics and department chair at Wichita State University.

Molly Bettie is lecturer in media and communication at the University of Leeds.

Benjamin Brady is attorney-adviser for the US Securities and Exchange Commission, Office of Market Supervision.

Alessandro Brogi is professor and director of undergraduate studies at the University of Arkansas.

Frédérick Gagnon is professor at the Department of Political Science at the University of Quebec in Montreal.

Alice Garner is adjunct in history at La Trobe University.

Justin Hart is associate professor and associate chair of US foreign relations at Texas Tech University.

Hannah Higgin is faculty in history at Blair Academy.

Lonnie R. Johnson is executive director of the Austrian-American Educational Commission.

Diane Kirkby is emeritus professor at La Trobe University.

Carla Konta is postdoc lecturer at the Department of Italian Studies at the University of Rijeka in Croatia.

Sam Lebovic is associate professor of history and director of the PhD program at George Mason University.

David L. Prentice is adjunct professor at the University of Arkansas—Fort Smith.

Giles Scott-Smith holds the Roosevelt Chair in New Diplomatic History, Leiden University, and is the academic director of the Roosevelt Institute for American Studies.

David J. Snyder is faculty principal of the Carolina International House and clinical associate professor of history and global studies at the University of South Carolina.

Randall B. Woods is distinguished professor of history at the University of Arkansas.

Guangqiu Xu is chair professor of Jinan University in Guangzhou and Xi'an International Studies University in Xi'an, China, as well as visiting professor of history at Lingnan University in Hong Kong.

Index

Studies in Conflict, Diplomacy, and Peace

Series Editors: George C. Herring, Andrew L. Johns, and Kathryn C. Statler

This series focuses on key moments of conflict, diplomacy, and peace from the eighteenth century to the present to explore their wider significance in the development of U.S. foreign relations. The series editors welcome new research in the form of original monographs, interpretive studies, biographies, and anthologies from historians, political scientists, journalists, and policymakers. A primary goal of the series is to examine the United States' engagement with the world, its evolving role in the international arena, and the ways in which the state, nonstate actors, individuals, and ideas have shaped and continue to influence history, both at home and abroad.

Advisory Board Members

Books in the Series

Obama at War: Congress and the Imperial Presidency
Ryan C. Hendrickson

The Cold War at Home and Abroad: Domestic Politics and US Foreign Policy since 1945
Edited by Andrew L. Johns and Mitchell B. Lerner

US Presidential Elections and Foreign Policy: Candidates, Campaigns, and Global Politics from FDR to Bill Clinton
Edited by Andrew Johnstone and Andrew Priest

Paving the Way for Reagan: The Influence of Conservative Media on US Foreign Policy
Laurence R. Jurdem

The Conversion of Senator Arthur H. Vandenberg: From Isolation to International Engagement
Lawrence S. Kaplan

Harold Stassen: Eisenhower, the Cold War, and the Pursuit of Nuclear Disarmament
Lawrence S. Kaplan

JFK and de Gaulle: How America and France Failed in Vietnam, 1961–1963
Sean J. McLaughlin

Nixon's Back Channel to Moscow: Confidential Diplomacy and Détente
Richard A. Moss

Breaking Protocol: America's First Female Ambassadors, 1933–1964
Philip Nash

Peacemakers: American Leadership and the End of Genocide in the Balkans
James W. Pardew

The Currents of War: A New History of American-Japanese Relations, 1899–1941
Sidney Pash

Eisenhower and Cambodia: Diplomacy, Covert Action, and the Origins of the Second Indochina War
William J. Rust

So Much to Lose: John F. Kennedy and American Policy in Laos
William J. Rust